Classical Economic Growth

To Maureen

Classical Economic Growth
An Analysis in the Tradition of Adam Smith

Gavin Clydesdale Reid

Basil Blackwell

Copyright © Gavin C. Reid 1989
First published 1989
Basil Blackwell Ltd
108 Cowley Road, Oxford, OX4 1 JF, UK

Basil Blackwell Inc.
432 Park Avenue South, Suite 1503
New York, NY 10016, USA

All rights reserved, Except for the quotation of short passages for the purposes of criticism and review, no part of this publication may be reproduced, stored in a retrieval system, or transmitted, in any form or by any means, electronic, mechanical, photocopying, recording or otherwise, without the prior permission of the publisher.

Except in the United States of America, this book is sold subject to the condition that it shall not, by way of trade or otherwise, be lent, re-sold, hired out, or otherwise circulated without the publisher's prior consent in any form of binding or cover other than that in which it is published and without a similar condition including this condition being imposed on the subsequent purchaser.

British Library Cataloguing in Publication Data

Reid, Gavin C.
 Classical economic growth: an analysis
 in the tradition of Adam Smith
 I. Title
 330.15′3
 ISBN 0-631-16298-4

Library of Congress Cataloging in Publication Data

Reid, Gavin C.
 Classical economic growth: an analysis in the tradition of Adam Smith/Gavin C. Reid
  p. cm.
 Bibliography: p.
 ISBN 0-631-16298-4
 1. Classical school of economics. 2. Smith, Adam, 1723–1790.
 I. Title.
 HB94.R45 1989
 330.15′3 dc 19   88-37636

Typeset in 10 on 12 pt Plantin
by Colset Private Limited, Singapore
Printed in Great Britain by
T. J. Press (Padstow) Ltd, Padstow, Cornwall

CONTENTS

Preface		ix
1	The Classical Perspective	1
	1.1 Introduction	1
	1.2 The Evolution of Economic Systems	3
	1.3 The Operation of Self-Interest	13
	1.4 Competition, the Firm and Increasing Returns	19
	1.5 Natural Law, Natural Liberty and Harmony	25
	1.6 Conclusion	29
2	Allocation versus Accumulation	35
	2.1 Introduction	35
	2.2 Efficient Allocative Equilibrium	36
	2.3 A Simple Sectoral Model	42
	2.4 Accumulation and Growth	43
	2.5 The Macroeconomic View of Growth	44
	2.6 Conclusion	46
3	Theories of Smithian Growth	49
	3.1 Introduction	49
	3.2 Sectoral Growth Models	50
	3.3 Aggregative Growth Models	53
	3.4 Growth Paths and the Stationary State	64
	3.5 Conclusion	72
4	Growth and Accumulation at the Industry Level	75
	4.1 Introduction	75
	4.2 The Firm and its Pricing Policy	76
	4.3 Price Leadership and Followership	76
	4.4 Cost-Plus Pricing	77

	4.5	Technical Progress	79
	4.6	Trends in Profits and Concentration	82
	4.7	Constant Price and Stable Demand	83
	4.8	Constant Mark-Up and Stable Demand	84
	4.9	Constant Mark-Up and Expanding Demand	87
	4.10	Conclusion	89
		Appendix	90
5	The Division of Labour and Technical Change		93
	5.1	Introduction	93
	5.2	The Division of Labour	94
	5.3	Endogenous Technical Change	103
	5.4	Technical Change and the Production Function	106
	5.5	Conclusion	112
6	Fluctuations and Growth at the Aggregate Level		115
	6.1	Introduction	115
	6.2	Beyond the Short Period	116
	6.3	Keynes and the Classics	117
	6.4	Two Models of Fluctuations and Growth	118
	6.5	Existence and Stability of Equilibrium	120
	6.6	Comparative Dynamics	124
	6.7	Conclusion	125
		Appendix	127
7	Bargaining Power and the Division of Labour		129
	7.1	Introduction	129
	7.2	An Aggregate Classical Model	130
	7.3	A Parameterization of the Model	132
	7.4	The Division of Labour and Bargaining Power	133
	7.5	Some Numerical Examples	136
	7.6	Conclusion	140
		Appendix	140
8	Disequilibrium and Increasing Returns		143
	8.1	Introduction	143
	8.2	The Young-Kaldor Extensions of Smith	146
	8.3	The Implicit Production Function	148
	8.4	The Role of the Merchant	151
	8.5	Conclusion	153
9	Classical Economics in a Post-Industrial Society		155
	9.1	Introduction	155

9.2	Extension of the Division of Labour	156
9.3	The Competitive Process	160
9.4	Institutional Evolution	170
9.5	Alienation and its Amelioration	175
9.6	Social Obligation	181
9.7	Conclusion	183

Epilogue 189

References 191

Index 203

PREFACE

In yesterday's lecture I showed you how the division of labour increases the opulence of a nation.

Adam Smith, *Lectures on Jurisprudence*

I

So said Adam Smith, according to a student who attended his lectures at Glasgow University over 225 years ago. There is no better way of summarizing the intent, and one hopes the content, of this book than that quote from Adam Smith's *Lectures on Jurisprudence* (LJ(A), p. 349).* Our volume is rooted in the tradition of classical economics deriving from Adam Smith. However, its concerns and its methods are modern. What follows is not an exercise in the history of economic thought, though history is acknowledged when it is relevant, but rather a study in analytical economics.

The relatively primitive notions first formulated in what is now called Smith's *Lectures on Jurisprudence* laid the foundation for the fuller and more sophisticated analysis of *The Wealth of Nations*. It was this which started the science of economics as it is now understood, and established a research agenda of extraordinary fruitfulness which is still being explored with originality and imagination to this day.

---

*Throughout this book, where works of Adam Smith are cited, reference is made to the Glasgow edition, using the following system of abbreviations: WN, *The Wealth of Nations* (Campbell, Skinner and Todd 1976); EPS, *Essays on Philosophical Subjects* (Wightman and Bryce 1980); LJ, *Lectures on Jurisprudence* (Meek, Raphael and Stein 1978); TMS, *The Theory of Moral Sentiments* (Macfie and Raphael 1976); LRBL (Bryce 1983). LJ(A) refers to the jurisprudence lectures in the 1762-3 session, and LJ(B) to those in the 1763-4 session, University of Glasgow.

Two of the major components of that research agenda, as the quote suggests, were: the consequences of the division of labour; and the progress of material well-being (opulence) in a civilized society. Others include (using modern terminology): endogenous technical change, capital accumulation, sectoral disequilibrium, increasing returns to scale, and the functional distribution of income. They were, and are, central themes of economics.

Let me distinguish between two possible approaches to those central themes. The first, the approach of the history of economic thought, is concerned with determining the intellectual origins of these ideas, with relating them to the history of their time of original discovery, and with examining their intellectual coherence. Representative of this approach is the meticulous scholarship of Samuel Hollander's *Economics of Adam Smith* (1973). The second, the approach of the mathematical economists, takes ideas of central importance to classical economics, like endogenous technical change and increasing returns in the production of output, and uses them to characterize dynamic growth paths in a purely formalistic sense. This approach is exemplified by papers of considerable complexity, such of those of Dechert and Nishimura (1983), Majumdar and Mitra (1982) and, only slightly less technical, of Romer (1986, 1987) and Prescott and Boyd (1987).

This book adopts neither of these approaches, for they each in their different ways seem to diminish the energy of the classical approach by being too taxonomic in one case, and too abstract in the other. Our concern is to do something more workaday in approach. We intend to treat the classical approach deriving from Adam Smith as providing a serious research agenda. The purpose of activity directed in this way is to enhance our understanding of how economies of practically possible worlds function and evolve.

II

The book aims to make the material discussed self-contained, and with this in mind the first three chapters – on the classical perspective, allocation versus accumulation, and theories of Smithian growth – develop appropriate background in political economy, comparative economic modelling and modern growth theory in the classical mould. Chapter 1 considers a number of issues which are essential to an understanding of the classical perspective, but likely to be ignored in an age of much narrower specialization when an economist may well never read the Ancients, and might fail to see the relationship between moral philosophy, jurisprudence and political economy. Adam Smith's *Wealth of Nations* grew out of his lectures on jurisprudence to

Glasgow University students; and the treatment of self-love (or self-interest) and justice in *The Theory of Moral Sentiments* has an important bearing on his political economy. The analysis of the evolution of society in terms of stages is something that is often associated with Marx, or more recently with Rostow, Hicks or Bell. However, a serious claim could be made that Smith was the originator of stadial analysis. Our own analytical treatment of this is entirely new, and is intended to extend the Smithian analysis in a novel way. The harmonious aspect of economic activity, the guidance of 'the invisible hand', has been overemphasized in popular views of Smith. This has concealed the extent to which he thought in terms of processes rather than equilibrium. The process of competition, for example, is significant both as an engine of economic growth and as an equilibrating mechanism. Finally, 'vulgar Smithism' would represent market activity as an unbridled free-for-all. It is therefore important to view the market as one of several social institutions for controlling self-love in a way which leads to a virtuous rather than pernicious outcome.

Chapter 2 begins to develop a number of key analytical points arising from these broader issues. Schumpeter, no great admirer of Smith, and arguably a rather poor student of him too, put the full weight of his authority behind the view that important economics was general equilibrium economics. One hundred years after Walras, one might question the wisdom of this. Certainly Smith *is* a precursory general equilibrium theorist, but his greater concern was with processes of growth and accumulation. That point needs to be made, even repeated, because growth theory has been worked at (perhaps too hard) by superior analytical economists – but frequently without illumination. This is a great pity, because probably growth, rather than redistribution, offers the more tangible prospect of welfare improvement in many economies. The shift of focus is therefore from allocation to growth in this chapter. A facilitating device is to deal with growth in macroeconomic terms. This is also in keeping with the aggregative approach to growth in Smith, with its emphasis on social product per head as an index of social welfare. Chapter 3 concludes the scene-setting with a reasonably rigorous modern account and critique of Smithian growth models, and some anticipation of our own methods of analysis.

Starting with chapter 4, new ground is progressively broken. Here, the analysis is sectoral and emphasizes the outcome of a competitive process in which firms are subject to dynamic increasing returns. The focus of attention is on the circumstances in which competitive pressure of the sort analysed leads to cumulative growth. The division of labour, made so much his own device by Smith, turns out to be crucial, not only within the firm but between firms and, by logical extension, between industries. This suggests an important theme for chapter 5. Here, unusually, a complete chapter is devoted to the analytics of the division of labour. This lays the foundation for several technical devices which are used in much of the subsequent theorizing, including the modelling of the division of labour by a technical progress term in an aggregate production function, and the construction of growth trajectories in the social product variable. Chapter 6 takes a step further in dynamic analysis by constructing a classical model, subject to the division of labour, for a comparative modelling exercise in which a Keynesian growth model is the alternative. In chapter 7 the emphasis is on equilibrium values, which may be interpreted as outcomes of a growth process, in a model which introduces two new parameters: the propensity to the division of labour; and the bargaining power of capital. Of particular concern are the consequences that variations in these parameters have for wage and profit rates, the functional distribution of income, and indices of potential distributional conflict, like the ratio of the aggregate wage bill to aggregate profits. Again, the methods used are aggregative. The analytical chapters of the book conclude with chapter 8, which recurs to the sectoral methods of chapter 4. This time more explicit attention is given to the way in which the division of labour modifies sectoral production functions. As a result, a more complete analysis is possible of the way in which increasing returns create disequilibria which generate cumulative growth.

Finally, in chapter 9, we return to political economy. Adam Smith anticipated but did not analyse industrialism. Beyond this stage of economic growth, we have the post-industrialism identified by Daniel Bell. In it, services, which Smith classed as deriving from unproductive labour, are the dominant form of economic activity. What further analysis shows is that the tertiarization of the economy is actually a consequence of the advanced division of labour, with intellectual specialization being crucial to the further growth of a service-based economy. In the same way as Adam Smith convinced the reluctant Physiocrats that industrial activity created value just as much as agricultural, so modern political economy must convince unreconstructed classical economists that services are as value creating as manufactures. We conclude with a relatively optimistic view of the ultimate consequences of the division of labour, and an analysis of social obligation – that grey area of virtuous conduct which goes beyond strictly legal obligation, but can make so much difference to the quality of everyday life.

III

The origins of this book are two fold. Firstly, in one direction, they lie in a period prior to my career as an academic. As a schoolboy, volume 1 of the

Everyman edition of *The Wealth of Nations*, edited by E. R. A. Seligman, came into my hands. I had found it myself browsing through volumes collected by my father, a Glasgow University graduate of the 1930's. The book had been passed to my father by A. Kerr Pringle, his life long friend and his contemporary at Glasgow University, and subsequently Professor of Applied Geology at Strathclyde University (1967–74). The book marker was a Glasgow tram ticket, and the subject – not quite a serious, still less a scientific one to my father, a biologist – was described with mirth in my household as 'Polly Conn'. Well, I subsequently met that lady in person as a student at Aberdeen University, with Kerr Pringle again coming back into the picture as my neighbour in St Swithin Street. The romance started and political economy ('pol. econ.') and I have been together ever since. With an academic prize I acquired volume 2 of the Everyman edition of *The Wealth of Nations* and so started my youthful interest in economics. Today I have the splendid large volumes of the Glasgow edition at my disposal, by now much marked by my own textual notes and emphases. However, the tough little volume 1 of my schooldays, with 'Kerr Pringle' inscribed on the front next to 'Everyman I will go with thee and be thy guide in thy most need to go by thy side', accompanies me on holidays or long train rides, and still provides what is, for me, the most beautiful exposition of the larger part of the truly significant statements about economics.

Secondly, on a less personal level, the origins of this book lie in a long-standing research and teaching interest in the history of politial economy and classical economic analysis, largely cultivated during my long association with the Department of Economics, University of Edinburgh. Sometimes one has to go away to find out what one has been thinking about, and so it has been with this book. The notion of writing it first occurred to me in a delightful year spent in the Department of Economics at Queen's University in Kingston, Ontario in 1981–2. Important to the further development of ideas was a two-semester period in 1984 spent in the Department of Economics, University of Denver, Colorado. It was my privilege to be able to complete a first draft of much of the material of this book whilst on sabbatical at Darwin College, University of Cambridge in 1987–8. I should acknowledge a grant from the Carnegie Trust in 1988 which greatly facilitated the completion of this book in Edinburgh.

Finally, the presentation to many seminar groups of the ideas expounded below has encouraged me in my belief that classical economic growth has the capacity to generate intellectual excitement. Indeed, I am still taken by surprise now and then at the very energetic response one can get to the exposition of analytical ideas which have their roots in the classics! I should particularly mention the useful opportunities I have had to test out ideas in the Scottish

Universities seminar 'circus' on which I have presented many papers on classical themes in recent years. Also of help in the speculative stage of this project were responses to my seminars at Denver University, Uppsala University and the London School of Economics.

I should also acknowledge the comments or advice received, at various points over a period of years, from the following people: Paul Anand, Marcellus Andrews, Carlo Benetti, Adam Crowther, Phyllis Deane, Walter Eltis, Alec Gee, Brian Hilton, Jan Kwiatkowski, Brian Loasby, Tom McCurdy, Geoff Meeks, Dennis O'Brien, David Raphael, Charles Rowley, Donald Rutherford, Neri Salvatore, David Simpson, Andrew Skinner, Tony Thirlwall, Vivian Walsh, Ian White, the late Nat Wolfe, David Wright and Athina Zervoyianni. None, however, is responsible in any way or form for the ideas expressed in this book.

Parts of the material contained in the chapters below have previously appeared in various issues of the *Scottish Journal of Political Economy* and the *History of Political Economy*. I wish to thank the Scottish Economic Society and Duke University Press for permission to use this material.*

G. C. R.
Edinburgh

---

*See Reid (1979, 1985b, 1987a, 1989) in References.

1
The Classical Perspective

1.1 INTRODUCTION

Our emphasis in this chapter, and indeed throughout the book, is on Adam Smith as the central figure of classical economics. Here in chapter 1 we make three principal points, the first two of which are strictly economic in character.

Firstly, we argue that economic systems are in continuous evolution and that this is closely associated with the pursuit of self-interest within a certain pattern of property rights. We need not necessarily assume that exchange is market mediated,[1] though this is of course the way in which it occurs in the system with which we shall be very much concerned, the free enterprise economy. For analytical purposes it is convenient to regard this evolution of economic systems as leading to a sequence of stages, of economic orders or systems. This is the *stadial view* of economic development.

Secondly, we argue that in those stages of economic evolution in which exchange is mediated by the market (e.g. Adam Smith's 'commercial society'), progress is achieved by a kind of competition which is best likened to a *race* or tournament. Economic agents who participate in this competition, be they consumers, producers, merchants or capitalists, do so out of self-interest. Their actions may have unintended beneficial consequences for society as a whole, but this is not a part of their design. This view of competition is contrasted with one that sees it as a kind of *structure* which displays certain optimality properties. The structure of a competitive system in this sense would imply features like all markets being cleared, with firms pricing at marginal cost and factors being paid their marginal value products. We cannot deny that this structure may be the *outcome* of competition.[2] However, it is a mistake to confuse the *act* of competition (i.e. the competitive process) with its *consequence* (i.e. the competitive structure). Indeed the competitive structure need have no reference to a free enterprise economy, for it can be achieved by a variety of planning mechanisms.³ The competitive process is by its nature a market-based activity. One cannot mimic a competition: economic agents do or do not compete, and if the latter, the competition is over. It has always struck the author as a peculiar use of words (be it ever so common) to describe as a competitive structure one in which all competition has ceased.

Our third point is less strictly economic in character. It is that self-interest, to which we have alluded on several occasions already, is not unbridled. It is regulated by justice. Adam Smith in *The Theory of Moral Sentiments* looked at the nature and operation of self-interest within an ethical framework. In it, justice links a social philosophy which respects the preferences and aspirations of individuals with a political economy which sees individual conduct as being self-seeking. Provided self-interest is regulated by justice, as Smith suggests, there is a moral basis for emphasizing liberty. Achieving such a system of liberty is itself an issue of institutional design, and is an aspect of the stadial view of societal evolution.

When J. K. Galbraith (1987, p. 286) recently wrote 'classical economics will endure because it solves the problem of power in the economy and polity', he was not being polite. His claim, on further inspection, was that the endurance of classical economics was attributable to what, in his view, was a variety of intellectual blindness. It consisted in wantonly refusing to see economic power relationships as exercised, for example, by corporate oligopolies, and emphasizing instead the so-called 'democracy of the market place' in which no economic unit has significant economic power, and each is in a sense equally individually powerless. By contrast, Galbraith sees power relationships, as between consumer groups, government agencies and corporations, for example, as being reality, and the 'democratic market' as being an abstract, intellectual contrivance which can be an impediment to perceiving reality. Put bluntly, he would claim that classical economics solves 'the problem of power' by ignoring it.

What would one make of Galbraith's view in the light of the writings of that greatest of classical economists, Adam Smith? Ironically, earlier in his work Galbraith (1987, p. 71) himself had quoted from *The Wealth of Nations* Smith's observations on the tendency to monopolistic price-fixing by cartels and the incentive problems which arise in large enterprises when the management of resources is not directed by the owners of resources. These provide two, amongst many other, examples of Smith's analysis of power or authority. Perhaps it is petty to expect mere consistency in an intellectual, even in the span of 200 pages. More important, possibly, is the fact that others too, apart from Galbraith, would restate the shibboleth that classical economics ignores aspects of reality which are important, including: the exercise of market power in goods markets; bargaining between oligopsonists and oligopolists in factor markets; and the consequences of technical change for growth and distribution. However, this misinterpretation largely arises from imputing what is essentially a *neo*classical general equilibrium view to a body of economic analysis of a rather different construction. Arrow and Hahn (1971), in their now classical statement of this brand of theory, start by making reference to Adam Smith's 'invisible hand' and by suggesting (p. 2) that 'Smith was a creator of general equilibrium theory.' This is a view which has also been endorsed by writers in the history of political economy, such as Hollander (1973).[4] Whilst Smith did indeed provide an analysis of how all markets would ultimately operate harmoniously, and in this sense he was, if you will, concerned with general equilibrium, his greater emphasis was actually on processes of adjustment of the sort that neoclassical general equilibrium theorists only model as a means of establishing propositions concerning the stability of general equilibrium. In Smith it is the process itself that is the competition.[5] Further, this process of competition is part of an analysis of growth.[6] It is with these issues that we shall be concerned, rather than with general equilibrium theory in the neoclassical vein which Galbraith, rightly or wrongly, finds so distasteful.

We turn now to the agenda of this chapter: stadial analysis; the process of competition; and the regulation of self-interest by justice.

1.2 THE EVOLUTION OF ECONOMIC SYSTEMS

The classical economists as a group favoured a stadial view of societal, and in particular of economic, evolution. This regards the development process as being made up of a distinct set of stages or epochs. There may be a measure of continuity between these stages in some, or even in many, respects, but each stage has certain distinctive, qualitative characteristics. Karl Marx is of course best known for his stadial analysis, but there is also one in Adam Smith.[7] Since then writers like Rostow (1960) and Hicks (1969) have revived the notion of a stadial view of societies or economies. In Smith, the stages of development are from hunting through pasturage to farming and finally, in his day, to commercial society. More recently David Simpson (1983), using a classical framework, has suggested that a new stage of society is emerging, namely the post-industrial, of the sort first analysed by Bell (1974).

As Ranadive (1977) has correctly stated, the basic unit of analysis in Smith is society. However, Reisman (1976) perhaps goes too far in arguing that Smith's concern to analyse society in a comprehensive way, considering not just economy but community, authority, status, the sacred and alienation, amounts to sociology. Though we would generally accept that each stage of society should be viewed in sociopolitical terms, when one considers the emphasis in Smith on the economic characteristics of each stage it seems sensible, for the moment, to concentrate on these to the exclusion of the political and sociological.[8] In doing so, we are accepting Smith as something of an 'economic determinist', who would regard economic activity as shaping, or determining, institutions and society.[9]

To be more precise, we shall emphasize here the path taken by social product (denoted Y_t at time t) over time. We do so because there is a tendency in Smith to identify social product, or social product per head, with welfare,[10] so this choice is more than a mere convenience. In later chapters we shall show how detailed classical models of varying degrees of complexity can be used to determine a *growth trajectory* of social product over time, given any specific stage of society.[11] For example, in modelling late commercial society in chapter 5 we have specified an aggregate production function for the whole economy, which is subject to technical progress caused by the division of labour. This can be used to construct a relationship (or, more precisely, a mathematical function) connecting social product this year (Y_t) with social product last year (Y_{t-1}).[12] What we now wish to do is to generalize this idea, saying that for any specific societal stage there exists (i.e. it is possible to construct) a model which will imply a certain growth trajectory for social product. Though more complicated cases are possible, we shall confine attention to equations which link just Y_t and Y_{t-1}. Formally, if we denote the stages of society by I, II, III, ... using the index i, then the growth trajectory for the ith stage will be defined by the equation

$$Y_t = \xi_i(Y_{t-1}) \qquad i = \text{I, II, III} \ldots \qquad (1.1)$$

The structure of the economy in each societal stage will determine the form of the function ξ_i, and specific examples are given in the chapters that follow (especially chapters 5, 6 and 7). Suppose, for the sake of argument, that one identified stage I with feudalism, stage II with mercantilism, stage III with industrialism, and stage IV with post-industrialism.[13] The growth trajectory for mercantilism is indicated by the function ξ_{II} figure 1.1. It has been drawn as a concave relationship between axes of social product this year (Y_t on the vertical axis) and social product last year (Y_{t-1} on the horizontal axis). Also drawn on the diagram is a 45° line which has the property that along it $Y_t = Y_{t-1}$: that is, social product this year is equal to social product last year. If this is true for arbitrary adjacent years it is true for all years. In other words we have a *stationary state*, with no growth, and no decline, in the value of social product. This is an equilibrium value of social product in the sense that this value, once it is achieved in a certain period, will be achieved indefinitely afterwards, in the absence of any disturbing influences. In the diagram, values of social product have an asterisk superscript when an equilibrium or stationary state is indicated, and a subscript which denotes the societal stage. The initial equilibrium value from the present historical perspective is denoted by Y_I^* for feudalism (stage I) and is associated with the equilibrium point A in figure 1.1.

How one emerges from stage I is not something that this book is concerned to analyse in any detail, for in general our interest is to investigate not a sequence of stages but rather certain stages in particular (e.g. stage III, the industrial, where this includes an interest in the beginning *and* end of the growth trajectory defined by ξ_{III}). However, briefly, the argument would be that the institutions of feudalism limited the possibility of growth beyond Y_I^* and created incentives for a new social and economic order. Skinner (1979, p. 81), in commenting on Smith's stadial analysis, observed that the agrarian stage that preceded feudalism had itself led to a 'state of conflict . . . which gave the proprietors some incentive to alter the pattern of landholding'. Once a new feudal pattern had emerged it led to growth (as along a trajectory like ξ_I), but this too was self-limiting, as the previous social order ultimately had been. Typically, these limits are set by institutions, especially those relating to property rights. For example, in the feudal case the laws of primogeniture were an impediment to the sale and division of land (WN, pp. 382, 384; LJ(B), p. 466). Further, tenants were obliged by custom to render arbitrary services to the feudal landlord (WN, p. 393), and the landlord himself taxed his tenants in a way that provided a disincentive to productivity improvements (WN, p. 390). As Skinner (1979, p. 80) has emphasized: 'While Smith did describe the feudal as a higher form of the agrarian economy, he also took some pains to emphasize the limited possibilities for economic growth which it presented; limitations which were themselves the reflection of the political institutions.'

Given the tendency for a particular social order ultimately to lead to stationarity, one must next enquire what consequence this prospect will have for the social order itself. We mentioned earlier how conflict had attended the transition from agrarian to feudal society. Whilst Smith, unlike his contemporary Adam Ferguson, did not emphasize the significance of sharp social conflict, he did not neglect the possibility. Thus Smith, talking of the transition from feudal to commercial society in his own stadial analysis, commented (WN, p. 422):

> A revolution of the greatest importance to the publick happiness was in this manner brought about by two different orders of people, who had not the least intention to serve the publick. To gratify the most childish vanity was the sole motive of the great proprietors. The merchants and artificers, much less ridiculous, acted merely from a view to their own

interest, and in pursuit of their own pedlar principle of turning a penny whenever a penny was to be got. Neither of them had either knowledge or foresight of that great revolution which the folly of one, and the industry of the other, was gradually bringing about.

The historical changes wrought are thus the consequences of individual self-seeking behaviour, but entail essentially *unintended consequences* which may be of revolutionary significance. Smithian revolutions are not necessarily, or intrinsically, bloody. They are however, concerned with a hiatus in the way society is organized. They are conceptual rather than armed revolutions. Much of the growth trajectory of each societal stage will be concerned not with revolutionary possibilities for change, but rather with enjoying the benefits of progressive growth; and therefore it was intellectually sound for Smith to give little emphasis to sharp social conflict.[14] It is only likely to be a feature of a society in the neighbourhood of a stationary state, as at A or B in figure 1.1.

The general argument concerning the demise of old stages and the emergence of new ones would be along the lines that Reisman (1976, p. 14) has suggested: 'To an economic determinist such as Adam Smith, the institutional and normative framework of society cannot simply be dismissed with a *ceteris paribus* assumption: economic activity itself is alone enough to prevent *ceteris* from remaining *paribus*.' That is to say, economic forces would encourage institutional evolution. The detailed argument is more lengthy and can be assisted by the use of figure 1.1.

The ultimately confining consequences of feudalism, some of which we have indicated above, led, as Skinner (1979, p. 81) has put it, 'once again [to] a state of instability [which] was to produce some change in the outlines of the social system'. From this instability emerged a mercantile stage (stage II), which is represented by the function ξ_{II} in figure 1.1. The arrowed step-like lines show one way of representing the adjustment of social product to a new equilibrium level of Y_{II}^* at B. This stage saw the emergence of cities, and the extension of trade to overseas market. The old feudal order, represented by the trajectory of ξ_I, was rejected. Economic forces had sown the seeds of its decline. The great feudal proprietors neglected the maintenance of their retainers (WN, p. 418), preferring to convert the surplus into newly available city manufactures rather than to return it to their retainers. In seeking to maximize a surplus that could now be disposed of for commodities, in an emerging exchange economy, they actually encouraged an increase in productivity by reducing the excessive number of retainers[15] (WN, p. 420) and creating a new class (of tenants), who agreed to a bargain that rents could only rise if they were able to cultivate land which was secure in their possession for a sufficient time to undertake those improvements which would raise productivity (WN, p. 421).[16] As Smith so

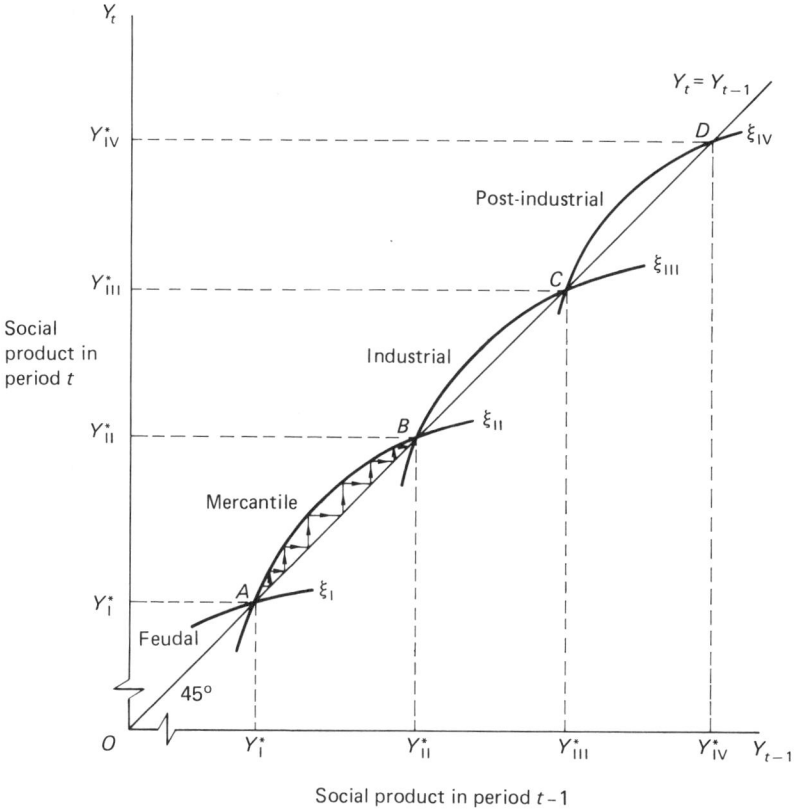

Figure 1.1 A sequence of societal forms (ξ_i denotes the ith societal growth trajectory)

colourfully put it (WN, p. 421): 'Having sold their birth-right, not like Esau for a mess of pottage in time of hunger and necessity, but in the wantonness of plenty, for trinkets and baubles, fitter to be the play-things of children than the serious pursuits of men, they became as insignificant as any substantial burgher or tradesman in a city.' More prosaically, Skinner (1979, p. 87) describes the change arising from the *quantitative* development of manufacturers undertaken in the cities, as leading to *qualitative* changes involving the creation of the institutions of an exchange economy. We observe that technically the relevant equilibrium established by ξ_{II} at A is unstable (with the property $\xi'_{II}(Y^*_I) > 1$), and mercantile society has been started off on an expansionary path by the new order which is reflected in the form of the function ξ_{II}.[17] We have chosen to call this society mercantile, meaning by this the stage between feudalism and industrialism.

8 *The Classical Perspective*

There is an overlap between our mercantile period and Smith's 'commercial' society. Indeed, Smith's first chapter of book IV of *The Wealth of Nations* is entitled 'Of the Principle of the commercial, or mercantile System', and here the two are regarded as synonymous. Smith starts this book IV (WN, p. 428) by saying: 'I shall endeavour to explain both as fully and distinctly as I can, and shall begin with the system of commerce. It is the modern system, and is best understood in our own country and in our own time.' Now the idea that Smith was analysing the economy of his time presents some problems to the modern reader. The reason is that Smith was both a critic of the restrictive aspects – what one would today call the mercantilist aspects – of his contemporary society and an admirer of the workings of competitive forces within it, which we would now certainly not associate with mercantilism. Smith spoke against mercantilism in that it put artificial restraints on apprentices (WN, p. 470), labour mobility (WN, p. 152) and imports (WN, p. 453), and in other ways diverted trade from natural channels, yet he also had confidence that self-interest would overcome 'impertinent obstructions', that competition would prevail. Thus (WN, p. 540): 'In Great Britain industry is perfectly secure; and though it is far from being perfectly free, it is as free or freer than in any other part of Europe.' Clearly Smith lived in a post-feudal age, yet the mercantilist restrictions he argued against in his time negated the principle of economic liberalism which was to be the credo of industrialism. Equally, whilst living at the beginning of the Industrial Revolution, and having some insight into the emergence of a new industrial society, Smith was essentially observing, drafting and writing before this epoch.[18] It might perhaps have been simpler to call stage II commercial society, as Smith did (it would have been the fourth of his stages), but that would have been to invite confusion in the mind of the modern reader with a society which Smith did not fully anticipate, the industrial, and indeed in which he did not live long enough to gain very much direct experience.

At the end of the growth trajectory of stage II, which we call mercantile, a new equilibrium is reached at B where ξ_{II} cuts the 45° line at a value of social product equal to Y_{II}^*. This equilibrium is stable, having the attribute $0 < \xi'_{II}(Y_{II}^*) < 1$. But having been reached, it is in a sense *undesirable*, for it offers no further prospect of growth.[19] However, as it is also stable, deviations from this equilibrium point, in either direction, will set up forces tending to return social product to its equilibrium value. Thus in terms of existing arrangements of society, the level of social product at Y_{II}^* is difficult to augment. This stable but undesirable equilibrium can only be circumvented by changing the form of society. This in turn would be reflected by a change in the form of the relevant function. Hartwell (1976, p. 40) put the matter well when he wrote: 'To Smith the limiting factor in growth was the constitution; the motivation for growth was timeless and universal.'

The switch from mercantilism to industrialism (which can be variously dated from the 1740s to the late 1780s)[20] can be represented formally in figure 1.1 by the switch from ξ_{II} to the ξ_{III} function. Though both ξ share the same equilibrium point at B, the one is stable (for ξ_{II}, the mercantile trajectory) and the other is unstable (for ξ_{III}, the industrial trajectory). Essentially, what we are arguing is that the emergence of a new stage involves converting a state of stable but undesirable equilibrium into one of unstable but desirable growth. The latter is achieved provided society ends up on the 'right side' of the unstable equilibrium – that is, the cumulative growth side.[21] The stable equilibrium at B, once achieved at the end of stage II, is undesirable in that it 'locks' a society previously accustomed to growth into a fixed level of social product which cannot be altered under the organization of this societal stage. By contrast, the unstable equilibrium at B is desirable in the sense that, provided one can initially disturb equilibrium in the 'right' direction[22] (which is not implausible given the general benefits of, and hence desire for, growth) the new society has the prospect of enjoying further growth along the trajectory ξ_{III} until a new, stable equilibrium is reached at C.

Disenchantment with the approach to B along the ξ_{II} trajectory of mercantilism is something that Smith gave widespread voice to in *The Wealth of Nations*. Reisman (1976) has provided a detailed collation of Smith's arguments in favour of a new social order which would limit state power in eighteenth-century Britain (i.e. limit mercantilism). There are five main points, namely that the state: (1) was necessarily ignorant of economic matters, because market information was too extensive to be knowable; (2) selected inappropriate economic goals, like the maximization of treasure, rather than of social product per head; (3) wasted revenues on luxuries and the employment of unproductive labour; (4) encouraged a bureaucracy which was negligent, corrupt and arrogant; and (5) imposed arbitrary laws which flew in the face of natural propensities and encouraged a mentality of evasion and avoidance. The attack which Smith mounted on the mercantile system was not particularly directed at mercantile theorists.[23] However, O'Brien (1975, p. 35) has argued that by constructing a general case for free trade Smith effectively destroyed the theoretical foundations of mercantilism. This is to be considered alongside Smith's account of Hume's price/specie-flow mechanism, as expounded in the *Lectures on Jurisprudence* (e.g. LJ(A), pp. 386–7), which undermined mercantilist balance of payments analysis. That is, it was not by intellectual confrontation with the theory of mercantilism that Smith persuaded others, but by construction of a coherent alternative with superior properties. To the extent that Smith engaged in attack it was, as La Nauze (1937) has indicated, with contemporary popular notions and the current private interests of merchants and manufacturers, as expressed through Parliament, for example. Whether Smith himself brought about the demise of mercantilism, or even hastened its demise, is somewhat at dispute. Fay (1934, p. 315) has argued that Smith went along with what was coming to be. In rather similar vein, Kindleberger (1976, p. 7) is of the opinion that 'his originality was in how vividly and graphically he expressed views which were common currency.' Perhaps the leading authority, Hollander (1973, p. 241), puts the matter with greatest subtlety. Smith perhaps did not literally *forecast* the Industrial Revolution, but in a variety of ways he did *anticipate* it. His remarks were perhaps not startlingly *prophetic*, but on the basis of knowledge at his disposable and his own analysis, he did show real *insight* into the emerging industrialism. It would, of course, be entirely consistent with our view that no one man, and no single book, could change the course of history. It was, rather, economic forces that prompted the emergence of the industrial stage (stage III). Koebner (1959) has argued strongly that Smith was unaware of some of the forces that were leading to the Industrial Revolution. There is a neglect of inventions, of external finance capital for firms, and new ventures, for example. However, Smith's neglect of these factors does not exclude an extension of his stadial analysis to embrace the emergence of industrialism. He died in 1790, and as economic historians tend to emphasize the two decades after 1785 as being the period when the Industrial Revolution undeniably took hold, Smith's neglect to give a detailed analysis of it before it really got started can perhaps be forgiven!

Concerning aggregate measures of output, of the sort that our growth trajectories of figure 1.1 refer to, Deane and Cole (1967, p. 80) have written:

> Before 1745, when total output grew very slowly, the population also changed very little, with the result that average real output rose slowly ... At the end of the century, however, there was a crucial change. After 1785, both total output and population were growing much faster than before, but the former now began to draw decisively ahead of the latter. For the first time, per capita output started to increase by nearly nine per cent per decade – or at more than three times the average rate for the rest of period.

What we seem to have here is a description of near stationarity, as at the end of the trajectory of ξ_{II} at B, followed by rapid cumulative growth, as in the start of the trajectory of ξ_{III} from B. Our stylization is of course heroic, but is indicative of the way in which stadial analysis of the Smithian variety can introduce some kind of formalism 'to lend order and coherence to what would otherwise have appeared to be a chaos of unconnected events' (Skinner 1979, p. 89).

We therefore see societal development proceeding along a secular path like that indicated by the segments of the ξ_i curves from A to B to C to D (and so on) in figure 1.1. Given the increase of welfare that attends growth in social product, the movements from A to B to C etc. are desirable. However, from the viewpoint of any given societal order, whilst C would be preferred to B, the prospect of actually arriving at *C and remaining there indefinitely* is not desirable. Growth of social product provides a means of resolving conflict about how it should be distributed. If, over time, all can have more than they once had, there is less bitterness in disputes over who should have more than whom at any point in time. Further, the experience of growth can lead to expectation of further growth, and a reluctance to accept decline, in a manner reminiscent of the 'ratchet effect' discussed in the theory and measurement of the consumption function. One can provide a more detailed account than above of the factors that would discourage the acceptance of a stationary state at B, as this point is approached. This requires a fuller elaboration of the relevant economic model (as it would for points A, C, D and so on). Under plausible assumptions, as the societal stage B was approached one would expect, for example, a decline in the real wage rate and rate of profit, an increase in rent, and a decrease in population growth.[24] This is all a matter of explicit modelling, of which chapter 3 provides many examples. As Smith would have put it, we have a decline from the 'cheerful' condition of growth to the 'dull' condition of stationarity in the course of the growth trajectory. The approach of the dull state, or indeed the entrapment within the dull state, is an inducement to revolutionary changes of the sort that Skinner (1979) has identified in Smith's writing. The movement from A to B to C and beyond involves rises and falls in the growth rate and characterizes long-term secular movements as proceeding by a *growth cycle*. Shorn of details of construction, this is illustrated in figure 1.2. The assumption here is that new societal forms will be progressive, involving cumulative growth rather than cumulative decline. This essentially requires an initial impetus that moves the economy in the right direction at the point when a new societal order is being established.

Much of modern growth theory has been concerned with equilibrium models of steady growth. However, that great exponent of growth theory Robert Solow (1988) has recently argued that more attention should be paid to disequilibrium departures from the steady growth path. Joan Robinson (1963, p. 7), also a significant contributor to the literature on equilibrium growth models, were she alive today would have appreciated the irony of the similar statement she made a quarter of a century earlier: 'To make the argument

12 The Classical Perspective

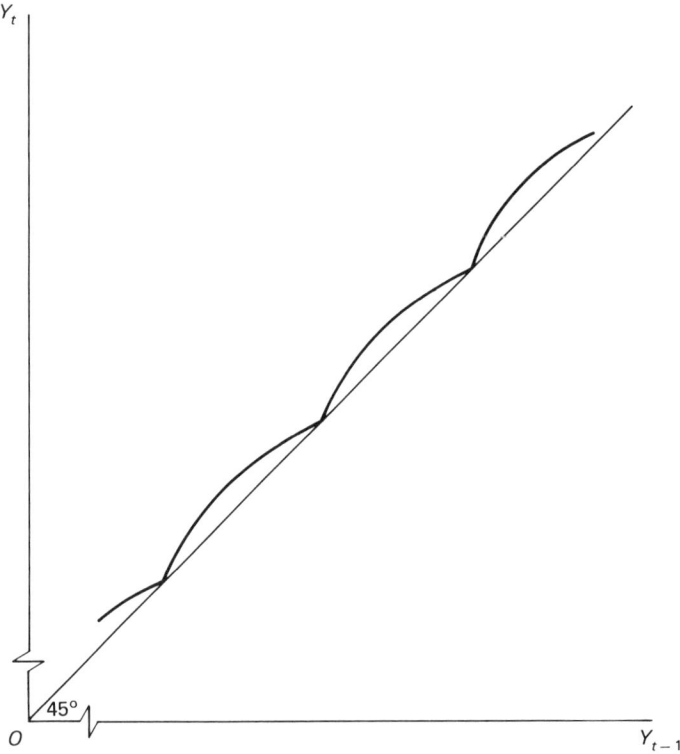

Figure 1.2 A growth cycle in social product

applicable to actual situations, we have to leave equilibrium analysis behind and approach the problem in terms of an historical process, the system continually lurching from one out-of-equilibrium position to another.' This statement perhaps best captures what we have aimed to do in this section. The stadial view of the progression of economies, as we have developed it, certainly does depict growth as lurching from one disequilibrium to another. But perhaps even Joan Robinson, in her desire to develop arguments which were applicable to real situations, expected too much from any growth theory. It will have been apparent in this section that what has been written is but part of a wider historical analysis. The aim of the theory constructed is to help make more sense of what history records as having happened, or what historians would have us believe has happened. Hicks (1960, p. 132) saw the role of exercises of the sort we have been engaged upon as follows:

> All we ought to hope to get from our analysis is a better understanding of

what did happen ... at that time. It is worth our while to construct theoretical models in order to improve our understanding of such phenomena. But the theorist, as such, is only a toolmaker; the explanation of what happened is the historian's business, not his.

Economic theory, and nowadays econometrics as well, are adjuncts to that form of historical analysis which attempts to explain the flow of past events. Stadial analysis provides one such adjunct: the rest is up to the economic historian.

1.3 THE OPERATION OF SELF-INTEREST

We have seen how one of the important factors driving Adam Smith's stadial analysis is the pursuit of individual self-interest. But we have not yet attempted to understand the nature of self-interest. This we will need to do if our subsequent discussion of the competitive process is to be at all adequate. Though *The Wealth of Nations* takes self-interest as an important force in the economy, rather little is said about the motive itself. To get further illumination on this we must turn to *The Theory of Moral Sentiments* (TMS). Although some of the mid- and late-nineteenth-century literature on Adam Smith made rather much of supposed shifts of position, or even inconsistencies, between the two works,[25] modern scholarship now takes the view that the one is a complement to the other.[26] Certainly we shall proceed on this basis, and thus will take the relatively detailed analysis of self-interest in *The Theory of Moral Sentiments* as our starting point.

Smith makes it quite clear that man is self-interested or self-loving.[27] He is 'recommended to his own care' (TMS, p. 82),[28] which is no bad thing, for who is more fit to care for the interests of an individual than he himself? Man is more interested in matters that impinge directly on himself than in those which generally affect his fellow citizens. However, he is aware that viewed from the perspective of others, he has no special claim to favoured treatment. If entirely governed by 'the selfish and original passions of human nature' (TMS, p. 138), man will rate his small gains or losses as more important than much greater gains or losses by his fellows. However, he can by experience learn to make a proper comparison between his own fortunes and those of others. Smith helps to explain this acquired capacity by using an analogy. He considers a scholar working in a study which has a window. Looking out from the study he can see an extensive wooded landscape, all of which is framed within the dimensions of the window. The window is small in relation to the study itself and the objects within it, like the table. However, this does not lead the scholar to be tricked by perspective, and into believing that the table is larger than the church or the oak tree he can see from the window. By practice we, like the scholar, acquire the capacity to compare the dimensions of the study, and the objects within it, with other locations we can imagine ourselves to be in, elsewhere on the landscape. Similarly, Smith would argue, we can correct the natural tendency to judge our own affairs to be more important than those of others. However, this corrective capacity requires cultivation and is itself fragile.

Smith (TMS, p. 136) considers how a European man of humanity would react to the news that a huge earthquake in China had killed millions of people. At first he might feel great sorrow for the misfortunes of the Chinese, and reflect on the transitory nature of life. Then he might start to consider what consequences the disaster would have for world trade and, ultimately, European commerce. However, Smith argues, 'when all this fine philosophy is over' (TMS, p. 136) the man might go about his daily business with no further worry at all. Indeed, it is possible that his own narrow interest might overshadow even the earthquake disaster. Thus in a memorable phrase Smith writes: 'If he was to lose his little finger tomorrow, he would not sleep tonight; but, provided he never saw them, he will snore with the most profound security over the ruin of a hundred million of his breathren.' Given this, that our passive feelings are so sordid and selfish, Smith asks: how can our actions sometimes be generous, even noble?

His answer is that reason, principle, conscience, 'the inhabitant of the breast' or 'the man within', is the judge of our conduct. His most widely used term for this was *the impartial spectator*.[29] One might well ask why it should exist, and why it should emerge as a judge of our actions, and a limiting force on the consequences of our self-interest or self-love. Smith would start by arguing that love of one's own character and of what is honourable is a greater love than self-love. But more important than this, the pursuit of our own self-interest, the gratifying of our self-love in an unrestrained way would make us objects of contempt to other men. Smith gives the example of a soldier who, though possibly flawed in some aspects of his character, may be noble and brave in certain circumstances because of the contempt in which he would be held for being ignoble and cowardly. Rather than put this directly to the test, the soldier appeals to the impartial spectator, to 'the man within'. Like the scholar looking out of the window, he tries to 'locate' himself elsewhere by the exercise of imagination.

Smith himself realizes that there are limitations to the impartial spectator. It is sometimes hard for him to act, as it were, at a distance. Selfish passions can lead him to lodge a false report. If the wrong act is *about* to be performed, in such circumstances, one has no more than a glimmer of the light of the impartial spectator. Once a wrong act has *actually* been performed, we are in retrospect unwilling to think ill of it, and may persist in injustice, defying the judgement of the impartial spectator rather than admitting to having been unjust. But, Smith argues, we can appeal to experience, and through it we can attempt to formulate general rules. Thus in his view the general rules of morality are ultimately founded upon experience (TMS, p. 159). By appeal to these general rules, misrepresentations of self-love or self-interest may be mitigated or eliminated.[30]

Now Smith's analysis of self-love is but one part of a larger analysis of moral systems. In part VII of *The Theory of Moral Sentiments* he provides a twofold classification according to the *nature* of and the *motive* for morality. Concerning its nature, Smith argued that virtue consisted in propriety, prudence and benevolence.[31] The motives were analysed under headings of self-love, reason and sentiment. It would involve too much digression from our purpose to give these categories a full analysis, but it is important to recognize that self-love or self-interest is embedded in a set of categories for the analysis of morality. Here we can only explore these categories very briefly.[32] Propriety involves the balancing of affections or dispositions. Prudence involves actions which ease the body (temperance) and the mind (justice). Benevolence involves the disinterested pursuit of the happiness of others. Whilst different schools have emphasized any one of these over the others, it is Smith's contention that positive virtue is captured by the exhaustive categories of propriety, prudence and benevolence. Motives for morality, or, perhaps more descriptively, the ways in which moral judgements can be made, are analysed under the headings of self-love (which we are equating with self-interest), reason and sentiment. Self-love enables us to distinguish between our own advantage or disadvantage; reason, between truth or falsehood; and sentiment, between the satisfaction or disgust that certain acts inspire in us.

Self-interest, or self-love, is part then of an ethical system designed to provide a theory of moral judgement. *The Theory of Moral Sentiments* is primarily a work in moral philosophy and a very major one at that, which should be considered as entire in itself. It does, however, bear a relationship with *The Wealth of Nations*, though this book too need not be read in conjunction with others to be understood. Perhaps the reason for reading both, apart from the manifest genius of each, is to guard against the 'vulgar Smithism'[33] which would see in *The Wealth of Nations* an analysis of 'economic man' as a rational utility maximizer. Such a view, though espoused even by distinguished theorists like Arrow and Hahn (1971), is faulty.

Self-interest in both *The Wealth of Nations* and *The Theory of Moral Sentiments* is not part of a set of *a priori* axioms. It is a description of one facet of 'man as he actually is' (Coase 1976, p. 546). Now the life of man in society is determined by many forces, of which self-interest is only one. In the market place, however, most other forces fall away. Benevolence has limited significance, or none at all, and the market provides a means of ensuring that cooperation, in the sense of agreeing to voluntary exchanges, is achieved amongst self-interested individuals. These individuals participate in a market order which is only coherent because the market is a type of power structure. Thus Rosenberg (1960) sees the market as a coercive institution which ties the consequences of self-interest to national welfare. Samuels (1973) regards it as a device for achieving controlled freedom, operating within certain societal norms. These norms constrain the operation of self-interest. Thus voluntary exchange, which is a kind of freedom, only takes place within the bounds of legal and moral rules, which involves a kind of coercion. Controlled in this way, self-interest is one aspect of virtue.

Smith's reason for adopting self-interest as an empirically valid postulate of his system derived from those works of the Ancients through to the mercantilists which did likewise, as Hollander (1977) has shown. In discussing Newton's system in *The History of Astronomy*, Smith commended the mathematician's adoption of *familiar* premises (EPS, p. 98). In applying his own methods of analysis to the 'immense machine' (TMS, p. 316) of human society, Smith similarly employed familiar premises, of which self-interested behaviour was one. Narrowing down from human society in general to the economic order, Smith saw the market place as leaving little room for the wider range of social or worldly sentiments, with self-love or self-interest being dominant. We are told: 'It is not from the benevolence of the butcher, the brewer, or the baker, that we expect our dinner, but from their regard to their own interest. We address ourselves, not to their humanity, but to their self-love, and never talk to them of their own necessities but of their advantages' (WN, p. 27).

Finally, one further aspect of Smith's moral philosophy must be referred to. It concerns his special use of the term 'sympathy'. It is of course introduced on the very first page of *The Theory of Moral Sentiments*, where sympathy is defined as the capacity to have a disinterested involvement in the fortunes of others. It is contrasted with selfishness, though it is obvious that Smith regards *both* as being part of the complete nature of man. It is perhaps no coincidence that cruder comparisons of what is supposed to be the one Adam Smith against the other were based on the view that the one emphasized sympathy and the other self-love, each of which is discussed in the first chapter of *The Theory of Moral Sentiments* and *The Wealth of Nations* respectively. However, this impressionable emphasis on the early part of each work is misleading, for sympathy is introduced as a way of explaining how self-love can be restrained. It provides the psychological basis for acts like invoking the impartial spectator. Sympathy works by using the imagination to put oneself in another man's predicament. It enables us to experience horror at the distress of innocent sufferers, and a sense of fitting or proper action when the perpetrators of that suffering are contained or punished. Man, according to Smith (TMS, p. 77), is 'endowed with a desire of the welfare and preservation of society', and sympathy is of use towards this end. Through it, we approve of punishments directed at perpetrators of 'unmerited and unprovoked malice' which may threaten the welfare of society, or in extreme cases its very existence. Conversely we would approve of actions which fostered the welfare and preservation of society.

Wilson (1976) has taken the logic of this part of Smith's work to its limit by arguing that moral judgements based on sympathy provide a basis for the welfare state and consumers' sovereignty. That the two are commended in tandem excludes, of course, central planning. But it embraces many possibilities for mixed economy variants, though the presumption is in favour of market mediation as a means of controlling possible excesses arising from self-love. Wilson (1976) regards public disapprobation as a powerful sanction on those who do not play the game of market competition fairly. What, however, if the public never find out? Then the argument would be that a person contemplating a sharp or dishonest business practice, which might be undetectable by law and veiled from the public eye, would nevertheless be restrained by a desire to be praiseworthy. Such a person would appeal to the impartial spectator, using his capacity for sympathy. The trouble with this argument, as Raphael (1985) has indicated, is that it is not clear how much operational significance the sympathy (or lack of it) of the impartial spectator actually has.[34] Smith gave a vivid account of the torment of a man of bad conscience (TMS, p. 118); but what if a man has no conscience, or ignores the judgement of the impartial spectator? The advantage of Smith's approach is surely that it identifies the very important role that social norms play in human conduct. The huge array of social protocol that most of us handle so deftly is not buttressed by any law, and frequently not by any agreed moral code of the institutional sort (e.g. a religious code, or a professional code of conduct). No law requires us to be polite and cheerful, to help old ladies on to buses, and to send Mothers' Day cards. But there is no doubt that if we all do these things, life is easier to conduct and more pleasant. If a man were to wantonly disregard all these things *and* it were known, no doubt he would attract disapprobation. But nobody goes in pursuit of an individual to check exhaustively on these things, and instances of rudeness or sourness, of neglecting old ladies and of forgetting Mothers' Day are therefore infrequently observed, in the very nature of things. However, to judge by indicators other than the life history of a given individual, like the cordial atmosphere in a restaurant frequented by businessmen concluding contracts, and the high volume of sales of Mothers' Day cards, social norms usually are widely adhered to, and herein lies the strength of Smith's analysis. We must conclude that the impartial spectator is not usually ignored. If he *is*, and the violation of good conduct is damaging to others, then clearly a different method of sanction arises. The sympathy of man is generally with those who are disadvantaged, and in favour of protection of the innocent and punishment of the wrongdoer.

Defining policies of the welfare state as those which are 'designed to assist the less fortunate members of society by the provision of benefits in cash or in kind', Wilson (1976, p. 88) argues that sympathy could provide the basis for supporting transfers by the state. If transfers are merely administered by the state, but essentially voluntary, then the role of sympathy in bringing this about is unambiguous.[35] If transfers are compulsory then the principal weakness of voluntary action, the emergence of 'free riders', is removed. But the elimination of free riders is not the same as accepting that some people, on principle, may not want to give at all, or that many people with largely similar circumstances may nevertheless have very different proclivities to give. Though Wilson does not use the argument, it seems that it would be compatible with Smith's moral philosophy to argue that the welfare state acts on social norms which would meet with the approval of the impartial spectator. Now one person's impartial spectator is not assumed to be different from another. If the device is to make any sense at all, there must be confluence of the judgements which the impartial spectator of each citizen makes. This is how norms emerge. The impartial spectator then provides a way round the requirement for unanimity, and therefore a basis for action. Compulsory state transfers then have the appearance of according with the wishes of an agreed-upon and unique impartial spectator.[36]

Though sympathy can be used to justify transfers, it implies not collectivism but rather individualism. Wilson (1976, p. 93) expresses it as follows: 'Sympathy leads to some degree of commitment to permissiveness . . . freedom for the individual to dispose of his income as he likes, to work where he likes and to choose the job he likes.' This is because sympathy inculcates a respect for the feelings of individuals, their rights to exercise personal moral judgements and to be free from oppression. Thus Smith says (TMS, p. 90) that we have 'general fellow-feeling . . . with every man because he is our fellow-creature'. Fellow-feeling is, of course, based upon our capacity for sympathy. But this sympathy is not expressed towards a collectivity of individuals. Rather 'our regard for the multitude is compounded and made up of the particular regards we feel for the different individuals of which it is composed' (TMS, pp. 89–90). He explicitly excludes the possibility that 'regard for the individuals arises from our regard for the multitude.' This is not to rule out socialization, which is an aspect of belonging to groups or being a member of society. Samuels (1973) argues that self-love or self-interest go hand in hand with socialization – indeed, that socialization works through sympathy and the impartial spectator, these acting as internalized social controls.

To conclude, sympathy provides a basis for individualism. It would endorse certain forms of redistribution by transfer, certainly by charitable acts but more contentiously, as Wilson (1976) would argue, through government transfers to those who are disadvantaged and with whom the impartial spectator has sympathy, including those whose interests have been damaged by aspects of the pursuit of self-love or self-interest.[37] However, sympathy also endorses individual rights, and a danger of too frequent recourse to the state for the execution of transfers and other activities is that it might create a burgeoning bureaucracy, which has the unintended effect of stifling individuality and limiting scope for personal freedom and self-expression. This would tend to imply a loss of sympathy.

1.4 COMPETITION, THE FIRM AND INCREASING RETURNS

As we hinted in the introduction to this chapter, there is something distinctively different about Adam Smith's theory of competition, compared with the prevailing orthodoxy. Though apparently heterodox,[38] the approach has many merits, and in a sense is more advanced in concept than the theory of perfect competition which is dominant today and is intrinsically an equilibrium theory. In the next chapter we shall give a fairly full treatment of the classical analysis of allocative equilibrium, so we shall not devote too much attention to it here. At an intellectual level, Smith did understand the concept of equilibrium systems in a fashion which, for its day, was very deep and precise, as we know from *The History of Astronomy* (EPS, pp. 33–105). There, the inspiration was Newtonian.[39] He also had a philosophical theory of balance or equilibrium (a part of which we have just finished discussing) in *The Theory of Moral Sentiments*. There he explained how, as Myers (1976) has put it, the moral faculties are balanced by the principle of sympathy. In this case, the balance or *equilibrium* cannot be treated with the precision of a mechanical or planetary system. In his political economy, Smith realized that data are uncertain, and our knowledge of cause and effect relationships is very imperfect. For this reason, concepts of equilibrium which are appropriate in the physical sciences do not transfer readily to political economy. Thus Smith was not sympathetic to the formalisms of the Physiocrats, which anticipated later mathematical developments of general equilibrium theory. Commentators on Smith like Myers (1976) have therefore concluded that Smith's manifest unwillingness to organize his theories tightly along equilibrium lines was entirely intentional. Such too would be the view of economists like Kaldor

(1972) and Richardson (1975). Our own view would be much in sympathy with this, but there are powerful minds that have reached opposite conclusions. Schumpeter (1954) regarded Smith's analysis of equilibrium as his best economic theory, pointing the way to the work of his own beloved Walras. Stigler (1976) rated Smith's analysis of allocative equilibrium, implying equal rates of return to resources in various uses, as 'still the most important substantive proposition in all of economics'. Even Hollander (1973, 1987), with his carefully explored analysis of the many facets of Smith, would emphasize allocative equilibrium as the core principle.

We will return to this view in section 2.2, but here our emphasis will be on the *process* of competition, rather than the *outcome* of competition, which is the achievement of equilibrium. That competition is a process rather than a state implies, of course, that we are dealing with disequilibrium. And because it is the process that we are interested in, and which characterizes the typical behaviour of the system, our normal object of analysis is the disequilibrium itself. Smith's first important piece of economic analysis in *The Wealth of Nations* is of the consequences of the division of labour. Its implications for competition are that the usual stable, individual equilibrium for the firm cannot exist, because of the increasing returns within the firm that the division of labour implies. The static equilibrium condition, price equal to marginal cost, of perfectly competitive analysis must immediately be abandoned. However, the point can be pushed further, to consider the consequences of the division of labour between firms, between industries, and finally between sectors. As the division of labour advances, so also does the pervasiveness of increasing returns. In turn, this eliminates the stable equilibria that usually emerge beyond the scale at which returns no longer increase. This, in outline, is the argument.

Detailed technical analysis of the division of labour is deferred until chapter 5, so until then the concept will be handled informally. In Adam Smith's pin-making example, and indeed as he would have it 'in every art', the introduction of the division of labour, with the extra specialization within the workplace that this implies, 'occasions . . . a proportionable increase of the productive powers of labour' (WN, p. 15). Technically, the division of labour within the firm is the cause of increasing returns. This will be experienced in terms of falling unit production costs. Now Smith himself had no 'theory of the firm' as such. This was really not established as a theoretical area at least until the work of Cournot (1838). If we want a Smithian theory of the firm, we cannot therefore rely upon Smith himself. Recently, Negishi (1985) has attempted to provide such a theory using the device of the kinked demand curve.[40] The argument is illustrated in figure 1.3. The curve $p_n \equiv AC$ (where AC is average cost) denotes the way in which 'natural price' p_n falls with output Q.[41] The

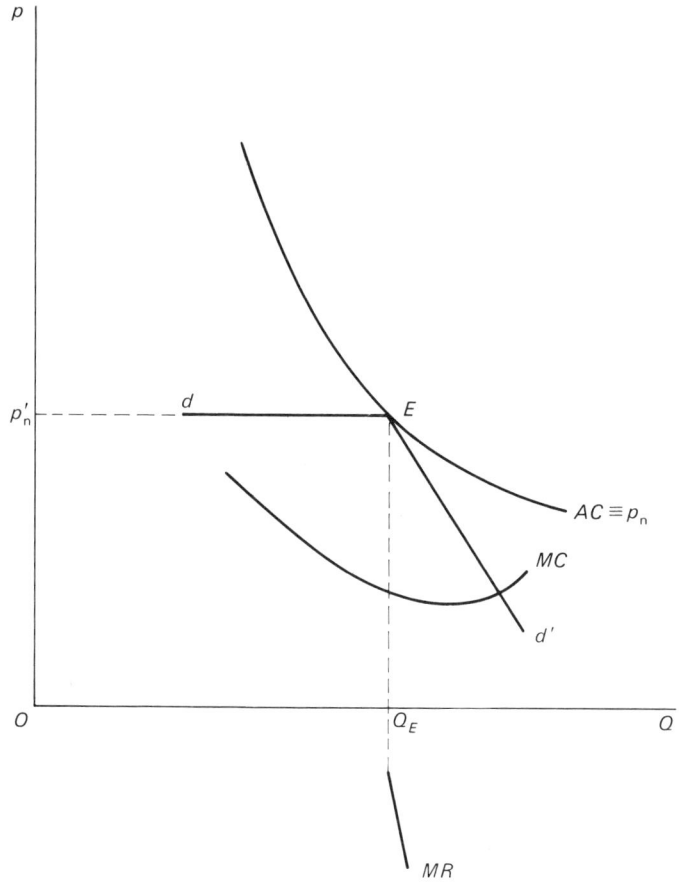

Figure 1.3

natural price is usually defined for some stage of development: advancing, declining or stationary. That is, p_n is specific to some point on a growth trajectory for a societal stage, as illustrated in figure 1.1. As such it should be taken as constant. The detailed composition of natural price will be analysed in chapter 2; here it suffices to say that its three constituent parts are the natural rates of wages, profit and rent. A number of writers, including O'Brien (1975, p. 79), have indicated that Smith's natural price is related to Marshall's long-run normal price. This comparison is helpful in the sense that it conveys the important fact that Smith's natural price is a unit cost of production, taking account of the long-run average values that have to be paid for wages and rents, and the average profit that must be earned if production is to be continued.

As the first step to exploring the consequences of the division of labour for the process of competition, let us follow Negishi (1985) by starting *within* the firms. Intrafirm division of labour, which operates by the division of operations within a firm producing a certain product, will in general lead to a reduction in unit costs. The incentive for such division of labour is the process of competition, which takes the form of a race to capture the extra demand created by cost reductions. Smith gave this explicit attention (WN, p. 748), writing of 'the competition of producers, who, in order to undersell one another, have recourse to new divisions of labour and new improvements of art, which might never otherwise have been thought of'. This sort of progressive reduction of unit cost of production for competitive advantage is given detailed attention in the industrial analysis of chapter 4, where the effect is looked at in discrete terms, with improvements taking place period by period. Within a certain period, the division of labour may be taken as given. Negishi, by contrast, treats the effect of the division of labour as continuous; hence his smoothly falling p_n curve. To emphasize the relationship between natural price and unit, or average, cost of production, the p_n curve has also been labelled AC. In free competition of the Smithian kind, entry is unimpeded; hence equilibrium, if achieved, will entail no profit above the natural rate. Thus average revenue and average cost will be equal (at E) as in figure 1.3. Given the marked differences in elasticity in the upper and lower segments of the dEd' curve, the jump in the marginal revenue curve MR which is characteristic of such a kinked demand curve will be sufficiently large that the segment of MR relevant to Ed' will lie below the horizontal axis. Further, given the general criterion for profit maximization, expressed in inequality terms, Q_E is a profit maximizing level of output.[42] From the viewpoint of the firm, the extent of its market is given by dEd' and the division of labour reduces unit costs according to the schedule $AC \equiv p_n$. Thus the point of contact E establishes the limit to the division of labour which is set by this firm's market. Hollander (1973, pp. 209, 239) has properly indicated that Smith's analysis of the subdivision of labour in terms of plant size was the basis for his 'extent of the market' result. What Negishi (1985) has tried to do is to give this modern expression.

There are difficulties with his approach, however. Richardson (1975) too had noted the relationship between an extended division of labour analysis and the theory of imperfect competition. An *inter* firm division of labour leads to rival firms offering similar, but not identical, goods under increasing returns. Richardson (1975, p. 355) writes that 'Chamberlin's theory of monopolistic competition does presume an inter-firm division of labour the extent of which is limited by the size of the market; to that extent it corresponds much more

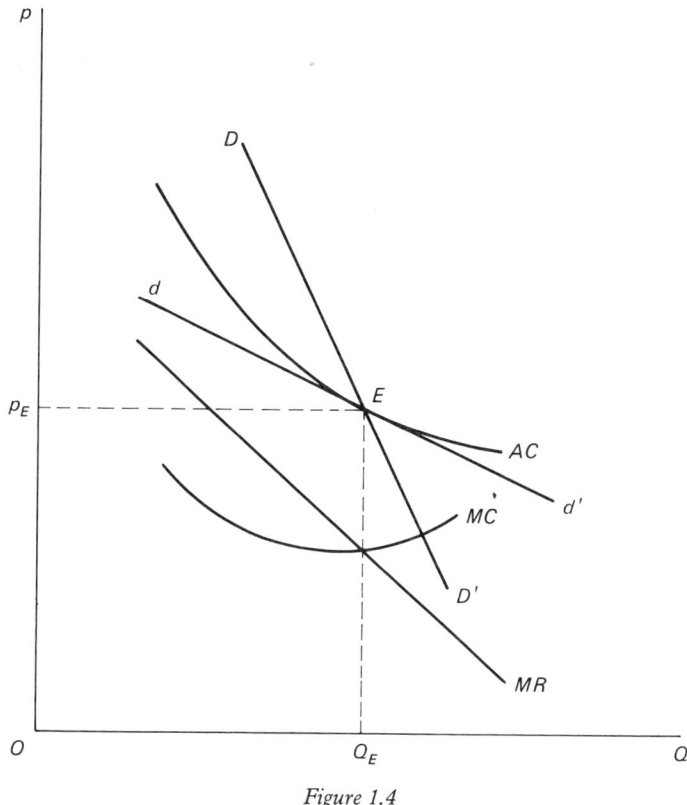

Figure 1.4

closely to Smith's vision than does the perfectly competitive model. Nevertheless, it retains a static character foreign to Smith.' What Richardson had in mind was a diagram like figure 1.4. Here, DD' and dd' denote the *pari passu* and *ceteris paribus* demand curves of Chamberlin. MR is the marginal revenue curve for the average revenue curve dd' (i.e. the inverse of this demand curve). The unit or average cost curve AC is tangential to dd', implying zero supernormal profit (i.e. entry is unimpeded). The close relationship between this construction and Negishi's (figure 1.3) is apparent if one regards dED' as the demand curve 'proper' for the firm. Of course, figure 1.3 relates to intrafirm and figure 1.4 to both intra- and interfirm division of labour. Both devices ultimately fall down, however, because of their static character. They fail to capture the process of competition by suggesting a stable equilibrium of price and output. In chapter 4 this disadvantage is avoided by letting unit cost be fixed within a period, but falling through technical progress between periods.

This traces out a *locus* which lies along a curve like the falling AC schedule. Each point on this curve, for firms which are able to produce up to capacity, represents a current-period profit maximizing equilibrium, by analogy with each of the points E in figures 1.3 and 1.4. This idea of a *moving* equilibrium is probably more satisfactory than either of the types discussed above.[43]

To develop a Smithian idea of process competition, however, one has to go beyond even interfirm to interindustry and intersectoral division of labour. This was the important step suggested by Allyn Young (1928, pp. 533–9). It continues to be the case that the extension of the division of labour leads to increasing returns, but now the consequences of increasing returns in one industry or sector have important external effects, because of the demands thereby created in other industries or sectors. We develop this point in further detail in chapter 4. Essentially it is that the division of labour is both the basis for, and the result of, economic growth. To use a very simple formalism by way of illustration, if T is technical progress, and output is Y, there are two directions of causality. On the one hand, the extent of the market, as measured by output Y, is dependent in an increasing fashion on technical progress: $Y = Y(T)$. On the other hand, technical progress is dependent in an increasing fashion on the division of labour: $T = T(Y)$. In $Y(.)$ causality runs from T to Y; and in $T(.)$ it runs from Y to T. More fully specified, these effects would operate through some form of lag structure,[44] as a basic methodological principle is that cause is prior to effect. A point that Young (1928), Kaldor (1972) and Richardson (1975) do not seem to have grasped, and this simple formalism helps to demonstrate, is that the endogeneity of technical change and the two-way causality between it and the extent of the market as represented by $Y(.)$ and $T(.)$ do not rule out the possibility of equilibrium. In this case, equilibrium (T^*, Y^*) would have the property that simultaneously $Y^* = Y(T^*)$ and $T^* = (Y^*)$.

The endogeneity of technical change, caused by the division of labour, becomes, as it were, internalized within the process of adjustment. This process of adjustment *is* the disequilibrium that Young, Kaldor and Richardson talk about. It may well terminate in equilibrium. Indeed if it did not, one would have to accept either that one had deliberately only modelled a part of the process, or else that one had an unacceptable model of adjustment.[45] Certainly Adam Smith himself saw his process of competition as leading to a variety of equilibria. It established natural price, and natural rates of rent, wages and profit. It also ultimately propelled the economy towards a stationary state.

Let us conclude with an example of the market process that Smith was concerned with, and one which has been rather controversial: the analysis of investment priorities. In Smith's original analysis (WN, II v) of investment priorities, sectors were ranked in the order of agriculture, manufacturing, trading and distribution.[46] He thought that this ranking was also according to the productivities of productive labour. O'Brien (1975, p. 208) suggests that Smith derived his argument from the Physiocratic emphasis on agriculture. However, Hollander (1971, 1973) argues that Smith's apparent 'agricultural bias' derived not from the view that agriculture had an advantage over manufacturers in an *absolute* sense, but rather from the judgement that there were *relative* economic advantages to agricultural investment. For example, the risk was lower. Furthermore, factor endowments and factor prices played a role. Thus with abundant land in the North American colonies, and cheap uncultivated land, investment tended to flow to the purchase and improvement of land. Hollander (1973, p. 281) concludes: 'It would, therefore, seem to be the *market process*, as reflected in the relative price of land which assures that, whilst land remains cheap, the profit rate in agriculture will exceed that in industry, so that investors will prefer the former.' Actually Smith's argument about the priority of agriculture was meant to do no more than caution against the government deliberately intervening in favour of manufactures as against agriculture, when profit rates suggested this was inappropriate. Quite correctly, Hollander (1973, p. 304) argues that there are no logical grounds for suggesting any priority in the allocation of capital if profit rates are equal across sectors – a point Adam Smith would not have disputed. In this sense, Hollander is right to argue that in Smith there is *in logic* no sectoral investment priority. It should be made clear, however, that this is a statement about equilibrium. Smith's analysis of investment priorities was about disequilibrium, and the flow of capital to sectors with relatively high profit rates. Thus investment priorities are a reflection of differentials in rates of profit before equilibrium is established. It is the competitive, or market, process that encourages the appropriate flows of capital.

1.5 NATURAL LAW, NATURAL LIBERTY AND HARMONY

In the previous section we have emphasized the disequilibrium aspect of the market or competitive process. Though Smith actually gave less emphasis to the equilibrium aspect of competition, it is this that has subsequently received greater attention, and this too that is, properly speaking, part of his harmonious view of society. It is in turn derivative of a natural law philosophy, with natural liberty – the right freely to pursue one's interest – being a means of attaining a harmonious outcome. The issues raised in this section can only be adequately treated by a trained philosopher, so we cannot hope to do justice to them in a deep scholarly sense.[47] They are important, however, and we will proceed to examine them partly because they have received the attention of many economists, and also because they help us to understand Smith and classical economics that much better.

Natural law philosophy has its roots in the writings of the Ancients, particularly Aristotle, and can be traced through the writings of St Thomas Aquinas, and the other scholastic writings of the Middle Ages, to the Physiocrats. Quesnay, for example, talked of a *droit naturel* which governed human action and ultimately was above laws made by men, *droit légitime*.[48] However, we know that Adam Smith formulated both his moral philosophy and political economy *before* becoming familiar with Quesnay's works and, indeed, before meeting the man himself.[49] However, through the writings of Protestant natural law theorists, including Grotius, Pufendorf and most notably Hutcheson, Smith would have had one possible source of influence. Perhaps as important was Smith's study of the Ancients themselves, particularly of Roman writers on the Stoic doctrine, among whom Smith frequently referred to Epictetus, Marcus Aurelius and Cicero. Indeed, Macfie and Raphael (1976, p. 7) have identified many passages and phrases from the writings of Marcus Aurelius that have a Smithian ring to them. They concern the benevolence of an all-wise being who conducts the machinery of the universe and brings about cosmic harmony. Smith had himself been a student of Francis Hutcheson whilst at Glasgow University, and subsequently held his former Chair from 1752 to 1764, so the influence from this quarter was inevitable.[50] Macfie and Raphael (1976, p. 6) regard Smith's ethical system as a combination of Stoicism and Hutcheson. From Hutcheson, the influence came through the analysis of benevolence, which corresponds in philosophical terms to the Christian ethic of love. From Stoicism the influence came through the concept of *self-command*, which Smith regarded as necessary for any virtue. At points, Smith himself consciously joined these two, as in: 'As to love our neighbour as we love ourselves is the great law of Christianity, so it is the great precept of nature to love ourselves only as we love our neighbour' (TMS, p. 25). This combination of Christian love with Stoic self-command is described here as 'the great precept of nature' by Smith, and is consonant with the Stoic view of nature as a harmonious force.

Now although harmony arises out of the operation of the law of nature, this does not mean that individual vices and follies are excluded. This point is important, because the Stoic view that good could come out of evil provided the basis for Smith's 'invisible hand' result. In *The Theory of Moral Sentiments* (TMS, pp. 184–5) we are told that, despite the 'natural selfishness and rapacity' of the rich, 'They are led by an invisible hand . . . without intending it, without knowing it, [to] advance the interest of the society, and afford means to the multiplication of the species.' Whilst here, the selfishness of individuals is presumed to manifest itself by an attempt to gain distinctions of class, the argument carries over to the economic sphere. Indeed, there is a remarkable congruence between this quote and the famous passage from *The Wealth of Nations* about the unintended harmonious consequences of an individual seeking his personal gain:

> By directing . . . industry in such a manner as its produce may be of the greatest value, he intends only his own gain, and he is in this, as in many other cases, led by an invisible hand to promote an end which was no part of his intention . . . By pursuing his own interest he frequently promotes that of the society more effectually than when he really intends to promote it. (WN, p. 456)

It should be clear from these passages just how naturally Smith's analysis of the harmonious consequences of market activity, despite individual self-interest, derives from his moral philosophy. It would therefore be quite improper to accept the view popularized by Arrow and Hahn (1971) that the technical analysis of general equilibrium systems casts any light at all on this implication of Smith's moral philosophy. Rather we would accept the evaluation of Macfie (1959) that *The Wealth of Nations* works out the economic case of the philosophy implicit in *The Theory of Moral Sentiments*. In this sense it is a special case – albeit an important one – of a wider ethical system.

The natural law tradition also embraced the concept of natural liberty. In its original form it had the connotation of the freedom which a man enjoyed in a state of nature. In Adam Smith's political economy it meant freedom from artificial restrictions on, or inducements to, trade. It consisted in 'allowing every man to pursue his own interest his own way' (WN, p. 664). Smith particularly referred to natural liberty in the context of the system which would emerge in the absence of intervention. This 'system of natural liberty' was regarded as desirable, in contrast to the baleful system of mercantilism. In a famous passage in *The Wealth of Nations* (p. 687) Smith wrote:

> All systems either of preference or of restraint, therefore, being thus completely taken away, the obvious and simple system of natural liberty establishes itself of its own accord. Every man, as long as he does not violate the laws of justice, is left free to pursue his own interest his own way, and to bring both his industry and capital into competition with those of any other man, or order of men.

It implies not that there is, as it were, no work for the economic system to do in the absence of intervention, but rather that order would emerge through the pursuit of self-interest. This order would be harmonious. An important part of that famous passage is the reference to 'laws of justice'. These laws determine the framework within which competition takes place. They moderate self-interest. Billet (1976) has correctly perceived that *The Wealth of Nations* argues not against all restraints on economic liberty, but rather against *unjust* restraints. Smith is concerned that the pursuit of *legitimate* economic ends be unrestrained by systems that favour certain groups, and suppress others. But *illegitimate* economic ends would be ruled out. As Billet (1976) would have it, justice implies liberty, but not a free-for-all. In accepting justice, defined as that part of the morally desirable which can be attained by public force, one is stopping far short of the ideal of today's libertarians which would see even justice as being market mediated. To Smith, natural justice was derivative from human nature, and normative in content. Positive law was deliberately founded on natural law, and its administration was therefore ultimately intended to buttress natural law. Government, the monarchy or the state is responsible for the enforcement of law,[51] and should not put arbitrary restraints on natural liberty. However, some restraints may be necessary in order to ensure a *just* liberty. Thus it should not permit one citizen or group of citizens to oppress another. Other duties of the sovereign power under a system of natural liberty are the defence of society against aggressors and the undertaking of certain public works. Smith suggested four major reforms to bring about a system of perfect liberty: free occupational choice, which would abolish restrictive apprenticeships and settlement laws; the repeal of laws restricting the transfer of land; domestic free trade, which would involve the abolition of local taxes and customs; and international free trade, which would involve the abolition of mercantile restrictions, duties, bounties etc. However, he was not a freetrader of the sort that later became identified with the Manchester School.[52] Furthermore, as Viner (1927) has detailed in a dispassionately accurate fashion, Smith identified many exceptions to the doctrine of natural harmony. For example, there could be a conflict between masters and workmen over wages; merchants might extract unnaturally high profits; risky ventures might be too readily undertaken; and so on. There is no doubt, however, that these *are* exceptions; the general principle is that a system of natural liberty leads to harmony.

Viewing natural liberty within an allocative framework, Buchanan (1987) has recently pushed analytical argument to the limit by proposing that the allocation of liberty can be treated by analogy with the allocation of any other good. What Buchanan suggests is that individuals place a value on the 'liberty to purchase' another unit of a good. Indeed market exchange can be interpreted as the exercise of a liberty to buy or to sell a good. Buchanan then shows that the maximization of individual liberties in his sense leads to the maximization of the sum of consumers' and producers' surplus. This is one version of the invisible hand result, with its implied socially beneficial consequence following from free, self-seeking, individual action. However, the result is actually much narrower in scope than Smith's, because it has lost sight of the notion of liberty as it relates to a system of moral philosophy. In Smith, there were many aspects of virtue that were not expressed in the market place. Indeed the market was seen as a kind of social control on just one particular moral sentiment, self-love, which within bureaucracy, for example, could have damaging results if uncontrolled. When the market is viewed as part of a larger social system, the concept of natural liberty is seen to be broader than that of simply the right to buy or sell.

1.6 CONCLUSION

Our discussion in this chapter has been wide ranging, and necessarily incomplete as an account of the background to Adam Smith's economics, let alone all of classical economics. However, it intended to do no more than offer a perspective. In developing this perspective we have had an eye very much on the structure and content of the rest of the book. This is its main purpose. It might also serve to give a fuller treatment of topics which are perhaps neglected or underdeveloped, like stadial analysis. Finally, it attempts, albeit from the perspective of an economist rather than a philosopher, to remind the reader that the Smithian position is very broad, embracing a number of areas of inquiry. Though we necessarily go on in the rest of this book, as an aspect of specialization itself, to develop more detailed technical arguments deriving from Adam Smith, it is always necessary to return periodically to the wider view to put this new work into perspective. We must be like Adam Smith's scholar viewing a wooded landscape from a study window. The imagination must be used to view the landscape from points outside the study.

NOTES

1 For example, under feudalism, a well-defined economic system with specific property rights and self-interested individuals, market mediation is relatively unimportant.
2 So it is analysed in the approach to competition adopted by economists of the Austrian school (see also note 38 to this chapter). They describe the *structure* (as distinct from the *process*) of competition as the 'evenly rotating economy', a term due to Mises. However, it is not regarded as a state of actual economies. These, rather, involve various degrees of adjustment to the evenly rotating economy.
3 Including those discussed under the general heading of Lange-Lerner socialism. The planning mechanism is concerned with achieving a desirable outcome which mimics that

30 *The Classical Perspective*

which would *result* from competitions in various markets. It does not mimic the competitions *per se*, and it is these which are the typical situations in markets. Influential statements of trial-and-error methods for mimicking competition in a socialist economy are Lerner (1944) and Lange (1936). For a critique see Hayek (1940) and the very comprehensive analysis in *Economic Calculation in the Socialist Society* by Hoff (1949).

4   Thus Hollander (1973, p. 114) says: 'Smith's formal treatment of value may best be appreciated if envisaged as an attempt to achieve a conception of long-run *general* equilibrium.' The insertion of the words 'long-run' is significant here, for Hollander is also aware of the importance of Smith's process analysis. Thus he talks shortly afterwards (p. 116) of 'the treatment of the allocation *process* in the *Wealth of Nations*' and again of 'the remarkable chapter "Of the Natural and Market Price of Commodities" ' (WN, book I, p. vii) which presents 'process analysis relevant to the complex case' (p. 117).

5   See chapter 4 for the author's own analysis of the process of competition.

6   Growth, of the sort which is impelled by the division of labour, is a principal concern of this book. Chapter 4 explicitly links the competitive process to growth. Later chapters suppress the sectoral (or industry-level) analysis of competition for simplicity and deal in aggregate terms, but the competitive process is still assumed to be in operation.

7   In both LJ and WN. There is the strong possibility that Adam Smith was the codiscoverer, with Turgot, of the stadial approach. Meek (1971), in a fascinating account of his detective work on this issue, dates the joint discovery to 1750–1. Turgot's analysis was complete in respect of hunting, pasturage and agriculture but only briefed at the fourth stage, which Smith analysed under the title of 'commercial society'. Smith appears to have been the forerunner by fifteen to twenty years of the four-stages theories central to the writings of Adam Ferguson, William Robertson, John Millar and Lord Kames. However, there is the possibility that in the jurisprudential, rather than the political economy, literature, anticipations of the stadial approach may be found.

8   Some of these broader issues will be returned to in section 1.5 and, further, in chapter 9. We note here that Meek (1971) has argued that Smith's is essentially a materialistic view of societal evolution, which again justifies our emphasis on the economic.

9   See Reisman (1976, p. 10) for further comment on this view.

10 See Myint (1948), O'Brien (1975, ch. 2), Ranadive (1977), and chapter 7 for further discussion. The older term 'social product' is synonymous with 'national income', but seems more felicitous in view of our concern with the product of various societal forms.

11 See especially chapters 3, 5 and 6.

12 This provides us with a non-linear first-order difference equation (see Chiang 1974, ch. 16). Many variations on this theme are possible. For example, in chapter 6 a second-order linear difference equation in social product is obtained from another classical model which is constructed for comparison with a Keynesian model due to Pasinetti. For the moment, the details are unimportant; the point is that such models can be constructed (for a survey see chapter 3). The treatment of Adelman (1962) is notable for its derivation of an expression for the growth trajectories of social product. It uses a first-order differential equation rather than a difference equation.

13 These categories differ somewhat from Smith. That is not particularly problematic to our analysis as we are really most concerned with the transformation from mercantilism to industrialism (the stage that was heralded in by *The Wealth of Nations*), and the *possible* transformation from the latter into the post-industrialism of today. Whether feudalism and mercantilism are distinct, or significantly overlap, are detailed issues of economic history which we could not begin to address here. Fortunately, it is not necessary to do so in order to convey the sense of our argument.

14 Though as we shall see in chapter 7, the resolution of social product into rent, wages and profit components, particularly if these categories relate to incomes of social classes or 'orders of society' (like rentiers, workers and capitalists), is likely to imply 'distributional conflict'. That is, bargaining will take place to resolve rival claims over the way in which social product is split up. To the extent that rent, wages and profit incomes arise from certain types of

The Classical Perspective   31

activities (e.g. backing a business enterprise, becoming an employee) rather than the *roles* of certain types of individuals (e.g. being a capitalist, or a member of the working class), the intensity of distributional conflict will be diminished, for some individuals will be involved in several activities which cut across rigid social roles (e.g. a man might be both a waged employee *and* a stockholder in a number of firms, not excluding the one for whom he works).

15 Before the development of exchange relations to a reasonably sophisticated level, physical commodity surpluses could not so readily be converted into objects of wealth. An aspect of the display of wealth therefore became the mere scale of the proprietor's operations, as reflected in number of retainers. Many retainers, of course, would have led totally unproductive lives.

16 Needless to say, tenants negotiated as long leases as they could, arguing that the greater the rent increase, the longer the period of time required to implement the necessary improvements to meet the higher rental. The important effect of this bargain was to secure the property rights of the tenant over the land he worked.

17 See Chiang (1974, ch. 16), Goldberg (1958) or Baumol (1959, ch. 13) for a statement of stability conditions for non-linear first-order difference equations of the sort given by (1.1).

18 See Kindleberger (1976), who generally argues against Smith having been aware of the Industrial Revolution, though he doubts whether it is necessary to make this case anyway.

19 Skinner (1979, p. 87), paraphrasing Smith, writes: 'The drive to better our condition, allied to the insatiable wants of man (referred to in *The Theory of Moral Sentiments*) provides the maximum possible stimulus to growth.' If this drive is thwarted by the arrival at a stable equilibrium, the equilibrium reached is 'undesirable'.

20 See Kindleberger (1976, p. 2) for various datings by economists and economic historians of the Industrial Revolution. Rostow's (1960) idea of 'take-off' has analogies with our analysis of the emergence of unstable equilibrium leading to growth, from a stable equilibrium characterized by stationarity. Rostow looks at exports and imports to determine a date for the take-off which started the Industrial Revolution. He chooses the date 1783, which was only seven years before Smith died, and seven years after the publication of *The Wealth of Nations*, a book which had a very long period of gestation.

21 It will be observed that, to the right of the unstable equilibrium of the intersection of ξ_{III} with the 45° line at B the growth is initially cumulative. Towards the end of the trajectory, as C is approached, growth slows down. Being on the 'right side' of the unstable equilibrium at B is important, as falling short of B but still on ξ_{III} would lead to progressive decline. This possibility was appreciated by Smith. It corresponds to the search for a new social order going tragically wrong, and is not an essential error in the vision of a new society (for ξ_{III} could indeed improve well-being) but an error in setting up the initial conditions. Informally, the system initially must be pointed in the right direction. After this, growth is self-reinforcing.

22 That is, to $Y_{II}^* + \epsilon$, where ϵ has a small positive value.

23 Meaning by this writers like Montchrétien, Colbert, Mun, Sena and von Hornick. For a compressed summary treatment, see Gray (1931, ch. 3). Smith did make *some* reference to the theorists of mercantilism. He excuses Colbert in some measure from departing from reason in favouring retaliatory duties by saying (WN, p. 467): 'Mr Colbert . . . seems in this case to have been imposed upon by the sophistry of merchants and manufacturers.' Thomas Mun's *England's Treasure by Forraign Trade* (1664) is quoted in *The Wealth of Nations* (WN, pp. 431-2) on the analogy between foreign trading and the time from seed to harvest in agriculture, and Smith wrote (LJ (A), p. 381) of mercantilist theory that 'Mr Mun was the first who formed it into a regular system – many writers have since adopted it.' Other mercantilists directly mentioned include Joshua Gee, author of *The Trade and Navigation of Great-Britain Considered* (1729) (WN, p. 392).

24 For formal modelling of this see, for example, Samuelson (1978).

25 This was especially true of some of the German literature which chose to stylize *The Theory of Moral Sentiments* as a book which suggested social conduct was driven by sympathy, whilst *The Wealth of Nations* suggested it was driven by egoism.

26 See the treatment by Macfie and Raphael (1976, pp. 20-5) in the Glasgow edition of TMS. A more modern view than the superficial German *Umschwungstheorie* would be that moral

32 The Classical Perspective

judgements could be explained in terms of sympathy, but motives to action are governed in other ways and, amongst other things, by self-interest.

27 In this context, self-interested and self-loving behaviour are regarded as synonymous.

28 Indeed, later Smith appeals (TMS, p. 272) to the Stoic philosopher Zeno for the view that every animal is recommended to its own care and endowed with the principle of self-love.

29 Thus 'the natural misrepresentations of self-love can be corrected only by the eye of this impartial spectator' (TMS, p. 137).

30 In modern parlance, one would say that Smith was providing an analysis of the development of conscience. Raphael (1985, ch. 3) has compared Smith's attempt favourably with Freud's later psychoanalytic theory. The advantage of Smith's approach is that it embraces a wider range of influences than Freud's. In the latter, parental attitudes are emphasized, whereas in the former these are put alongside other important influences like teachers, schoolfellows and neighbours.

31 Smith also recognized licentious systems (TMS, part VII, ch. IV), though they were regarded as pernicious. He introduced it mainly to take issue with Bernard Mandeville's *The Fable of the Bees: or, Private Vices, Publick Benefits* (1714).

32 A fuller analysis, written from the perspective of an economist, is contained in Skinner (1979, ch. 3).

33 A term due to Samuels (1973).

34 The impartial spectator may remove doubts about partiality of one's judgement, but may not assist in moral choices between a variety of relatively good, or relatively bad, options. As Raphael (1985, p. 40) puts it: 'If your attitude is hesitation between conflicting goods, each of them affording some valid ground for choice, it does not help to know that the impartial spectator sympathizes.' Thus the impartial spectator assists objectivity, but not moral choice. Indeed, it is not entirely clear that the approval of the impartial spectator must entail any form of moral guidance, for it may be based on other grounds, such as the aesthetic or the intellectual (see Raphael 1985, p. 41).

35 The simplest case, voluntary transfers through charities, is obvious. They afford direct, individual means of expressing sympathy. Some might argue that the transfer mechanisms may not be as efficient as when the state is involved. It should be said that this justification of transfers on supposed Smithian grounds would be regarded as a very controversial position by many Smithian scholars.

36 Sugden (1986) has a different view: that norms, once established, can acquire moral force, but the establishment of such norms can be a process innocent of moral considerations. In our case, moral judgement is the starting point, and norms agreeable to the impartial spectator reflect this.

37 That is, a basis is laid for payment of compensation, in certain cases (e.g. where markets have failed to provide a compensatory mechanism which is litigable).

38 Though certainly not to economists of the Austrian school, i.e. followers of the economic writings of Menger, Böhm-Bawerk, Hayek, Mises, Rothbard and Kirzner – to select some of the major figures.

39 See Skinner (1972) for an analysis of the essay on astronomy as an exercise in philosophical history, which seems to me to put this work in its proper setting. The essay on astronomy may have been an inspiration for Smith's later system building (or model building as we say today) based on a limited number of premises, but I would dispute that the Newtonian system itself (or any earlier cosmological theory) provided an appropriate analogy for the working of an economic system. In this respect, I am at one with the conclusion of Myers (1976), that attempts by philosophers and political economists to establish a *close* connection between Newtonian principles and Smith's analysis of society are misconceived.

40 See Reid (1981) for a detailed account of the origins and development of this model.

41 This falling natural price curve is somewhat contentious, for it is normally drawn as a horizontal straight line (as in O'Brien 1975, ch. 4). When it is, however, there is no doubt that intrafirm division of labour effects are being ignored. That is, the horizontal natural price curve is relevant to a *given* division of labour.

42 See the discussion in Reid (1981, ch. 2).
43 It perhaps best represents the sort of conceptualization that Young (1928, p. 535) had in mind.
44 For example, $Y = Y(T, T_{-1}, T_{-2}, \ldots)$ and $T = T(Y, Y_{-1}, Y_{-2}, \ldots)$, which implies a distributed lag structure on both the technical progress term and the output term. T might be an index of productivity advance, and Y the value of output. Of course, other measures are possible, but that does not affect the illustration.
45 In the sense that explosive disequilibrium behaviour is not typical of most economic systems, though a local tendency to increasing disequilibrium may be.
46 Smith's argument was really empirical. Even today it appears to be well confirmed by facts. See the figures in Nusbaumer (1987, p. 83).
47 For an introduction to such an approach by an eminent moral philosopher, see Raphael (1985), and the more exacting treatment in Macfie and Raphael (1976), this being the introduction to the Glasgow edition of *The Theory of Moral Sentiments*.
48 See Gray (1931, pp. 1-105) for the necessary background from Greece and Rome, through the Middle Ages, to the Physiocrats.
49 Smith had originally intended to dedicate *The Wealth of Nations* to Quesnay, who had acted as physician to the Duke of Buccleuch during a serious illness in Paris in 1766. The Duke was under Smith's tutelage during a Grand Tour of Europe.
50 Indeed, in his early incumbency of the Chair of Moral Philosophy, Smith had even tried (unsuccessfully as it turned out) to emulate Hutcheson's lecturing style.
51 See chapter 5 for Smith's argument in favour of this. He would not go so far as arguing that law and order should be subject to market provision.
52 See Grampp (1960, ch. 2).

2
Allocation versus Accumulation

2.1 INTRODUCTION

This chapter seeks to contrast two important themes in Adam Smith's economic analysis. In the first, the consequences of competition are viewed as equilibrating, with the outcome of the process of equilibration being socially desirable.[1] In the second, the stress is on growth and accumulation. Competition is in the nature of a contest and the economy is regarded as being propelled forward by technical progress, the driving force of which is the division of labour. The former view is emphasized by authorities like Samuel Hollander (1973) and given even-handed treatment by scholars like Andrew Skinner (1979). The latter view is emphasized by figures like George Richardson (1975) and Nicholas Kaldor (1985), who characteristically direct attention to the forces making for disequilibrium in a growing capitalist economy.

Whilst suggesting no inherent inconsistency between these two stances – for they are indeed compatible, and each in its own right is important and legitimate – we shall argue in this chapter that an emphasis on accumulation is now appropriate. It is by far the most underdeveloped part of Smith's research programme. Furthermore the process of accumulation, rather than that of optimal allocation, offers the greatest potential insight into prospects for material improvement in society.

As Skinner (1979, ch. 7) indicates so clearly, Smith's view of the economy has both sectoral (or microeconomic) and aggregate (or macroeconomic) aspects. In this chapter we shall start at the sectoral level, introducing matters of concern in later parts of the book, most notably in chapters 4 and 8. Though the view we shall advance is that sectoral analysis is ultimately what one should aim to employ, there is no doubting the advantages of the aggregate approach

36 *Allocation versus Accumulation*

for isolating specific theoretical features, like the consequences of increasing the extent of the division of labour. This issue is explored using aggregate models in chapters 6 and 7.

2.2 EFFICIENT ALLOCATIVE EQUILIBRIUM

In a Smithian system of free competition in which economic agents seek their own interests and factors of production (including enterprise) are mobile, rent, wages and profit will be determinate. In the first instance we shall develop this analysis for a single market. Later, we shall move from this partial equilibrium analysis to general equilibrium analysis.

Following Dasgupta (1960), we need an appropriate interpretation for what Smith called the 'real price'. It will be the 'price in labour'. Denoting the contribution to price of wages by w, of rent by r and of profit by π, then

$$\frac{w + r + \pi}{\bar{w}} \tag{2.1}$$

will denote the amount of labour that can be purchased from the sale of a unit of a commodity with nominal price equal to $w + r + \pi$. In (2.1) $\bar{w}$ is an appropriate index used to make this conversion from nominal to real values. Dasgupta suggests it can be identified with the subsistence wage, reasoning that this measure of wages per unit of labour provides a suitable invariant index. In this sense $\bar{w}$ is different from a *numéraire*, which merely establishes relative values. By contrast, $\bar{w}$ establishes absolute values and permits comparisons of value to be made over time and space (Hollander 1973, pp. 127–9). In his original treatment, Dasgupta (1960) argued that $\bar{w}$ was fixed, but later (1961) he appeared to be shifting his ground. It seems to this author that his later argument is in reality about a quite different issue, namely the possibility of growth raising wages above the subsistence level almost indefinitely. This we would not dispute. But what is missing from consideration by Dasgupta is the possibility of defining subsistence in a socially determined way, with $\bar{w}$ being subject to some sort of 'ratchet effect', rising over time, but never falling. We will not attempt here to solve index number problems of the sort suggested by this paragraph. By and large, relative prices will not been important part of the analysis of this book, which deals for the most part in aggregate variables. If price equals the cost of production, and is therefore determined in each market by an expression like (2.1), then $\bar{w}$ *facilitates* the derivation of relative prices but is not essential to it, as we know from modern marginal analysis.

If we aggregate across markets, given a constant $\bar{w}$ (or, more generally, a *determined* $\bar{w}$), then real national income, or the real value of social product, may be written

$$\frac{\Sigma(w + r + \pi)}{\bar{w}} = \frac{\Sigma w + \Sigma r + \Sigma \pi}{\bar{w}} = \frac{W + R + \Pi}{\bar{w}} \tag{2.2}$$

where W, R and Π are aggregate wages, rent and profit, respectively. Thus we have a way of measuring the magnitude of, and hence real changes in, social product. We would not today use Smith's method, but we would still wish to use the concept of real social product, and to compare its various values along a growth trajectory. This, however, is to anticipate the aggregate framework of chapters 5, 6 and 7. The important point is that by the choice of an appropriate index, value (as Dasgupta 1985 would have it) is expressed as an absolute magnitude and not a ratio in the classical framework. This absolute value is always in relation to the index chosen.

Now let us look further at the decomposition of value, as in (2.1), into wage, rent and profit components. We are back at the individual market level, with p referring to the price of one unit of a commodity. Smith distinguished between the *natural* rates of rent, wages and profit (denoted here r_n, w_n and π_n) and the *market* rates of rent, wages and profit (denoted here r_m, w_m and π_m).[2] Natural rates are determined by long-run considerations, and may be regarded as given in the short period. Let us make this assumption provisionally. Market rates deviate from natural rates according to the play of the forces of supply and demand. In Smith, demand has a special connotation. It is *effectual demand*, meaning the demand of those willing to pay the natural price. Supply in the short period is fixed. It implies a totally inelastic (vertical) market supply schedule. But supply is dependent on capital, labour and land inputs, and should these factors shift, then supply will shift. A good is *usually* sold at the market price p_m, which in general will deviate from the natural price. Given that rent, wages and profit are also market determined, the typical situation is

$$p_m = r_m + w_m + \pi_m \tag{2.3}$$

with all magnitudes being *market* magnitudes. Equation (2.3) represents the typical situation in actual markets. We now wish to investigate the way in which the natural price will emerge, this being

$$p_n = r_n + w_n + \pi_n \tag{2.4}$$

The natural price and the natural rates of rental, wages and profits are to be thought of as average values in a particular state of societal organization (or, as we put it in chapter 1, 'societal stage'). Dmitriev (1904) was the first to show in a mathematical sense how a valid decomposition of natural price could be

38 Allocation versus Accumulation

performed: essentially because prices of intermediate commodities could in turn be so decomposed. Dmitriev's formulation was deficient, however, as Larsen (1977) has shown, in its neglect of the rental component. Here we proceed with the full decomposition of (2.4). In Smith, natural prices (or rates of wages etc.) constituted 'centres of gravity' about which market values fluctuated.[3] He had therefore the concept of 'negative feedback' in market adjustment, meaning that when natural and market prices were out of line the corrective economic forces always moved market prices in the proper *direction* (though not necessarily by the required *amount*). His argument may be illustrated by reference to figure 2.1. Expressed formally, the relationship between market supply S, effectual demand D, market price p_m and natural price p_n is

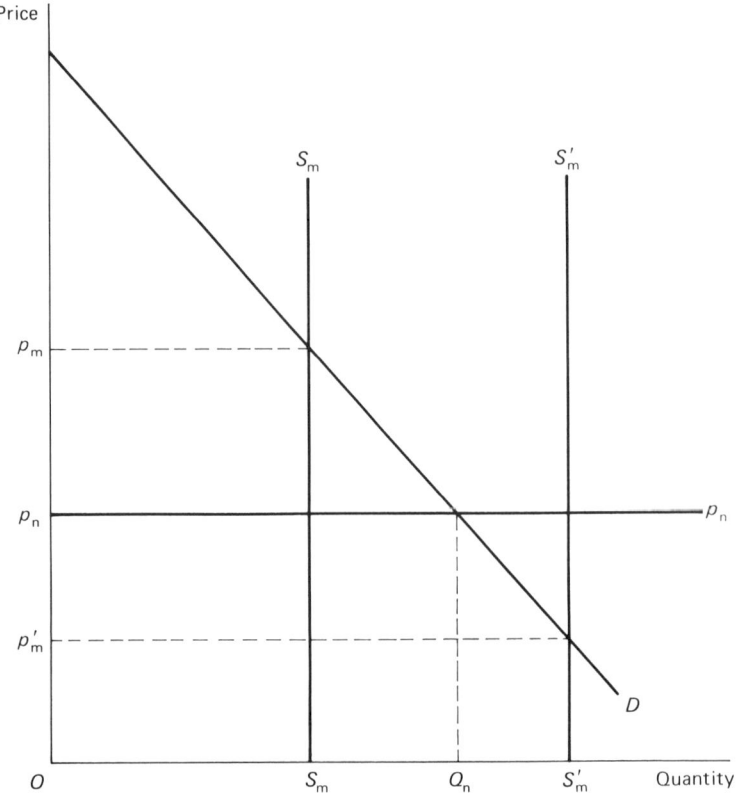

Figure 2.1 Market prices p_m and natural price p_n

$$p_m \gtreqless p_n \text{ as } D \gtreqless S \tag{2.5}$$

Whilst Smith gave little attention to demand compared with his mentor Francis Hutcheson, we know from the scholarship of Hollander (1973, ch. 4) that Smith did indeed make use of a demand schedule such as D in figure 2.1 and was aware of such niceties as variations in the elasticity of demand, and shifts of, as opposed to shifts along, the demand schedule. The schedule D is really a set of potential effectual demands. A specific one has been picked out for a certain natural price p_n, and is indicated by Q_n on the horizontal axis. Those willing to pay the price p_n for the commodity generate a total or effectual demand at that price of Q_n. If market supply is less than effectual demand (e.g. as in the diagram $S_m < Q_n$) then the immediate effect is to increase market price above natural price (to p_m). This arises not simply from competition in the abstract, but literally from 'a competition' between the surfeit of customers who wish to acquire the good. Their willingness to compete depends upon influences like wealth and the perceived luxuriousness of the good. If market supply exceeds effectual demand (e.g. with $S'_m > Q_n$ as in the diagram) another competition will emerge, this time between sellers. They are seeking to entice more customers to buy the good than would do so at the natural price. It can only be done by reducing market price below the natural price (i.e. $p'_m < p_n$ in the diagram). Notice in both these procedures the active price-setting roles taken by traders.

However, this is to emphasize temporary equilibrium adjustment by variations of the market price above or below the natural price. It is an extreme form of partial equilibrium analysis with price variations clearing the market, and considerations of market linkages being ignored. Let us first extend the analysis to further market linkages. If $p_m > p_n$, the factors supplying the good will share in a positive surplus above their natural rates of

$$p_m - r_n - w_n - \pi_n > 0 \tag{2.6}$$

Assuming, as is sensible, positive relationships between factor supplies and their rates of remuneration, a consequence of the surplus indicated by (2.6) is that greater amounts of factors will be channelled towards the production of this good, for which market price exceeds the natural price. This will have two consequences. Firstly, market rates of rent, wages and profit will tend to be reduced in the markets for the appropriate types of land, labour and capital. Secondly, through what we would now call a production function relationship, the augmentation of factors in turn augments the commodity supply, bringing supply closer to effectual demand. As a consequence, reduced competition amongst the diminished number of disappointed customers leads to a lower market price. This process continues until the supply is equal to effectual demand. If the converse inequality to (2.6) held, factors would be withdrawn from the relevant markets, and their market rates of remuneration would rise in the face of this diminution in supply. The reduced availability of these factors would lead to reduced commodity supply, and suppliers of the commodity would need to compete less vigorously to find more customers than would arise at the natural price. The process continues until commodity supply has been reduced to the level of effectual demand. The adjustments of factor supplies, commodity supply, and the movements of market price and market rates of rent, wages and profit described above, are all part of the process of competition. Notice that equilibrium is achieved by the competition of suppliers or customers to find an equilibrating market price in the short run, but that it is variations in *supply* that achieve equilibrium in the long run.

The process of competition is endemic, and practically speaking there are almost invariably disturbances that keep this process alive. There is always a 'target seeking' character to the process, but the speed at which movement towards the targets of natural price and natural rates of rent, wages and profit occurs depends on the flexibility of the system. Thus two factors contribute to keeping *natural* and *market* values distinct. Firstly, disturbances to the market may be caused by a new pattern of market possibilities, like: new commodities; alternative employment opportunities;[4] the availability of new land; and the right to engage in previously proscribed economic activities. One must not neglect to mention that an aspect of a new pattern of market possibilities is the discovery that something is no longer worth doing (e.g. producing an outmoded fashion good, training in an obsolescent skill). This situation too is an aspect of a new pattern and will stimulate market activity, or a process of competition. Secondly, impediments to trade can make the process of competition protracted. Smith's free competition is not like perfect competition in all its dimensions (e.g. it permits price-making behaviour by economic agents), but it does have one crucial characteristic in common – the free mobility of factors of production. Restrictions to such mobility can take many forms: monopoly, trade secrets, market privileges,[5] apprenticeships, trade unions, trade associations and professional associations. These two factors which contribute to the process of competition are 'observationally equivalent', but can nevertheless be broadly interpreted as signs of good health and bad health, respectively, in the way competition functions. In the first case market activity is a healthy sign of adaptation to new circumstances. In the second case, market activity is an unhealthy sign of trying to circumvent artificial restrictions to the mobility of resources. Effectively it slows down the process of competition. Only in special circumstances, as indicated by Hirschman (1970), is this likely to be beneficial.

In the course of a complete growth trajectory the consequences of innovations can be substantial and one would expect the natural values of variables like price and the wage rate to be themselves subject to change. For example, over the full growth trajectory from cumulative expansion to the stationary state one would expect the natural wage to rise and then fall, though perhaps not to as low a level as it attained at the end of the last stage of society. All this is best treated in terms of long-run secular growth. Here the quantity adjustments by which the natural price is attained are shorter-run effects, with the natural price itself being a datum. Such adjustments are the stuff of normal competitive market activity and are at the core of Adam Smith's allocative analysis. Papola (1967) characterizes this part of Smith's analysis as a partial, comparative-static system of equilibrium, and this is surely correct. Blaug (1968) too has favoured the partial equilibrium interpretation. To express it formally one would write necessary and sufficient conditions for market equilibrium[6] as follows:

$$
\begin{aligned}
S &= D \\
p_m &= p_n \\
w_m &= w_n \\
r_m &= r_n \\
\pi_m &= \pi_n
\end{aligned}
\qquad (2.7)
$$

It follows that when these conditions are satisfied we have

$$p_m = w_m + r_m + \pi_m = w_n + r_n + \pi_n = p_n$$

which is the equivalence of market and natural price not only in terms of levels, and hence in terms of labour, but also in terms of constituent parts with respect to rates of wages, rent and profit. This equivalence of p_m and p_n once the process of competition has worked itself out leads to a desired allocation of resources. It is also a *desirable* allocation of resources in the sense that if *all* markets are subject to those forces of competition which have been analysed here for just one market, the overall allocation of resources is optimal from the viewpoint of society as a whole, for competition will act to equalize rates of return on resources in various uses. This is Adam Smith's invisible hand result. The pursuit of private interest leads to a public benefit: the most efficient allocation of the resources of society. This is what we would call today a 'general equilibrium' result. The efficient allocation of resources as between all markets is a theme which has become important since the writings of Walras. Writers like Schumpeter[7] and Hollander[8] would regard Smith's major contribution as being the early statement of how a capitalist economy achieves this. They would characterize this general equilibrium as being a *set* of conditions such as (2.7).

42 *Allocation versus Accumulation*

2.3 A SIMPLE SECTORAL MODEL

The simplest way in which to illustrate the general equilibrium approach is to concentrate on a very elementary two-sector case as in Walsh and Gram (1980). Prices referred to here will be *natural* prices, and the allocative problem will be assumed to have been solved, in the sense that the market process referred to above has been completed and market prices have been brought into correspondence with natural prices. Suppose there are just two commodities, corn and iron, with unit prices denoted p_C and p_I and quantities denoted y_C and y_I. Then with no supernormal profit the allocative equilibrium has *price relations* of the form

$$p_C a_{CC} + p_I a_{IC} = p_C$$
$$p_C a_{CI} + p_I a_{II} = p_I \tag{2.8}$$

where a_{IC} denotes the amount of iron required to produce one unit of corn, a_{CC} the amount of corn required to produce one unit of corn, a_{CI} the amount of corn required to produce one unit of iron, and a_{II} the amount of iron required to produce one unit of iron. Equations (2.8) are best thought of as unit cost equations. Thus $p_C a_{CC}$ is the cost of corn to produce one unit of corn, and $p_I a_{IC}$ is the cost of iron to produce one unit of corn. The total cost of producing one unit of corn, using both corn and iron, is therefore $p_C a_{CC} + p_I a_{IC}$. Corresponding to this set of price relations is a set of *quantity relations*

$$a_{CC} y_C + a_{CI} y_I = y_C$$
$$a_{IC} y_C + a_{II} y_I = y_I \tag{2.9}$$

The left-hand side of the first equation indicates the amount of corn required in corn production ($a_{CC} y_C$) and in iron production ($a_{CI} y_I$), implying a total amount of y_C. Similarly, the left-hand side of the second equation denotes the amount of iron required in corn and iron production, this being equal in sum to y_I. What this pair of relationships (2.8) and (2.9) illustrates is an allocative equilibrium which rules out the possibility of growth and accumulation. The system merely reproduces itself period by period. Implied in the natural prices of (2.8) are natural rates of wages, rent and profit, but these are just sufficient to keep factors supplied at the requisite level for producing amounts of corn and iron that satisfy effectual demand. Surplus, and hence the possibility of *capital accumulation* (or investment), arises when the quantity relations of (2.9) take the form

$$a_{CC} y_C + a_{CI} y_I < y_C$$
$$a_{IC} y_C + a_{II} y_I < y_I \tag{2.10}$$

If this is the case, then corresponding to the physical surpluses of corn and iron

Allocation versus Accumulation 43

indicated by the inequalities of (2.10) are 'value surpluses' in the price relations, which involve re-expressing the equalities of (2.8) by inequalities of the form

$$p_C a_{CC} + p_I a_{IC} < p_C$$
$$p_C a_{CI} + p_I a_{II} < p_I$$
(2.11)

The existence of surpluses, whether identified by the quantity (2.10) or the price (2.11) relations, leads us away from issues of allocation to possibilities of accumulation and growth. Taking the above inequalities as our starting point, the next section will show how these ideas can be expressed formally.

2.4 ACCUMULATION AND GROWTH

We have seen from the set of quantity relations in (2.10) how a surplus economy may be defined. One may now ask how this surplus is disposed of. The way in which growth is best promoted is by using the surplus entirely for capital accumulation (i.e. investment). If growth completely absorbs the surpluses, we can rewrite (2.10) as

$$a_{CC} y_C (1 + g_C) + a_{CI} y_I (1 + g_I) = y_C$$
$$a_{IC} y_C (1 + g_C) + a_{II} y_I (1 + g_I) = y_I$$
(2.12)

where g_C and g_I are the growth rates in the corn and iron sectors respectively. We note that for a technology of the sort we have been presenting, with constant returns to scale, the situation of unequal growth rates between sectors ($g_C = g_I$) could not be sustained.[9] We shall return to this point in a more technical context in chapter 3. However, part of the surplus might be absorbed in 'luxury consumption' of corn and iron, which may be denoted $\lambda_C y_C$ and $\lambda_I y_I$. Then (2.12) may be modified to embrace this possibility, giving

$$a_{CC} y_C (1 + g_C) + a_{CI} y_I (1 + g_I) = (1 - \lambda_C) y_C$$
$$a_{IC} y_C (1 + g_C) + a_{II} y_I (1 + g_I) = (1 - \lambda_I) y_I$$
(2.13)

The introduction of the absorption of surplus by luxury consumption will *necessarily* lower the growth rates g_C, g_I in (2.13) below their values in (2.12). The greater is the consumption, the lower is growth and accumulation. One can give formal expression to this relationship by an appropriate consumption/growth trade-off equation.[10]

Walsh and Gram (1980) present a detailed argument for regarding the system of equations (2.13) as depicting Smithian growth. It is true that it is a useful stylization, and has the particular virtue of appearing to be an extension of Smith's allocative analysis. However, as we shall show in chapter 3, if the prices are indeed to be interpreted as 'centres of gravity' in a long-run framework, then one must perforce assume balanced sectoral growth. Further, retaining an analysis with constant returns to scale, this balanced growth rate will be uniform over time. A sectoral analysis that abandons all of this is fearfully difficult to construct, and will not be attempted in this book. However, a preliminary attack on the problem is developed in chapter 8. Another, more tractable, method of proceeding – and one which is very much in the classical tradition, as Dasgupta (1985) has recently observed – is to develop the growth analysis in *aggregate* terms, suppressing difficulties of sectoral analysis. In effect one is going to assume a growth rate which is uniform across sectors, but variable over the growth trajectory. A possible interpretation, and the one adopted in a Malthusian context by Costabile and Rowthorn (1985), is to assume one is dealing with a one-good economy (e.g. a corn model). On the whole, I am averse to this procedure and would prefer to adopt the sometimes uncomfortable intellectual compromise of dealing with a many-good economy, but one in which it makes sense to talk of a value of aggregate output like social product. Hicks (1972) has fortunately provided some theoretical comfort to those, like the author, who wish to proceed in this way.[11]

2.5 THE MACROECONOMIC VIEW OF GROWTH

Because of the considerable attention given to the 'invisible hand theorem' of general allocative equilibrium, the significance of the macroeconomic mode of analysis to Smithian analysis is often overlooked, though Henderson (1954), Dasgupta (1985) and most notably Skinner (1979) have reminded us of its importance. Unfortunately, there is some confusion in Henderson's analysis between Smith's system as general equilibrium analysis, and Smith's aggregative or macroeconomic analysis. Macroeconomics is not a synonym for general equilibrium economics. It is our view that it would be strictly correct to view Smith as having provided a detailed microeconomic analysis of *partial* equilibrium. He does also have a microeconomic theory of *general* equilibrium but, despite the attention focused on this by writers like Hollander (1973), the treatment is far less detailed. However, when it comes to macroeconomic analysis, particularly of growth and accumulation, Smith again was able to provide a very detailed account of how the whole economy moved forward. However, he did so by suppressing much detail. In particular, there is no growth analysis of prices. The role of prices is to achieve allocative equilibrium, and appropriate equilibrating adjustments will be made in the course of growth. However, income, investment and technical change caused by the division of labour are more important to growth than prices *per se*. Here too we follow Smith, as have so many writers since (including those concerned with the so-called neoclassical theory of growth, of which Solow 1988 provides a recent example) in suppressing concern for pricing in our growth analysis. The advantage of doing so is not only analytical tractability, but also the possibility of treating an entirely new problem which by its nature is characteristic of a higher level of aggregation than individual markets or industries: the problem of the distribution of social product. Its division into the macroeconomic aggregates of wages, rent and profit can be used, as Marx and his followers were to show, as the basis for an analysis of class conflict. Arguments about the distribution of product at the microeconomic level have a different character; they reduce to being technical *bargaining* problems. At the macroeconomic level, particularly if types of income can be uniquely attached to classes of individuals, what is merely a technical aspect of individual bargaining between employer and employee at the micro level, becomes the basis for a potential clash of classes as a whole.

Skinner (1979) particularly identifies book II of the *Wealth of Nations* with a macroeconomic model. He sees it as a kind of circular flow model in which the connection between *aggregate* income, output and expenditure is established. These flows, however, are not constant, for Smith was concerned with a growth process in the course of which the level of output produced in a given year was *more* than sufficient to replace the goods used up. That is, growth depends upon 'an additional capital', which is to say capital accumulation. This leads Skinner (1979, p. 177) to argue that the saving necessary for this capital accumulation to take place can lead to a process of cumulative growth. In it, the higher income and output generated in each successive year provide the means of further saving and capital accumulation: 'Once started, the process of capital accumulation and thus economic growth may be seen as self-generating, indicating that Smith's "flow" is to be regarded as a spiral rather than a circle of given dimension.' Finally, this process of growth can be linked with the division of labour: 'As the process of growth unfolds, so in turn the increasing size of the market gives greater scope to the division of labour, thus increasing productivity and at the same time giving greater scope to technical change in the shape of the flow of invention, so that the economy can be described as one subject to increasing returns' (Skinner 1979, p. 181). Although Skinner's representation of Smith is persuasive, it is incomplete. True, the growth analysis is essentially macroeconomic, and indeed we shall usually find it most simple to build models in this way. However, as Young (1928) first explained, the basis for growth in Smith is really microeconomic: it is the division of labour at the sectoral (i.e. industry) level. As Lauchlin Currie (1981, p. 53) has so aptly put it: 'There is interdependence of sectoral and overall growth rates.' As we shall see in chapters 4 and 8, one would ideally

46 *Allocation versus Accumulation*

look at Smithian growth in sectoral terms. It turns out, however, that one can go a long way using the most aggregative methods for modelling Smithian growth. This will be the method introduced in chapter 5, and used in various ways in chapters 6 and 7. It involves specifying an aggregate production function for the economy as a whole, which is subject to a form of technical change caused by the division of labour. This provides a relatively crude way of modelling the *process* of growth, but, it turns out, a rather useful way of modelling the *consequences* of growth.

2.6 CONCLUSION

Here, we have provided an introduction to two important concepts which will be useful for our further discussion: classical sectoral analysis, and classical aggregate growth. The sectoral analysis can be used for looking in a detailed way at the evolution of individual industries, and indeed even individual firms, as in chapter 4. It can also be developed to give an account of the cumulative growth process, as in chapter 8. The second concept, that of a classical aggregate growth model, suppresses sectoral detail but provides rewards in other directions. In particular, it provides a means of explicitly representing the growth path of a classical economy subject to technical change caused by the division of labour (chapter 6). It also enables one to look at a classical model in which capital is of both the fixed and the circulating varieties, and the size of the labour force is endogenously determined, with a view to exploring the sensitivity of equilibrium values of variables to shifts in parameters like the division of labour and the bargaining power of capital.

NOTES

1 This leads to modern 'invisible hand' theorems concerning the optimality, in a Paretian sense, of general competitive equilibrium, as discussed, for example, by Arrow and Hahn (1971).
2 A number of writers (e.g. O'Brien 1975, ch. 4 and Papola 1967) have perceived the relationship between the Marshallian analysis of equilibrium and that of Smith. The natural price corresponds to Marshall's *long-run normal price*. Note that the decomposition of commodity price into rent, wages and profit is a part of the Marshallian supply analysis (see Marshall 1890, footnote p. 344).
3 'Centre of gravity' also has the connotation of *stable* equilibrium. In figure 2.1 the equilibria discussed are indeed stable.
4 See Hollander (1973, p. 121) on the significance of retraining labour.
5 For example, franchises for exclusive rights of production in certain markets.
6 This is to ignore issues of the *stability* of equilibrium. For the sort of picture depicted in figure 2.1, stability is guaranteed.
7 Schumpeter (1954, p. 242) described Smith's analysis of market and natural prices as a

primitive way of explicating 'the universal interdependence of the magnitudes that constitute the economic cosmos'.

8   Hollander (1973, p. 114): 'Smith's formal treatment of value theory may best be appreciated if envisaged as an attempt to achieve a conception of long-run *general* equilibrium.' See also Skinner (1979, p. 161).
9   See Walsh and Gram (1980, p. 72).
10 See Walsh and Gram (1980, ch. 11). In the one-sector case, where only corn y_C is produced, with corn coefficient a_{CC}, the consumption/growth trade-off equation is $\lambda_C = -a_{CC}g + (1 - a_{CC})$, where λ_C is the proportion of output consumed and g is the growth rate. Note that $d\lambda_C/dg = -a_{CC} < 0$, the 'trade-off'.
11 As Hicks (1972, p. 161) put it: 'Suppose that the . . . goods are demanded, throughout, in fixed proportions. Analytically, therefore, they can be reduced to a single good, a "bundle" which I shall call output.'

3
Theories of Smithian Growth

3.1 INTRODUCTION

Adam Smith was not an economic theorist in the modern sense of the term. Theory and evidence are often developed alongside one another in his writings, and the relevant parts of his overall view on the process of economic growth are not gathered together in one place. Disentangling historical facts from analysis, and placing together the fragments of analysis, are no easy tasks. What one is left with seems from a modern perspective to be incomplete, for the convention today is to expound explicit models which can be shown to be determinate, and from which qualitative predictions can be unambiguously derived, given certain theoretical restrictions. One embarks on this enterprise with rather little help from Smith, for his method was different.

Nevertheless, it is possible to provide a distillation of Smith's growth analysis. Outstanding contributions include the work of Spengler (1959), Anspach (1976), Lowe (1975) and Hollander (1973, chs 6–8). Our purpose in this chapter, however, is to interpret theories of Smithian growth rather more narrowly. Whilst a distillation of Smith's original analysis is useful, it does not get round the difficulty that in its original form the analysis lacked coherence and consistency in a number of respects, and that no mere distillation can mask this. Therefore what is to be examined below is a set of theories which aim in a sense to be *reconstructions* and *extensions* of Adam Smith's growth analysis, in that they take certain common building blocks and use them to construct theoretical structures which meet modern requirements of coherence and consistency.[1] To be grand, one could contrast (and unfavourably at that!) 'mere' consistency with scope, breadth of vision, comprehensiveness, historical awareness, and much more besides, all of which are characteristic of Smith. Not that Smith had any difficulty with handling 'mere' consistency; far from it.

50 *Theories of Smithian Growth*

It is simply that this attribute was not revered then as it is now. Today, one would still hope for the breadth and scope of Smith, though this is now much harder to achieve; but before even attempting this, more attention must be paid to matters of humble detail of logic in a way which earlier writers like Smith might well have regarded as displaying an unhealthy preoccupation with formalism. The ultimate goal should still be to enfold analytical reasoning within a broader framework which respects historical context, and takes cognizance of institutions and ethics.

3.2 SECTORAL GROWTH MODELS

In chapter 2 the idea of a sectoral growth model was introduced, using the simple example of a two-sector model for the production of corn and iron in which growth rates of the means of production of both corn and iron differed, and there was luxury consumption of corn and iron. There is no doubt that Smith himself thought in sectoral terms, and this tradition has been reawakened by a new revivalist school, the modern classical, of which Walsh and Gram (1980) provide an exposition. They once again emphasize the sectoral approach of the classical writers, this time bringing to bear on traditional areas of enquiry the full arsenal of contemporary analytical methods. Modifying the corn-iron notation of Walsh and Gram (1980) introduced in chapter 2 to one which more readily lends itself to generalization, a two-sector version of this sectoral model may be written as

$$\left. \begin{array}{l} a_{11}(1+g_1)y_1 + a_{12}(1+g_2)y_2 = (1-\lambda_1)y_1 \\ a_{21}(1+g_1)y_1 + a_{22}(1+g_1)y_2 = (1-\lambda_2)y_2 \end{array} \right\} \tag{3.1}$$

where a_{ij} (the typical 'technical coefficient') denotes the amount of the ith commodity required to produce one unit of the jth commodity. Other symbols are: y_i (the output of the ith sector; g_i, the growth rate in the ith sector; and λ_i, the consumption proportion in the ith sector. In defining consumption proportions we follow the usual practice of treating minimum subsistence not as consumption, but as a cost of production. The λ_i relate to what Dorfman, Samuelson and Solow (1958, p. 325) call 'extraneous final consumption' and Walsh and Gram (1980, p. 72) call 'luxury consumption'. In the Von Neumann growth model as usually developed by modern economic theorists,[2] the λ_i are set equal to zero, and the growth rates are equalized across sectors, giving $g_1 = g_2 = g$. Then (3.1) can be rewritten as

$$\begin{array}{l} (a_{11}y_1 + a_{12}y_2)(1+g) = y_1 \\ (a_{21}y_1 + a_{22}y_2)(1+g) = y_2 \end{array} \tag{3.2}$$

which is the case of maximum balanced growth. If positive extraneous final consumption is permitted, a lower rate of balanced growth will be achieved. Generalizing (3.1) to the many-sector case we get

$$\mathbf{A}\,\mathrm{diag}(1 + g_i)\mathbf{y} = \mathrm{diag}(1 - \lambda_i)\mathbf{y} \tag{3.3}$$

where $\mathbf{A}$ is the technology matrix with typical element a_{ij}, $\mathbf{y}$ is the column vector of outputs, the g_i and λ_i are sectoral growth rates and consumption proportions respectively, and diag(.) denotes a diagonal matrix with elements as indicated on the principal diagonal and zeros elsewhere. Adopting the assumptions used in going from equations (3.1) to (3.2), of zero luxury consumption and uniform growth rates across sectors, expression (3.3) simplifies to

$$\mathbf{A}\mathbf{y} = \frac{1}{1+g}\mathbf{y} \tag{3.4}$$

If $\mathbf{A}$ is indecomposable, the eigenvector $\mathbf{y}$ corresponding to the dominant eigenvalue $1/(1 + g)$ is, by the Perron-Frobenius theorem, strictly positive.[3] This is the Von Neumann model of balanced growth, and clearly g is the maximum rate of balanced growth. It is an analytical framework of this modern classical type that Samuelson (1977) adopted in his remarkable 'vindication' of Adam Smith. It is to this model that we now turn our attention.

In Samuelson's (1977) model the basic assumptions are: goods are produced from land and 'doses' of labour and raw materials; consumption is what remains of gross production after intermediate requirements are satisfied; subsistence rations of each good are defined at a level which reproduces the population; workers do not save or invest; and perfect competition, with free entry, constant returns and rapidly diffused knowledge, holds generally. In Smith's 'rude state', as interpreted by Samuelson, rent and profit are zero, with the wage rate being determined at a level which just permits the purchase of subsistence requirements. Here land is assumed to be so abundant in relation to labour that no rent arises, and as production is assumed to be instantaneous, no interest or profit arises. In this case, competition implies that we can write $\mathbf{p} = w\mathbf{v} + \mathbf{pA}$, from which

$$\mathbf{p} - w\mathbf{b}$$

with

$$\mathbf{b} = \mathbf{v}[\mathbf{I} - \mathbf{A}]^{-1} > 0$$
$$= \mathbf{v} + \mathbf{v}\mathbf{A} + \mathbf{v}\mathbf{A}^2 + \ldots \tag{3.5}$$

where $\mathbf{p}$ is a row vector of competitive prices, w is the wage rate, $\mathbf{v}$ is the row vector of direct labour requirements, **I** is the identity matrix, **A** is the square technology matrix of technical coefficients a_{ij}, and **b** is a row vector of total labour requirements. For convergence of the matrix series in (3.5) it is required that every good must indirectly, if not directly, require some labour. This gives us a precise Smithian 'labour command theory of value', with

$$\mathbf{pm} = w = \mathbf{bm}w, \quad \mathbf{bm} = 1 \tag{3.6}$$

where **m** is a column vector of subsistence requirements per worker. Expression (3.6) assures us that the wage rate w is just sufficient to purchase the subsistence requirements of goods **m** at competitive prices **p**. Also

$$\mathbf{pc} = wL = \mathbf{bc}w = \mathbf{bm}wL \tag{3.7}$$

where **c** is a column vector of consumption amounts of the various goods, and L is total labour. This defines net national product in the 'rude state' as being equal to total wages or the subsistence consumption of workers.

The growth phase is initiated in a way which is not fully explicated in Samuelson, but the gist of his argument is that the division of labour will lower direct or indirect labour requirements. He is correct, technically speaking, that lowering subsistence requirements per worker will also do the trick. However, this is a purely formal possibility and not one which makes sense in a Smithian framework, where subsistence requirements – being culturally rather than physiologically determined – should if anything rise over time. Emphasizing, therefore, the consequences of the division of labour in decreasing elements of **v** and/or **A**, the growth phase is characterized by replacing the equalities of (3.6) and (3.7) with the following inequalities:

$$\mathbf{pm} < w, \quad \mathbf{bm} < 1, \quad \mathbf{c} \geq \mathbf{m}L \tag{3.8}$$

With the real wage rising above subsistence, population is assumed to grow at an exponential rate, and with it outputs at the same rate. This is the Von Neumann model with positive consumption. Without time-phased production, profit will not arise, but rent will make an appearance once labour has increased to the extent that fixed land becomes scarce. It is logically sound in such a model to resolve price into wage and rent components. Samuelson shows that the competitive solution that emerges from this model is equivalent to that which would emerge were a benevolent planner to minimize the labour required to produce any assigned consumption vector. In this sense, Smith's invisible hand theorem is proven at any point on the growth path. The distributional issue of how the components of the consumption vector **c** are allocated amongst members of society is, however, unresolved. No doubt some distributions of consumption, whilst socially efficient, might nevertheless be in violation of certain ethical standards.

Theories of Smithian Growth 53

Once production is viewed in a time-phased way, profit appears in the system. Capitalists save and accumulate by consuming less than the full amount of current profits. With population growth (because of a wage which is above the subsistence level) and capital accumulation proceeding apace, the fixed amount of land is finally fully utilized. The wage is pushed down again to the subsistence level and the rate of profit to a low level at which capitalists and rentiers spend all their incomes on current consumption. For such a model, balanced exponential growth is followed by a relapse into a 'dull' stationary state in which rent is maximized and wage and profit rates are depressed to minimal levels. For this stationary state there exists a factor/price frontier relationship indicating a trade-off between the wage rate, rent, and the rate of profit.

As Samuelson presents his model, invention of the sort implied by the division of labour provides a sporadic lowering of elements of **v** and/or **A**. This effect is regarded as presenting itself in a random fashion and, when it does appear, it will raise one or more of the real wage, the real rent or the profit rate. However, the effect is regarded as transient by Samuelson, and the economic system settles down again into a rent maximizing stationary state. This sort of approach is the subject of a critique in section 3.4. A crucial difference between invention as conceived by Samuelson in his version of Smithian growth, and invention as it is viewed in subsequent chapters of this book, is that in Samuelson it is *exogenous* whereas we would argue that it should be *endogenous*. A significant feature of many of the aggregative growth models along Smithian lines to be discussed in the next section is that they do view invention as endogenous. There is in principle no reason why this approach should not be generalized to the sectoral case. However, we defer discussion of this until chapter 8.

3.3 AGGREGATIVE GROWTH MODELS

The starting point for many classical macroeconomic models is the specification of an aggregate production function. This is true of early theorists in the field like Higgins (1959), Johansen (1969), Adelman (1962), and Barkai (1969) and is a tradition that has been maintained by contemporary theorists like Eltis (1984), Reid (1985a), and Costabile and Rowthorn (1985). We shall discuss the detailed specification of production functions subject to technical change in chapter 5, and concentrate here on the way in which such a component fits into a multi-equation model.

Higgins (1959) puts forward a mathematical growth model which aims to embrace the views of Smith, Malthus and Mill. It has eight equations. The first is an aggregate production function with output Y dependent on the labour force N, land T, capital K and the level of technique B. Marginal products are assumed positive, but diminishing. Thus the production function may be written

$$Y = f(N, K, T, B) \quad f_N, f_K, f_T, f_B > 0 \tag{3.9}$$

Variants of this device are to be used frequently in subsequent chapters, notably chapters 6 and 7. The approach adopted by the author differs from that of Higgins in that technical change is made a function of the division of labour, which in turn depends upon the extent of the market, whereas Higgins makes the level of technique B depend upon the level of current investment I. Thus

$$B = B(I) \quad B' > 0 \tag{3.10}$$

This simple formulation is slightly unconvincing. In Arrow (1962) the current level of technique is related to cumulative gross investment, and in Kaldor and Mirrlees (1962) technical progress is related to the rate of growth of investment per member of the workforce. The formulation in (3.10) seems to the author to be unconvincing because it ignores the role of the history of past investment in determining the current level of technique. Investment, the net addition to capital stock dK/dt, is driven by the profits Π which capitalists expect to make:

$$I \equiv dK/dt = I(\Pi) \quad I' > 0 \tag{3.11}$$

This, as we now know from econometric evidence, is not a bad form of investment function. It has also been favoured by economic theorists such as Kalecki who regard themselves as writing in the classical tradition. Profit is assumed increasing in the level of technique and decreasing in the labour force:

$$\Pi = \Pi(B, N) \quad \Pi_B > 0, \Pi_N < 0 \tag{3.12}$$

The restriction $\Pi_B > 0$ is unexceptionable, but the tendency of an increasing labour force to lower profits requires further scrutiny. The implicit assumption is that land is fixed at a level $\bar{T}$, in which case diminishing returns in agriculture would depress profits. The counterforce to this, indicated by (3.12), is the tendency of improvements in technique to raise profits – most obviously in industries, but probably also in agriculture. The aggregate approach that has been adopted, of course, does not permit us to distinguish differential effects at the sectoral level.

The size of the labour force in Higgins's analysis is assumed to depend on the wages fund W in an increasing fashion:

$$N = N(W) \quad N' > 0 \tag{3.13}$$

If the wages fund (or, after it is distributed, the wages bill) is sufficient to provide the existing labour force with more than subsistence, it will encourage further growth of the labour force. The sum W which must be put aside to hire labour arises from, and indeed increases with, saving, which is put into effect through an equivalent amount of investment. Therefore

$$W = W(I) \qquad W' > 0 \tag{3.14}$$

What is missing from Higgins's analysis is an explicit introduction of the classical condition that $I \equiv S$, one that is employed extensively in chapters 6 and 7. The functional distribution of income is captured in the requirement that total output Y be equal to total profit plus wages:

$$Y = \Pi + W \tag{3.15}$$

An important omission in this formulation is the appearance of rent, which Higgins (1959, p. 95) cavalierly regards as 'a bit of a nuisance'. Properly speaking, given his assumption of fixed land $\bar{T}$, rent R should be defined residually as

$$R = Y - \Pi - W \tag{3.16}$$

This is a significant omission, particularly in view of Higgins's wish to discuss long-run equilibrium with his model. Thus he adds a final relationship expressing total wages as the product of the subsistence wage rate $\bar{w}$ and the labour force N:

$$W = \bar{w}N \tag{3.17}$$

If land scarcity *has not* set in, then no rent arises; this is as in Higgins's analysis, here (3.15). However, then we would expect the wage rate w to be above its minimum (subsistence) level, and we would therefore write (3.17) as

$$W = wN \qquad w > \bar{w} = \min(w) \tag{3.18}$$

If land scarcity *has* set in, then we would expect rent to arise as in (3.16), which is not used by Higgins, and the wage would be pushed to the subsistence level as in the specification of (3.17). Technically, (3.15) should be paired with (3.18) or (3.16) should be paired with (3.17), but *not* (3.15) with (3.17) as in Higgins's analysis. The difficulty that arises with Higgins's model is that it improperly models the classical labour market. This is also true of the aggregative model of Haim Barkai (1969) to which we turn our attention later. Finally, considered as theory, we note that Higgins's model does no more than state a set of equations. This in itself does not get us very far. What one seeks is insight into the evolution of the system specified, as in the model of chapter 6 which goes 'beyond the short period' to define a trajectory of social product, or

56 *Theories of Smithian Growth*

(possibly less ambitiously) qualitative predictions about the sensitivity of steady state values of the variables to shifts in behavioural propensities like thriftiness, as explored in the model of chapter 7. Other ways of getting some grasp of the content of a model are possible, but clearly the mere enumeration of equations is no more than a starting point of the sort one must always establish as a prelude to theorizing.

Adelman's (1962) theory, like Higgins's, is largely an enumeration of equations, though it is an advance in that an indication is provided of how, in principle, an expression for the equation of motion of the system can be derived. The starting point is again with an aggregate production function for which output is, in this case, expressed as a function of labour, land and capital. It is argued that the marginal products of labour and capital depend on capital employed and the institutional framework. It is not clear what Adelman intends here, for marginal productivity relationships are functions which should have the same arguments as the function from which they were obtained by taking partial derivatives. Apparently what is intended is that the production function has labour, land, capital *and* a variable representing institutional form as its arguments. Land is assumed fixed, and the variable representing the institutional framework is in the nature of a shift parameter. In chapter 7 a production function of this type is adopted with the institutional framework being, as it were, subsumed under the form of the production function. Then, adopting a classical 'stages of society' view of economic evolution, a distinct production function will pertain to each stage of society (i.e. to each institutional framework). Land fixity, in the analysis developed there, plays the role of a 'rigidity' that ultimately brings about a stationary state, for a given societal form. In Adelman no presumption is made in favour of the equation of motion of the system leading to a stationary state, and indeed it is hinted that changes in the institutional framework can imply increasing returns which might indefinitely sustain growth. However, there simply is not enough detailed structure in her analysis to be sure what is intended. The treatment of the labour market is of interest, as this part of the classical model is often neglected or only modelled crudely. Labour supply growth is assumed to be proportionately related to the deviation between the actual wage rate and the subsistence wage rate. This is assumed to be matched by the growth in labour demand. The demand for labour itself is supposed to be determined by the wages fund doctrine, which Adelman expresses in a parameterized form with the growth in labour demand being related linearly to capital growth and output growth. The deviation of the rate of profit from its 'natural' level, and aggregate income, are the determinants of capital accumulation. The deviation of the rate of profit is itself assumed to be decreasing in capital stock, and a function of the institutional environment. By substitution, the Adelman system can be reduced to one equation in which capital accumulation is explained by income, capital stock and institutional environment, and another equation in which rate of growth of income is a function of the same variables. It is possible in principle to solve out a system like this, given certain initial conditions, but Adelman does not impose sufficient qualitative restrictions on her schema to make this possible. It is suggestive, however, of how an approximately specified dynamic Smithian model might be constructed. In section 3.4 we refer to the 'canonical classical model' of Samuelson (1978) which successfully formalizes and then investigates theoretically a model akin to the one Adelman merely stated. In particular, it specifies appropriate adjustment equations for the wage rate and profit rate, which enable stability properties of the model to be investigated and, as Reid (1987a) has indicated, possible trajectories in wage/profit space.

Let us turn attention now to possibly the most widely cited aggregate model of Smithian growth. Barkai (1969) presents what he quite properly describes as a 'formal outline' of a Smithian growth model. In view of the importance of this model and the relationship it bears to the author's models in chapters 6, 7 and 8 of this book, it will be given a fairly detailed treatment. The aggregate production function is written:

$$Y = F(K, N, B) \tag{3.19}$$

which is assumed increasing in all its arguments. This may be compared with the Higgins formulation (3.9), where land appears explicitly. It seems clear from a number of distinguished analyses of Smithian growth, and most notably that of Spengler (1959), that land is the 'ultimate limitational factor' in Smith's system, though the societal stage itself as implicitly embodied in the form of the production function is also important. Without some limitation the stationary state is not achieved, and a significant weakness of Barkai's approach is that he talks about the stationary state, but has no limitational factor like land or institutions to bring it about. In Higgins the level of technique B depends upon investment, which we have singled out as unsatisfactory. In Barkai, B depends upon two factors, the extent of the market m and the capital–labour function t:

$$B = B(m, t) \qquad B_m, B_t > 0 \tag{3.20}$$

with

$$m = m(Y) \qquad m' > 0 \tag{3.21}$$

and

$$t = t(K/N) \qquad t' > 0 \tag{3.22}$$

58 Theories of Smithian Growth

Barkai would dispute the idea of a fixed capital–labour ratio as favoured by many analysts of classical growth, including Samuelson (1977, 1978); hence his formulation of the $t(.)$ function in (3.22). The author himself is not quite agnostic on the matter, regarding the formulation (3.22) as permissible, but possibly not of crucial importance compared with the $m(.)$ function in (3.21). The $t(.)$ function does introduce an unnecessary complication into Barkai's analysis, for his account requires that K/N rises with growth, yet no clear mechanism for bringing this about is proferred. The point is important, because if a growing output causes a population explosion, but capital accumulation proceeds more gradually, the positive effect of the division of labour as embodied in the $m(.)$ function will be offset by the negative effect of a declining t as K/N falls.

In the author's own theories, developed in chapter 4 onwards, the division of labour effect (as represented by an $m(.)$ function), over whose significance there is universal agreement, is regarded as the prime force behind technical change.

In his treatment of profit, the fundamental relationship in Barkai's model is what he describes as a 'profit rate function' in which the rate of profit r is explained by capital stock K and the level of technique B. Thus we can write

$$r = f(K, B) \quad f_K < 0, f_B > 0 \tag{3.23}$$

This is regarded as embodying a 'law' of the falling rate of profit, $f_K < 0$. Strictly, the 'law' should relate to the time path of the rate of profit as the economy approaches the stationary state, with r eventually reaching a low level or subsistence rate, as in Samuelson (1978). The view taken is that competition both tends to equalize profit rates across sectors – an effect noted in chapter 2, but obviously masked in the aggregative approach being used in this chapter – and also lowers the profit rate in general through increased capital promoting an increased supply of the goods in question, thus depressing market prices for these goods and lowering profit rates. Barkai (1969, p. 407) writes that in Smith 'a relation between the profit rate and investment is to the best of my knowledge not explicitly mentioned', and then proceeds to formulate one! It has the form

$$r = g(I, B) \quad g_I < 0, g_B > 0 \tag{3.24}$$

Barkai's argument for the restriction $g_I < 0$ is that 'the profit rate is a decreasing function of capital and the latter is positively related to investment.' However, this seems to confuse a *behavioural relationship* (the tendency for competition to lower the rate of return on capital) with a *definition* (the rate of profit being defined as the ratio of a surplus, however defined, to capital employed). There seems no need to introduce the technical change variable B explicitly, as in (3.24), for the effect of technical change on the rate of profit will be felt via the production function (3.19) and the profit rate function (3.23). In most modern stylizations of the classical system, as in Hicks (1937) for example, savings and investment are each a function of the rate of interest and an equilibrium between the two is brought about by variations in the rate of interest. However, Smith recognized no relationship between savings and the rate of interest, and indeed even today the nature of such a relationship is by no means resolved. Rather, the principal determinant of savings in Smith is the level of aggregate income. This is well supported as a hypothesis in a number of places in *The Wealth of Nations*, and it is therefore appropriate to specify a savings function, as Barkai does, having the form

$$S = S(Y) \quad S' > 0 \tag{3.25}$$

In Smith, savings and investment are equal at both the individual and the aggregate level, implying the identity used by Barkai (and Higgins as noted previously)

$$I \equiv S \tag{3.26}$$

Barkai's complete system is specified by the set of equations (3.19) to (3.26), which for, convenience we summarize as follows:

$$Y = F(K, N, B) \tag{3.19}$$

$$B = B(m, t) \quad B_m, B_t > 0 \tag{3.20}$$

$$m = m(Y) \quad m' > 0 \tag{3.21}$$

$$t = t(K/N) \quad t' > 0 \tag{3.22}$$

$$r = f(K, B) \quad f_K < 0, f_B > 0 \tag{3.23}$$

$$r = g(I, B) \quad g_I < 0, g_B > 0 \tag{3.24}$$

$$S = S(Y) \quad S' > 0 \tag{3.25}$$

$$I \equiv S \tag{3.26}$$

Now this is apparently a set of eight equations in nine unknowns: Y, K, N, B, m, t, I, r and S. If K is interpreted as fixed capital, then, captail accumulation, or investment, is $I \equiv dK/dt$, and seven equations can be solved out for seven variables, leaving one equation relating any two variables one cares to nominate out of the set of nine. Supposing I and K are nominated, one can write

$$I \equiv dK/dt = \Phi(K) \tag{3.27}$$

which is a first-order non-linear differential equation in K, giving us the equation of motion of the system. Solution of this equation requires knowledge of the form of the function Φ, which is a complicated composition of the functions in (3.19) to (3.26), and an initial condition. The equation is directly analogous to one of the equations of motion in Adelman's (1962) model of Smith's system. A similar sort of idea is introduced in the simple model discussed at the beginning of the next section, where a phase diagram is used to illustrate a possible path to the stationary state and the requirement for stability of the stationary state. Rather than investigating the trajectory of the model, which can be difficult, one can focus on the stationary state alone. In Barkai's representation of Smith this is achieved by setting capital accumulation to zero:

$$I = 0 \tag{3.28}$$

This increases the number of equations to nine but introduces no new variables, which makes the system determinate.

To conclude this section, we turn our attention to the very important work of Eltis (1975, 1984). For almost two decades Walter Eltis has made the classical theory of economic growth the major focus of his intellectual curiosity. His writings have ranged over all the leading classical figures, but here we wish to limit attention to his analyses of Smith. The 1984 variant is a slight improvement on the paper prepared for the *Essays on Adam Smith* (Skinner and Wilson 1975). Discussion will therefore revolve around the more recent treatment.

As a background to understanding the contribution of Eltis, it is necessary to be aware of the simple but suggestive treatment of Smithian growth by Hicks (1965). He, as Eltis (1975, 1984), develops an aggregate 'corn model' of Smithian growth, taking the third chapter of the second book of *The Wealth of Nations*, on the accumulation of capital, as his inspiration. The model can be expressed by the equation

$$Y_t = \frac{p}{w} K_t = \frac{kp}{w} Y_{t-1} \tag{3.29}$$

Here Y_t is corn output in year t, w is the corn wage, p is output per worker, and K_t is circulating capital.

The logic of this relationship runs as follows. If Y_{t-1} is last year's output, then Y_{t-1}/w is the number of workers employed. Total output in year t, given a labour productivity of p, will be $p(Y_{t-1}/w)$. Thus $Y_t = (p/w)Y_{t-1}$. If some of last year's output is consumed by unproductive workers, the circulating capital this year K_t will be less than last year's output. Thus $K_t = kY_{t-1}$ with $0 < k < 1$. The number of workers producing corn is therefore K_t/w; hence the equalities in (3.29). From this equation one gets the rate of growth of corn output as

$$\dot{y} \equiv (Y_t - Y_{t-1})/Y_{t-1} = \left(\frac{kp}{w} - 1\right) \tag{3.30}$$

The smaller is k, the greater is consumption by unproductive workers, and hence the slower is the rate of growth of output $\dot{y}$. This is clearly a very simple model: indeed, it was developed for expositional purposes only. It confines attention to homogeneous circulating capital, and is really only formulated in quasi-dynamic terms, it being possible to view each year in isolation rather than as intrinsically a member of a sequence. If we appeal directly to Smith, the variables k, p and w of (3.30) should be regarded, properly speaking, as dependent on time. Their variations year by year will alter the growth rate $\dot{y}$. In this way, a trajectory of growth is specified for the economy. Possible shapes of such trajectories are investigated in the next section.

Another interpretation, and possibly one which more naturally occurs to the economist educated in the properties of the Harrod-Domar model, is to regard p, w and k as constant, in which case we get what Hicks (1965, p. 13) defines as a 'regularly progressive economy'. Though appealing, this approach leads to difficulties. If p, w and k are constant, it is necessary that additional workers should be employed as the economy grows at a fixed rate. If there is a pool or reserve of unemployed workers initially, growth at a uniform rate is possible. However, once labour scarcity occurs the real wage rises and with it the wages fund, which restricts the rate of growth of the economy. In a Smithian framework, one would want to argue, as we do frequently in later chapters, that in addition the growth of the economy might raise productivity through the increasing returns arising from further opportunities for the division of labour. This could offset the tendency to a falling rate of growth. Another factor operating in the same direction, though not emphasized by Smith, might be a decrease of unproductive workers' consumption amounting to an increase of k in (3.30). This possibility has been emphasized in a contemporary context by Bacon and Eltis (1976).

Let us turn now to the model of Eltis (1975, 1984), a close relative of the Hicksian model just discussed. It has three components, and is developed in two variants: one in which 'stock' is made up of circulating capital alone, and another in which 'stock' consists of both fixed and circulating capital. Turning to the pure circulating capital variant, the first relationship is a simple one-factor production function $Y = \alpha N_p^\beta$, where α and β are positive constants ($\beta > 1$), Y is output and N_p is productive labour. The restriction on β is intended to capture the increasing returns that arise from the division of labour. Unfortunately, there is no explicit modelling of the way in which this division of labour effect works itself through, and of its dependence on the extent of the market. Such considerations are central to the analyses of this book. Rather, in Eltis the value of β is exogenously assigned, and then the consequences are explored of its being at various predetermined magnitudes compared with other parameters. If Y and N_p are regarded as functions of time, then taking natural logarithms and differentiating with respect to time yields the formula

62 Theories of Smithian Growth

$$\dot{y} = \beta \dot{n}_p \tag{3.31}$$

where

$$\dot{y} \equiv (dY/dt)/Y$$
$$\dot{n}_p = (dN_p/dt)/N_p$$

The ratio of the rate of growth of circulating capital k_c to the rate of growth of the workforce is assumed to be greater than unity:

$$\frac{\dot{k}_c}{\dot{n}_p} = \gamma > 1 \tag{3.32}$$

Eltis (1984, p. 92) regards this as a 'population supply equation', but lack of reference to the real wage, or to the relationship between the real wage and the subsistence wage, does seem to the author to make this interpretation rather strained. In chapter 7 we have chosen to make the supply of the workforce increasing in the real wage – a simple but plausible hypothesis. Other interpretations are possible, including those of Adelman (1962) and Samuelson (1977, 1978)[4] which specify appropriate labour force adjustment equations. What Eltis's specification in (3.32) most resembles, in fact, is the relationship $t = t(K/N)$, $t' > 0$ of Barkai's (1969) model, here (3.22). Indeed, in Eltis (1975, p. 442) the same quote from Adam Smith is used as the one cited by Barkai (1969, p. 399) to justify the specification.

The third relationship in Eltis's pure circulating capital model says that only a proportion h of the circulating capital K_c is used to provide wages and raw materials W for each of the productive workers: $hK_c = N_p W$. In terms of growth rates, this can be expressed as

$$\dot{k}_c = \dot{n}_p + \dot{w} \tag{3.33}$$

The proportion h is also to be interpreted as the fraction of the labour force employed productively. If this is constant over time, then we can write $\dot{n}_p = \dot{n}$, the rate of growth of the total labour force. Then equations (3.31) to (3.33) can be rewritten as

$$\dot{y} = \frac{\beta}{\gamma} \dot{k}_c \tag{3.34}$$

$$\dot{n} = \frac{1}{\gamma} \dot{k}_c \tag{3.35}$$

$$\dot{w} = \left(1 - \frac{1}{\gamma}\right) \dot{k}_c \tag{3.36}$$

This set of relationships expresses each of the growth rates of output, population and the wage rate as determined proportionally by the growth rate of circulating capital. To close the system one uses Eltis's analogue to Hicks's equation (3.30), which can be written

$$\ddot{k}_c = h\left(\frac{Y/N_p}{W}\right) - 1 \qquad (3.37)$$

The rate of growth of circulating capital will rise if $(Y/N_p)/W$ rises, given h. This will occur if Y grows faster than WN_p. Now the rate of growth of output $\dot{y}$ is $(\beta/\gamma)\dot{k}_c$ from (3.34), and the rate of growth of WN_p is $\dot{w} + \dot{n}_p$, the latter being $\dot{k}_c$ from (3.33). Thus

$$\ddot{k}_c \gtreqless 0 \quad \text{as} \quad \dot{y} \gtreqless \dot{w} + \dot{n}_p$$

which implies

$$\ddot{k}_c \gtreqless 0 \quad \text{as} \quad \frac{\beta}{\gamma}\dot{k}_c \gtreqless \dot{k}_c$$

or

$$\ddot{k}_c \gtreqless 0 \quad \text{as} \quad \beta \gtreqless \gamma \qquad (3.38)$$

The technical restriction implied in (3.38) is clear enough. Expressed intuitively, it says that the rate of capital accumulation will rise if the productivity-enhancing effect of the division of labour is stronger than the drag on growth imposed by the requirement of an increasing amount of circulating capital per worker. If, following Eltis, one treats profits and rent as the excess of output over wage and raw material costs, growth in the ratio $Y/(N_pW)$ implies growth in profits and rents. The condition for this is given by $\beta > \gamma$. For a declining economy, approaching the stationary state, one has $\beta < \gamma$ and $\ddot{k}_c < 0$. Then, according to Eltis (1984, p. 95): 'The rate of capital accumulation, the rate of profit, and the share of "profits and rent" in output will fall continuously, while the capital–output ratio will rise continuously, until capital accumulation ceases, and once capital accumulation ceases, there will be no further change in the capital–output ratio, the rate of profit, and so on.' The major problem with this view of the final phase of the growth trajectory, as the stationary state is approached, is that it treats profits and rents symmetrically. The decline in the rate of profit, and indeed the fall of the profit share, are sensibly associated with the approach to a stationary state, but rent should be treated in a different fashion. As we indicate in a variety of ways in the next section, when stationarity is approached and land scarcity becomes marked, one would expect rents to *rise* as a share of output, rather than to fall symmetrically, as Eltis suggests, with profit. Ultimately, the difficulty with Eltis's model is its incompleteness.[5] Land, and the classical labour market, are

64 Theories of Smithian Growth

amongst the features that are only treated informally. By contrast, this book argues that these features should be *formally* included in a satisfactory treatment of Smithian growth.

3.4 GROWTH PATHS AND THE STATIONARY STATE

Towards the end of the last section, we started to emphasize the idea of a growth trajectory. There are many ways of developing an expression for the growth trajectory in mathematical terms, all of which necessarily give an incomplete picture of Smith. By way of illustration, no more, of how one might proceed, consider the following aggregate Smithian growth model which explicitly includes land and the labour market. Labour supply N_s is assumed to depend on the real wage rate w, and labour demand N_d on capital stock K and the real wage rate. Thus

$$N = N_s(w) \qquad N_s' > 0 \tag{3.39}$$

$$N = N_d(K, w) \qquad N_{d_K} > 0, N_{d_w} < 0 \tag{3.40}$$

Output Y is assumed to depend on the capital stock, labour, land T, and the division of labour M. The division of labour effect is represented by a function which is increasing in the social product variable Y, this variable being used to proxy the extent of the market. Thus

$$M = M(Y) \qquad M' > 0 \tag{3.41}$$

This device, which we introduce for the first time here without detailed justification, will be used repeatedly in the rest of this volume. Land will be assumed fixed at the amount $\bar{T}$. As Lowe (1954) and Spengler (1959) have emphasized, it is ultimately the limited supply of land in Smith's analysis that brings about the stationary state at the end of the growth trajectory. Now the production function can be written as

$$\begin{aligned}Y &= Y(K, N, T, M) \qquad Y_K, Y_N, Y_T, Y_M > 0 \\ &= Y(K, N, \bar{T}, M(Y))\end{aligned} \tag{3.42}$$

where marginal products are positive and output increases with the division of labour ($Y_M > 0$).

Effectual demand[6] D is given by the product of the real wage and the number employed:

$$D = wN \tag{3.43}$$

Profit Π depends upon social product (the revenue element) and the wage payments which generate effectual demand (the cost element). Thus the profit function can be written as

$$\Pi = \Pi(D, Y) \quad \Pi_D < 0, \Pi_Y > 0 \tag{3.44}$$

Finally, capital accumulation, denoted by $\dot{K}$, depends upon profit:

$$\dot{K} = \kappa(\Pi) \quad \kappa' > 0 \tag{3.45}$$

The variables of the system are now D, N, w, K, Y, M, Π and $\dot{K}$, with the land variable being eliminated through its assumed constancy. There are seven equations (3.39) to (3.45) involving these eight variables. There is thus one 'free' variable, and the system may be collapsed into a single equation involving any two variables. A convenient way of proceeding, as in the model of Adelman (1962) discussed earlier, is to condense the system down into one equation involving the capital stock K and capital accumulation $\dot{K}$ variables:

$$\dot{K} = \psi(K) \tag{3.46}$$

For a steady state solution we require $\dot{K} = 0$, in which case $\psi(K^*) = 0$, K^* being a root of ψ. Then K^* can be identified with the long-run level of the capital stock when the economy has reached the stationary state. For stability we require $\psi'(K^*) < 0$.

A possible growth trajectory is illustrated in figure 3.1. If K overshoots K^* it will decline to that level over time; and if it is less than K^* it will rise to it over time, as indicated by the arrows on the growth trajectory. The function ψ depends in a complex way on the functions (3.39) to (3.45), and we defer until later choices of specific functional forms which enable a more precise characterization of possible growth paths. It is clear, however, that we cannot necessarily assume that $\dot{K}$ is a single-signed derived function of K. If ψ' is not single-signed, multiple-root possibilities for $\psi(K) = 0$ arise. If for a distinct K^{**} we have $\psi'(K^{**}) > 0$, $\psi(K^{**}) = 0$ then the equilibrium at this level of capital stock is unstable. Such an unstable equilibrium can lead to a period of growth associated with positive capital accumulation, as represented by that segment of the growth trajectory between K^{**} and K^* in figure 3.1. In the case being discussed here it should be noted that by virtue of the labour supply and demand conditions (3.39) and (3.40), a market clearing level of employment at a real wage rate w is being assumed along the whole growth trajectory. Now capital appears explicitly in (3.40) and its variation over time will likewise imply variations in N and w.

Before turning to the more sophisticated model of Samuelson (1978) to explore such effects, it is helpful to pause and consider the original development of the idea of a growth trajectory in *The Wealth of Nations*. In his

66 *Theories of Smithian Growth*

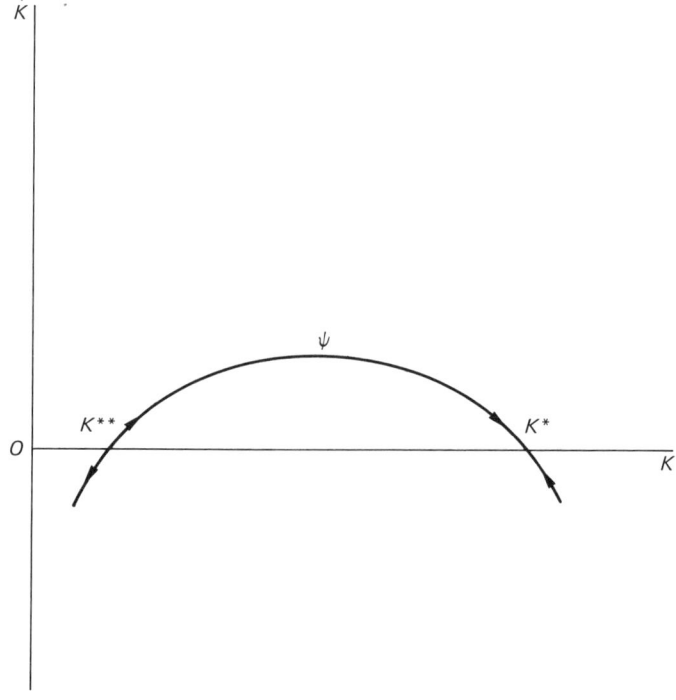

Figure 3.1

exposition, Smith started from the principle of the division of labour and moved on to an explanation of capital accumulation. However, in the words of Viner (1927, p. 116) Smith's model is 'a coordinated and mutually dependent system of cause and effect relationships'. This being so, we can enter the model at any point without doing violence to the logic. It is in fact highly instructive to take the role of parsimony in permitting accumulation as our starting point, moving on to the result that the division of labour is limited by the extent of the market. Growth takes place in an unplanned way and depends on the desire of individuals for betterment: 'An augmentation of fortune is the means by which the greater part of men propose and wish to better their condition. It is the means most vulgar and most obvious; and the most likely way of augmenting their fortune is to save and accumulate some part of what they acquire' (WN, pp. 341–2). This willingness to save leads directly to an augmentation of capital. In Smith's view there was an identity between saving and investment at both the individual and the aggregate levels:

Whatever a person saved from his revenue he adds to his capital, and either employs it himself in maintaining an additional number of productive hands, or enables some other person to do so, by lending it to him for an interest, that is for a share of the profits. As the capital of an individual can be increased only by what he saves from his annual revenue or his annual gains, so the capital of a society, which is the same with that of all the individuals who compose it, can be increased only in the same manner. (WN, p. 337)

The increase of capital arising from parsimony 'naturally tends to increase . . . the real quantity of industry, the number of productive hands, and consequently the exchangeable value of the annual produce of the land and labour of the country, the real wealth and revenue of its inhabitants' (WN, p. 337). Finally, this increase of annual revenue enlarges markets and provides the basis for the division of labour and hence an increase in productivity. When markets are small, there is no inducement to specialization, but as they enlarge 'the power of exchanging . . . gives occasion to the division of labour' and 'the extent of this division must always be limited by the extent of that power, or, in other words, by the extent of the market' (WN, p. 31). Thus 'the division of labour . . . as far as it can be introduced, occasions, in every art, a proportionable increase of the productive powers of labour' (WN, p. 15). This process of the progressive expansion of markets, with increasing scope for the division of labour, is not impeded by monetary restriction, for in Smith's view the money supply adjusts passively to the value of the annual produce: 'The quantity of money . . . must in every country naturally increase as the annual produce increases. The value of the consumable goods annually circulated within the society being greater, will require greater quantity of money to circulate them' (WN, p. 340). This increase of produce will not go on forever, and ultimately the economy approaches a stationary state which is 'consistent with the nature of its laws and institutions' (WN, p. 111). The characteristics of the stationary state were described by Smith as follows:

In a country which had acquired that full complement of riches which the nature of its soil and climate, its situation with respect to other countries, allowed it to acquire; which could therefore, advance no further, and which was not going backwards, both the wages of labour and the profits of stock would probably be very low. In a country fully peopled in proportion to what either its territory could maintain or its stock employ, the competition for employment would necessarily be so great as to reduce the wages of labour to what was barely sufficient to keep up the number of labourers, and, the country being already fully peopled, that number could never be augmented. In a country fully stocked in proportion to all the business it had to transact, as great a quantity of stock would be employed in every particular branch as the nature and extent of trade would admit. The competition, therefore, would everywhere be as great, and consequently the ordinary profit as low as possible. (WN, p. 111)

Figure 3.1 illustrates the case in which K^* is 'as great a quantity of stock [as] would be employed'. Using a more fully specified model, exactly conditions of this sort are described by Samuelson (1978) in his characterization of the limiting, long-run equilibrium position in a classical economy. Unfortunately, as in so much contemporary analysis, emphasis is on this stationary state, for modern economists are most attached to the properties of equilibrium positions. In Smith this equilibrium is discussed, as in the above passage, but only in the context of a growth trajectory: the path to equilibrium is as important as the attainment of equilibrium.

Samuelson's system can be represented by these relationships:

$$(K_{t+1} - K_t)/K_t = k(r_t - r^*) \tag{3.47}$$

$$(N_{t+1} - N_t)/N_t = n(w_t - w^*) \tag{3.48}$$

with

$$\lim_{t \to \infty}(N_t, K_t, r_t, w_t \ldots) = (N^*, K^*, r^*, w^*, \ldots) \tag{3.49}$$

and with $k(0) = n(0) = 0$ and $k', n' > 0$. The system is completed by relationships determining the rate of profit r on capital K and the wage rate w for labour N, a production function, and an adding-up relationship. Starred variables are long-run equilibrium values, and the system can be shown to be globally stable. In the absence of any form of induced technical progress, useful illustrations of possible dynamics of this system can be developed – an issue which Samuelson rather neglected in his enthusiasm for providing a rigorous analysis of stability. Consider figure 3.2, in which w^* is the subsistence wage rate and r^* is the minimal profit rate. Point A denotes some initial level of the wage and profit rates (w', r') and point B the stationary state (w^*, r^*), with $w' > w^*$ and $r' > r^*$. Paths ab and cb illustrate two different possible routes to the stationary state. Along path ab, the wage rate and the rate of profit fall steadily towards stationary state values, with population adjustment being assumed to take place relatively slowly. Thus the rate of profit reaches its minimal level before the wage rate has been depressed to a subsistence level. Along path cb, both the wage rate and the rate of profit initially rise, with r again adjusting more rapidly than w, starting to fall earlier, and attaining its

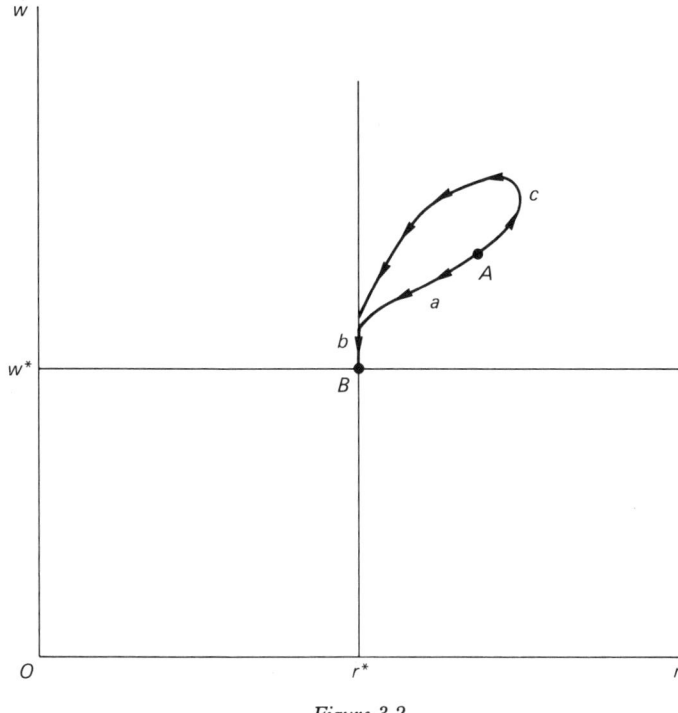

Figure 3.2

stationary state value sooner. The rationale of path *ab* is obvious, but that of path *cb* invites further discussion. Now in Smith technical change is endogenous, it being caused by the division of labour. By contrast, in Samuelson (1977, 1978) the process of technical change is exogenous to the system. In typical *ex cathedra* style, Samuelson (1977, p. 43) writes:

> Now let there be an invention . . . [it] must transiently raise one, or more probably both, of the profit rate and the real wage rate . . . but ultimately . . . the law of diminishing returns on fixed land operates. The system relapses into Smith's 'dull state' . . . If inventions keep recurring, the system goes through a Brownian motion in which profit rates and real wages average out above their subsistence levels . . . The model captures the general behaviour of economic history these last two centuries.

In a similar vein Samuelson (1978, p. 1428) talks of the way in which 'innovation plucks the DD string outwards' (i.e. the marginal product curve) as a consequence of which there is 'a Brownian dance or Schumpeterian fluctuation of real wages and profits at average levels above the minima'. The insertion of the word 'Schumpeterian' here is telling, and makes the application of Samuelson's analysis to Adam Smith very strained. Whilst Samuelson talks elsewhere of inventions being both spontaneous and induced, it is clear that the latter category is ignored in a formal sense. In his world, inventions are conceived of as impinging on the system from the outside, having been generated by some stochastic process. A modified version of his production function could be written as

$$Y = f(K, N, \epsilon) \qquad (3.50)$$

where ϵ is a random variable. Thus marginal products are themselves functions of this random variable, which implies, assuming perfect competition, that the real wage rate and the rate of profit are random variables:

$$w = f_N(\epsilon) \quad \text{and} \quad r = f_K(\epsilon) \qquad (3.51)$$

Samuelson talks of the economic system going through Brownian motion. By contrast, in Smith the emphasis is almost entirely reversed, with induced innovation being dominant and being achieved by the division of labour. To Smith, the principal determinant of innovation was undoubtedly the accumulation of capital, for 'labour can be more and more subdivided in proportion only as stock is more accumulated' (WN, p. 277). This is ignored in a formal sense by Samuelson, and indeed the specification of the production function (3.50) is, as even he seems prepared to hint, more Schumpeterian than Smithian.

The two approaches can be contrasted by reference to figure 3.3. For the purposes of geometrical illustration, inputs are regarded as being combined in fixed proportions so that it is therefore sensible to talk of a 'dose' of labour-cum-capital, and its corresponding marginal product. In period t the marginal physical product curve is MPP_t, and for the input level of Oa we can examine the breakdown into wages, rent, and profit. The subsistence wage rate is w^* and the wage rate in period t is w_t, and therefore total wage payments are $w_t caO$. Profits are given by area $w_t cde$, and rent by the area contained between ed and the MPP_t curve. Assuming that the MPP_t curve has not changed for a number of previous periods, the path of the point that determines the split between wages and profits is the negatively sloped arrowed line going through c. Invention of the sort Samuelson envisaged shifts the marginal physical product curve to the right. Such a new curve is labelled $MPP_{t+\tau}$ in figure 3.3. This can cause an increase in the wage rate along the path ch to a level $w_{t+\tau}$.

Theories of Smithian Growth 71

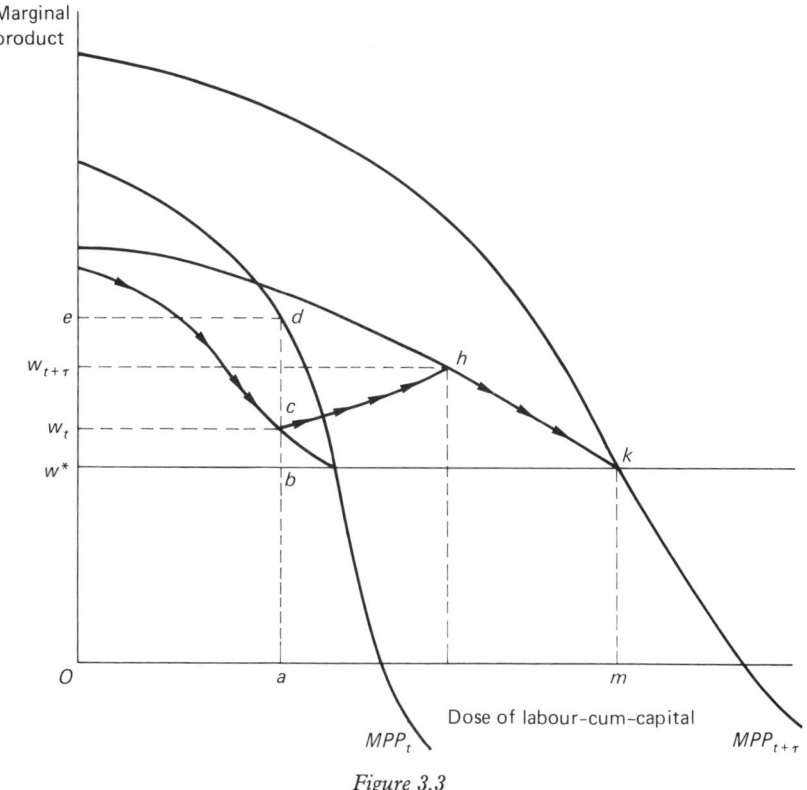

Figure 3.3

Thus if the $MPP_{t+\tau}$ curve remains stable for a number of periods – or, expressed more formally, no new ϵ term appears in the production function – the wage rate will fall along the path hk, eventually reaching the subsistence level w^* at input level Om if no new discoveries occur. An alternative representation of this trajectory is given by the path cb in figure 3.2. By contrast, in the Smithian approach, this random perturbation of the wage rate and rate of profit would not occur. The marginal product curve would shift *continuously* to the right as the economy expands, and scope for the division of labour increases, though growth would not necessarily proceed at a uniform rate. Furthermore, this growth would not be periodic or intermittent. If the growth rate were sufficiently rapid, and if the productivity gains from the division of labour were sufficiently great, then the real wage rate might move along an ascending trajectory for a while, as in figure 3.3.

Having considered a variety of paths to the stationary state, let us now examine the rate at which it occurs, and how adjustment takes place. Samuelson (1978, p. 1420), in analysing what he calls 'the canonical classical model of political economy', refers to 'long-run equilibrium and . . . *transient movement* towards equilibrium' (this writer's emphases). However, what might sensibly be regarded as transient in a physical system (and of course the theory of differential equations applied to such systems has been carried over to economics) is not so sensibly referred to as such for a social system, which might spend several centuries in this passage to long-run equilibrium. From the examples which Smith used to illustrate the final phase of the growth process, in which the stationary state is approached, it is clear that he envisaged the period of adjustment to this stage, in the absence of institutional evolution, to be very lengthy. As a result of Atkinson (1969) we know that the time scale on which growth models converge can be very long, for reasonable choices of parameters. Economic theorists are therefore faced with a considerable difficulty. Much of the theory is concerned with equilibrium analysis. This is neither mere expediency nor blinkered thinking. It arises almost of necessity, for the concept of equilibrium is more primitive, or essential, than the concept of adjustment to equilibrium. As Hahn[7] has put it:

> There is no 'primitive' account of the lag structure of all the error-correcting mechanisms we postulate; that structure is completely *ad hoc*. But the behaviour of the system is very sensitive to that structure . . . Equilibrium theory, even in its sequential and expectational form, is as robust as its sparse axioms; process theory seems totally unrobust and therefore strictly contingent. That is, while for equilibrium analysis functional form is almost inessential, it is almost everything for process analysis.

Essential to the viewpoint adopted in this book is the notion that Smith's analysis of growth is a *process* theory. Furthermore, whilst this process might in the long run culminate in a stationary state, the system must for a long time be exhibiting the characteristics of the process. The error-correction mechanisms postulated by Samuelson are familiar from the literature on passage to equilibrium in a Walrasian system. However, there is no doubting their arbitrariness.[8] Furthermore, these adjustment mechanisms do not begin to capture the sort of process of cumulative growth which is regarded as central to Smithian analysis in this book.

3.5 CONCLUSION

In this chapter we have been concerned to expound and criticize models of Smithian growth with the intention of suggesting new routes forward, analytically speaking. We have omitted consideration of purely literary theories, and also restatements in geometrical terms of literary theories as represented by the elegant diagrammatical treatment of Lowe's (1954) analysis provided by Thweatt (1957) and O'Brien (1975). What we have aimed to suggest is a number of theories which are ripe for further analytical exploration: competition as a process; the possibility of cumulative growth; the role of the division of labour in driving the growth process; and the importance of viewing the economy in sectoral terms. It is to these themes that we first turn in the next chapter.

NOTES

1 Here one is particularly thinking of contributions by theorists like Barkai (1969), Eltis (1984) and Samuelson (1977).
2 For a non-technical and accessible account see Walsh and Gram (1980, ch. 3). For a more advanced treatment, see Abraham-Frois and Berrebi (1979).
3 See Abraham-Frois and Berrebi (1979) for further technical details.
4 See, for example, (3.48).
5 This is also true of his fixed and circulating capital variant, which leads to a modification of (3.37) containing the ratio of fixed to circulating capital as an extra term. For this variant a lower growth rate is implied because of the requirement to provide extra workers with fixed capital.
6 WN, p. 73.
7 Quoted by Littlechild (from a personal communication) in Kirzner (1982).
8 Indeed, Samuelson (1947, p. 297) has himself suggested an alternative specification of the classical population adjustment mechanism.

4
Growth and Accumulation at the Industry Level

4.1 INTRODUCTION

We have seen that the emphasis in the classical approach has been on accumulation rather than allocation. Further, competition takes the form of 'a competition', in the sense of a race or contest, rather than of a static, efficient outcome (Stigler 1957). This process of competition need not involve very many firms, each small in relation to the market as a whole; though this is not ruled out for some markets. It may, rather, involve a moderate number of firms, with one or more having price-setting capabilities, engaged in rivalrous competition for market shares which are significant in relation to the market as a whole (Negishi 1985). In this chapter, firms are regarded as engaging in competition by seeking cost-reducing technologies. An essential component of any approach in the tradition of Adam Smith is that technical change, arising from the division of labour, is endogenous. We shall leave to later chapters explicit consideration of the way in which an advance of the division of labour brings about this technical change, but shall immediately start treating such technical change as the major force driving the competitive process.

The approach adopted requires the abandonment of many of the standard devices employed by the theorist concerned with the firm, including marginalism, Walrasian notions of equilibrium, and static analysis.[1] The model constructed is one of an imperfectly competitive industry in which technical progress is led by a firm which is said to be following an *aggressive pricing policy*, in a sense made clear in section 4.3. The model is presented in three versions for the purposes of exposition, proceeding from the simple to the more complex, with the final version involving consideration of interactions with other industries.

76 *Growth and Accumulation at the Industry Level*

4.2 THE FIRM AND ITS PRICING POLICY

If, as has been suggested, a number of basic tenets of traditional theory are rejected, including marginalism and static microequilibrium, it is incumbent on the critic to suggest alternative ground rules on which analysis can proceed. As Reid (1981, ch. 1) has shown, the classical economists had a healthy understanding of the realities of business conduct. This was clearly true of Adam Smith. For example, during his period as a professor at the University of Glasgow, he was well acquainted with the local business community including, most notably, Provost Andrew Cochrane, who assisted Smith in the acquisition of statistical and institutional information later to be used in *The Wealth of Nations*. In the same way, we would now wish to take a view of the industry and the firm which is founded on some understanding of the realities of business life. The approach adopted involves using more realistic assumptions than those conventionally adopted. They will be considered under three headings: aggressive price leadership, cost-plus pricing, and technical progress.

Unfortunately, it is not possible to relax all the unrealistic assumptions conventionally adopted in the theory of the firm. For simplicity, it will be assumed that all firms have a single plant (though perhaps with a very high capacity) with which one type of good is produced. The analysis is dynamic and is conducted in terms of periods which can be regarded as *seasons of production*. Within each season of production the price does not vary; nor does any firm alter its plant. Empirical evidence on the firm continues to confirm that this is a general practice. Price changes are relatively infrequent, and tend to occur at periodic (sometimes annual) price reviews. It is assumed that all firms have identical non-overlapping production seasons, and make revisions of plans at the beginning of each new season, having decided what plant they will use.

4.3 PRICE LEADERSHIP AND FOLLOWERSHIP

It is known that price leadership is common in oligopolistic industries, with one firm being dominant and taking on the price-setting role, and other firms acting as followers, which entails price-taking behaviour, with the leader's price being regarded as a datum. Price leadership may exist in oligopolies with either a homogeneous or a differentiated product. In the case of a homogeneous product all firms usually charge an identical price; whereas in the case of a differentiated product, the price of any follower tends to differ from the leader's price by a constant proportion. In the latter case, the price of a follower will often slightly undercut that of the leader, this being the only way in which a follower can overcome the reputational advantage of the leader and winnow away a share of the market. At a later point in this chapter a combination of these two situations will be introduced in which the mildest degree of product differentiation exists. This is sufficient to induce what is called a *priority pattern* in the purchases of customers.

A particular form of price leadership will be given emphasis in this chapter, which combines the role of leadership with an aggressive pricing strategy. The latter was first defined by J. M. Cassels (1936, p. 435) in the following words: 'What is meant by the individuals being aggressive in their price policies is that there is nothing in their psychological make-ups, or in their institutional arrangements, which will prevent them cutting price when the competitive situation calls for price cutting.' Clive Saxton (1942), one of the first contributors to the cost-plus versus marginalist pricing debate, devoted a considerable part of his classical study *The Economics of Price Determination* to what will be called here *aggressive price leadership*: this being, as the term suggests, the combination of an aggressive price policy with the role of price leadership. The term is applied to relatively new industries in which price leaders adopt systematic strategies for pushing capacity upwards at a rapid rate by changing the technical conditions of production, at the same time as progressively lowering price over successive seasons of production. Contemporary examples of this readily spring to mind, most notably in the electronics, electrical goods and pharmaceuticals industries.

4.4 COST-PLUS PRICING

The first assumption of the theory is that prices are determined on a cost-plus basis. That is, all firms will compute their selling price by adding a constant profit margin to their average costs under partial adaptation.[2] So many studies indicate that some sort of cost-plus pricing policy is followed by the majority of firms, that it is considered to be a vital element in any realistic theory of the firm. Also in line with empirical evidence, it will be assumed that average costs (and, by implication, marginal costs) are constant, under partial adaptation.

There are several versions of this cost-plus pricing technique, variously described as *mark-up*, *full-cost*, and *target* pricing. Probably the classical statement of this technique is given by Hall and Hitch (1939, p. 113), who wrote: 'Prime (or "direct") cost per unit is taken as the base, and a percentage addition is made to cover overheads (or "oncost", or "indirect" cost), and a further conventional addition (frequently 10 per cent) is made for profit.' Actually the technique as currently applied in highly technically progressive industries might entail a 'conventional addition' for profit which is substantially greater than 10 per cent, but this quote is in essentials a good guide to business practice. The simplest version of the technique will be adopted. Consider a particular firm (say, the ith) which is producing in a defined industry at a particular time (say t). Then

price = unit direct cost + unit gross profit

or, in symbols,

$$p(t) = c_i(t) + \pi_i(t)$$
$$= [1 + k_i(t)] c_i(t) \qquad k_i(t) > 0 \qquad (4.1)$$

where $p(t)$ is the price set by the leader; $\pi_i(t)$ is the gross profit margin; $c_i(t)$ is unit direct cost (average variable, or prime, cost); and $k_i(t)$ is the percentage gross profit mark-up, which is always positive and may frequently (though not invariably) be substantially less than unity. All variables are dated, as a dynamic analysis of industry evolution is to be undertaken. The distinction between the indirect cost and profit mark-ups has been ignored and the two have been lumped together into a gross profit mark-up. Gross profit will be used to meet indirect cost, together with any one or all of research and development expenditure, inventors' royalty fees and firm's production licence fees; the residual is regarded as pure profit. If we gave each item an individual mark-up this would probably result in a loss, rather than a gain, in realism, and furthermore would render the analysis unnecessarily intricate.

Some economists have been discomfited by the apparent inconsistency between the assumption of profit maximization and a mark-up pricing rule. It is easily shown that for the profit maximizing firm the ratio of the net profit margin to price is equal to the reciprocal of the elasticity of demand. A mark-up which does not vary with shifts in demand cannot therefore permit profit maximization. Three comments on this criticism may be made. Firstly, long-run and short-run profit maximization should be distinguished. A firm might prefer an apparently non-optimal short-run pricing rule which does not require too much knowledge of market conditions (e.g. elasticity of demand) or too frequent price revisions, such revisions being costly and inconvenient to customers and salesman alike. In the long run, it is argued later, firms seek increasing profits over time, even though they adopt a mark-up rule for any given plant. Secondly, it might not be unreasonable to suggest that the demand curve is iso-elastic - an assumption which is not particularly strong over the relevant range of price variation. Thirdly, the role of information and uncertainty should not be ignored. Information on costs is more easily obtained than information on demand conditions; for example, rules-of-thumb may often be adopted as a means of dealing with ignorance and uncertainty. In a world with no uncertainty about the future, and full information in the present, such rules may be non-optimal. But the practical requirements of making day-to-day decisions in an uncertain environment tend to foster such rules.

4.5 TECHNICAL PROGRESS

Aggressive price leadership is a common feature of oligopolies in which technical progress is pervasive, if not continuous. This technical progress is important to the achievement of persistent cost reductions by the leader. At the most general level its achievement is dependent on the division of labour, and particularly on the emergence of specialized activities within the firm exclusively directed at research and development. This is encouraged by a division of labour which advances to a 'division of thought'. Hollander (1973, pp. 142-3) remarks on the emphasis in Adam Smith on the adoption of cost-reducing methods by large firms. Smith's own words (WM, p. 277), though from an earlier age, are still telling: 'As the operations of each workman are gradually reduced to a greater degree of simplicity, a variety of new machines come to be invented for facilitating and abridging those operations.' Behind the innovation – which leads to the industrial application of new methods of production – lies the activity of invention. It is conventional to distinguish between product and process inventions. A product invention involves the discovery of a new type of good altogether, whereas a process invention is a technique for producing an existing type of good at a lower unit cost than hitherto achieved. As this chapter concentrates attention on the development through time of a particular industry producing a predefined product, it will discuss only process inventions. This is not so limiting as one might judge at first sight. If a product invention X is in fact a new type of capital good which is designed to produce a good Y, for which an established market already exists, then X should be regarded as a process invention with respect to Y even though it is a product invention in itself. Adam Smith himself talked about both product and process invention, and saw that the enlargement of markets was not just the extension of markets for existing commodities, but also the creation of entirely new markets for hitherto unavailable commodities (i.e. for new goods). Concentrating as we are on a predefined market, the latter effect is not yet a relevant consideration in our analysis, but it will become so once linkages with other markets are considered, as in section 4.9.

As evidence suggests, the aggressive price leader retains the initiative by achieving a higher rate of innovation than the followers. It will be assumed that the innovating leader always possesses the latest vintage of capital equipment, and the followers will be consigned to using plant which is at least one vintage behind the leader. Technical progress takes the form of *cost reduction* and *capacity extension*. The convention is adopted of calling the leader firm 1. Then the nature of the leader's technical progress may be described by the inequalities

$$c_1(t) < c_1(t-h)$$
$$a_1(t) > a_1(t-h) \quad h = 1, 2, 3, \ldots \quad (4.2)$$

where a_i refers, in general, to the capacity output of the ith firm. This is similar to the assumption about technology made in the work of Sylos-Labini (1969), but differs from that analysis in that it does not restrict analysis to a fixed number of technologies in the industry, but allows for the development of new technologies.[3]

A follower can obtain plant in three different ways: by purchasing second-hand plant either from a leader, or from another follower selling off a more recent vintage of plant than he possesses; by undertaking himself the research necessary to develop the lower-cost technique which the leader has already developed but kept secret; or by paying a licence fee to the leader in order to benefit from accomplished, but 'classified', unreported research.

Whichever method is used to obtain plant, it will be assumed that it is obtained by the payment of a lump sum, and that therefore marginal cost under partial adaptation is unaffected.

The fact that followers always operate later vintages than the leader may be expressed by the simple equations

$$c_i(t) = c_1(t-h_i)$$
$$a_i(t) = a_1(t-h_i) \quad h_i = 1,2,3, \ldots; i = 2,3, \ldots \quad (4.3)$$

for some positive integral h_i. The inequality $h_i > h_j$ implies that the ith firm has an older vintage of plant than the jth firm. That is, the ith firm has higher unit cost and smaller capacity than the jth firm. An elementary consequence of (4.2) and (4.3) is that

$$c_i(t) > c_1(t)$$
$$a_i(t) < a_1(t) \quad i = 2,3,4, \ldots \quad (4.4)$$

This state of affairs will be said to characterize the leader as being both *cost dominant* and *output dominant*.

To explain the conditions under which the leader will innovate, it is necessary to introduce the notion of a *valuable invention*. By this is meant a process which is potentially more profitable than the newest vintage of plant actually operating. It is assumed that a leader will innovate (i.e. adopt an invention) only if the invention will increase its gross profit.[4] This is an important point, because it means that the discovery of a cost-reducing invention is not sufficient in itself for that invention to be adopted; the scale at which the new plant would operate must be considered. The neglect of this point is a major weakness of the seminal discussion of cost-reducing innovation by Arrow (1962), who ignores the capacity problem and tacitly assumes that new plant can be replicated at will.

Assuming that the leader is always working at capacity, the gross profit before the introduction of a valuable invention is $\pi_1(t)a_1(t)$ and after is $\pi_1(t+1)a_1(t+1)$. It is required that

$$\pi_1(t)a_1(t) < \pi_1(t+1)a_1(t+1)$$

or, in simpler notation.

$$\Pi_1(t) < \Pi_1(t+1) \tag{4.5}$$

The rationale behind this condition is threefold. Firstly, if a firm is to have any incentive to change at all, there must be some compensation for the inconvenience of switching to new plant. Secondly, the process of innovation is subject to uncertainty, and compensation for this bearing of uncertainty is embodied in condition (4.5). Thirdly, because plant is expanding in capacity and presumably increasing in complexity over time, it is increasingly more expensive to purchase or build. If the leader is to maintain as smooth a rate of technical progress as is possible in an uncertain world, then the more modern the plant, the greater the amount he must be able to put aside per unit time towards the purchase (by a lump sum) of new plant. Now this contribution towards what we might care to think of as an ever-enlarging sinking fund must be drawn from gross profit; this provides another justification for (4.5).

Finally, the possibility of cost-reducing technical progress is not unlimited. There may be diminishing returns to research and development; and in order for an object to exist at all, it must be made up of material of non-zero cost. By contrast, there is no foreseeable limit to the growth in capacity of new plants. It seems probable that over time the major factor in maintaining the inequality (4.5) will be growth in capacity. It is assumed, therefore, that unit cost $c(t)$ is bounded from below and away from zero, whereas capacity $a(t)$ is not bounded from above. An interesting consequence of this, when considered in conjunction with (4.3), is that the leader's unit cost curve under 'total adaptation'[5] is L-shaped, in line with empirical evidence.

Strictly speaking, there is no continuous unit cost curve under total adaptation, but rather a series of points at capacity through which a flattened L-shaped curve could be drawn. A similar relationship holds for those followers

82 *Growth and Accumulation at the Industry Level*

working at full capacity. Expressed another way, firms are subject to dynamic increasing returns. This relationship has been anticipated by the falling natural price curve of figure 1.3.

To summarize: (a) the leader is innovating faster than the followers, and is both cost dominant and output dominant as a consequence; and (b) only valuable inventions, capable of providing higher profit than existing plant, will be adopted by the leader.

4.6 TRENDS IN PROFITS AND CONCENTRATION

In the ensuing pages, the behaviour of profits and concentration over time will, for the purposes of convenience and clarity, be analysed under three headings:

1 Constant price and stable demand

2 Constant mark-up and stable demand

3 Constant mark-up and expanding demand.

The conclusions will differ, depending on what is assumed about prices and demand. To take price first, evidence suggests that the leader would tend to keep his mark-up constant, and hence would allow price to fall with cost. This conclusion was first admirably expressed by Andrews (1949, p. 272):

> As it grows, a business will let any actual fall in costs influence its price through the operation of the normal pricing policy . . . an expanding business will tend to fix its costing margin on the basis of average overheads on the last account plus an allowance for normal profit. It will, therefore, tend to reduce its price. Granted a rapidly expanding market, it may even look ahead a little and take account of the lower costs which it expects at the larger outputs.

Initially this complication is avoided but, under the second and third headings, this realistic assumption is incorporated into the analysis.

Concerning demand, the main point to put forward is that it may take the form of either derived demand or final consumer demand. For this reason, we shall always talk of 'customers' for the product of the industry, meaning either firms or consumers. Whether or not one assumes demand is stable depends on the perspective one takes. In a partial equilibrium analysis, the assumption of a stable demand schedule is acceptable. For reasons which will become apparent, the only important alternative assumption in a general disequilibrium analysis of industries is that demand is expanding over time.

The case in which both price and industry demand are given is the least realistic, but the simplest to study. It is used as a starting point merely to introduce the model in action. Modifying this simple case, by allowing price to fall but maintaining demand conditions constant, brings the argument into the familiar realm of partial equilibrium analysis, in which effects beyond the industry are ignored. Finally, the third and most realistic case analyses the interplay between industries under the assumption of general dynamic increasing returns.

4.7 CONSTANT PRICE AND STABLE DEMAND

Suppose that both market demand and the price set by the leader were stable over time. This implies that the leader has an increasing mark-up over time (see A.4.1)[6] and effectively defines the oldest vintage of plant which can operate profitably. It is assumed that if the price set by the leader is below any follower's unit direct cost, then that follower will go out of business. Any such price for which $p < c_j(t)$ holds has been called an *elimination price* by Sylos-Labini (1969). He points out that even prices above $c_j(t)$ may prevent entry in the long run if they permit only a low level of profit. This is true, but it introduces an unnecessary complication which even Sylos-Labini elected to ignore in much of his analysis. The concept of an elimination price is less important in this section, where price is constant, than in the next section, where price is falling.

No follower will go out of business if it is selling at above unit direct cost and operating at capacity. However, as technical progress proceeds, the total capacity of industry becomes greater, even though customers' demand is unaltered at the constant market price. This implies that over time an increasing number of firms will be forced to work below capacity.

At this point it is convenient to extend the analysis by assuming a mild degree of product differentiation exists: sufficient, at least, to establish what we shall call a *priority pattern* of customers.[7] Customers follow a priority pattern in that, *ceteris paribus*, they will purchase the good produced by the most recent vintage of plant. As a uniform price prevails other things are indeed equal, and customers may be thought of as having the mildest preference for the product of a recent rather than a later vintage. But if the former is not available, they will be content to purchase the latter, rather than having to queue, register on a waiting list, or accept a delay in delivery. There may be several reasons for this priority pattern. For example, the possession of a good from the new vintages may confer a certain prestige upon the customer, even though the product is

84 *Growth and Accumulation at the Industry Level*

homogeneous in a physical sense. It implies that customers tend to buy from firms with the greatest turnover, which is rather plausible. As will shortly be discovered, the newer the vintage of plant, the greater the profit. Hence firms with newer vintages are capable of undertaking greater advertising expenditure than firms with older vintages, and in this way too a priority pattern could be established.

Thus the leader will always operate at capacity because he has a 'first-purchase' advantage; whereas firms with older vintages already working with relatively low profit margins may have their miseries compounded by having to operate below capacity. In terms of the strict logic of the model, only firms with the oldest vintage of plant which can be profitably operated at the prevailing price will have to work below capacity, but in practice it is unlikely that customers will follow a priority pattern with complete consistency, and there will be merely a tendency for excess capacity to be greater for firms with older vintage of plant.

Because price is constant, and unit cost is falling over time, unit profit for each firm, and the leader in particular, is increasing over time. This fact, when considered in conjunction with the extension of capacity caused by technical progress, means that the gross profit of the leader is increasing over time (see A.4.2). Thus the condition for an invention to be valuable (cf. (4.5)) is automatically satisfied. At least some of the followers will work at capacity. Because followers employ plant which is at least one vintage behind the leader, they will all have lower unit profits and smaller capacity outputs; indeed, some may even operate below capacity. It follows that the leader's gross profit exceeds that of any follower (see A.4.3). In other words, it is automatically true that the leader is cost, output and profit dominant: this firm is in a position of total hegemony.

The leader's position with respect to market share will also be dominant in the long run. As technical progress proceeds and firms expand capacity, the firms with the oldest vintage of plant will find themselves losing their market shares. They may try to counteract this tendency by buying or developing more modern plant, but in fact this will only exacerbate the situation. There is a fixed quantum of demand at the prevailing price but an increasing aggregate capacity caused by technical progress. Only the leader cannot lose. Eventually he will become the sole producer after a period of increasing, and probably accelerating, concentration.

4.8 CONSTANT MARK-UP AND STABLE DEMAND

As suggested by the quotation in section 4.6 from Andrews (1949), it is more realistic to assume that the percentage profit mark-up remains constant over time, rather than price itself.

If the leader maintains a constant mark-up and demand is stable over time, there are two immediate consequences. Firstly, if unit direct cost is falling and the mark-up is constant, then price per unit and unit gross profit will fall (see A.4.4). Such a conclusion is very Smithian. He wrote (WN, p. 260): 'It is the natural effect of improvement, however, to diminish gradually the real price of almost all manufacturers ... In consequence of better machinery, of greater dexterity, and of a more proper division and distribution of work, all of which are the natural effects of improvement, a much smaller quantity of labour becomes requisite for executing any particular piece of work.' Secondly, only the leader is in a position to maintain a constant mark-up because it is not to be expected in general that the rate of diffusion of cost-reducing innovations to followers will exactly offset the rate of decrease in the price set by the leader. In fact, because the unit direct costs of the followers are always above the leader's, the leader must have the greatest mark-up and the greatest gross profit (see A.4.5). Unlike in the previous case, it is no longer true that any cost-reducing invention is valuable (see A.4.6). We now require that the cost-reducing effect must be outstripped by the capacity-extension effect. This means that the rate of innovation will be slower than in the constant price, stable demand case. It will be assumed that although inequality (4.5) does not automatically hold, the leader will be sufficiently prudent to ensure that any innovation it makes will meet this criterion. If this is true, then by definition the leader's gross profit is increasing over time. It is of interest to note that firms may be subject to a classical falling rate of profit even if they observe this valuable invention criterion. In so far as capacity is a measure of capital employed, the value of capital is the cost per unit of capacity times the capacity. Then the rate of profit is:

$$\frac{\text{unit gross profit} \times \text{capacity}}{\text{cost per unit of capacity} \times \text{capacity}}$$

or, more simply, the ratio of unit gross profit to cost per unit of capacity.

It has been shown that unit gross profit is falling over time (see A.4.4), so the behaviour of the rate of profit depends on cost per unit of capacity $\kappa(t)$. No particular assumption has been made about this, and the evidence is not clear-cut. On the one hand there is the engineers' '0.6 rule' (described by writers like Moore 1959), which says that the increase in capital cost of a plant is given by the increase in capacity raised to the 0.6 power. In other words, cost per unit of capacity falls as capacity increases (see A.4.7). This rule is based on production processes in which the amount of material required to enclose a given volume (e.g. in boilers, gas tanks, compressors) is the basic cost–capacity ratio. As Moore (1959, p. 127) puts it: 'Area varies as the volume to the 2/3 power, or in other language, cost varies as capacity to the 2/3 power.' On the other hand, Moore (1959, p. 128) admits that 'complicated industrial machinery does not

86 *Growth and Accumulation at the Industry Level*

necessarily exhibit the same relationship between area (cost) and volume (capacity) as do simple structures like tanks and columns.' If a process invention involved a fair degree of automation and/or computerization of the production process, then it is probable that the 0.6 rule would be violated, and cost per unit of capacity might well increase. In such cases, the rate of profit must certainly fall (see A.4.8). The rate of profit will only rise if something akin to the 0.6 rule is working sufficiently strongly to offset falling unit gross profits. This analysis suggests that a falling rate of profit may be merely a mechanical consequence of pursuing a constant mark-up policy in an environment of persistent innovation. One could argue that this is not undesirable. Firms increase their gross profits as they innovate, and customers enjoy the benefits of this innovation through the falling price of the good produced by the industry.[8]

Another point of considerable interest in this constant mark-up, stable demand case is that followers are always at a competitive disadvantage in the innovatory process. The argument is as follows. Each follower is using plant of a type which the leader used several periods previously. But in those past periods, price was higher. Hence any follower is operating plant which had earlier yielded a higher profit to the leader (see A.4.9). If a firm's capability for introducing new plant is an increasing function of its gross profit, then a follower's position is clearly weaker than the leader's. For, if the level of gross profit which the leader has earned in each period is always necessary to achieve the next innovation, then followers may simply be debarred from undertaking their own research and development. However, it is unlikely that this in itself will prevent them from adopting new plant. Second-hand plant should be available, and even new plant of an older vintage will be less desirable than when first introduced and hence will command a lower price.

Unlike the situation discussed under the constant price, stable demand heading, firms will continually be exiting from the industry as the leader's price falls below the unit direct costs of followers with the oldest vintages of plant. Previously, firms only shut down when they were forced to work well below capacity. This effect will still exist, but will now be supplemented by one of greater importance, namely, a persistently declining 'elimination price' whittling away the profits of marginal firms. As before, this will mean that there is a tendency to increasing concentration over time, and the priority pattern of customers implies that eventually the leader will become the sole producer. However, in contrast to the previous case, price will be lower and output greater in this more realistic case, as a consequence of the leader's falling profit margin.

Several of the characteristics of the constant price, stable demand case carry over to the constant mark-up, stable demand case: output and profit dominance of the leader;[9] increasing concentration over time, terminating with monopolization by the leader; and the continuous exiting of firms as technical progress proceeds. There are some important differences, however, and two in particular are noteworthy. Firstly, profit margins and price are falling over time, and as a result there may be a tendency for the leader to experience a falling rate of profit. Secondly, the leader, by adopting a constant mark-up policy, always has a competitive advantage over the followers in the innovatory process. Indeed, this may be regarded as the rationale for adopting such a policy.

4.9 CONSTANT MARK-UP AND EXPANDING DEMAND

So far the analysis has proceeded in dynamic but, nevertheless, partial equilibrium terms. It remains incomplete until our particular theory of the firm is integrated into a theory of all industries.

Notable contributions by Kaldor (1972) and Richardson (1975), both of which emphasize the significance of increasing returns in the process of industrial growth, provide a suitable starting point. Here the emphasis will be on the Kaldorian analysis. Building on a famous paper by Allyn Young (1928), Kaldor argues that theorists should reinstate increasing returns as an economic 'axiom', because it is more realistic than the assumption of constant returns which lies at the heart of general equilibrium analysis in the Walrasian tradition. As we shall see, if we follow Kaldor and Young, the notion of equilibrium in an industry becomes meaningless. If increasing returns prevail in all industries, then in the words of Young (1928, p. 528): 'No analysis of the forces making for economic equilibrium, forces which you might say are tangential at any moment of time, will serve to illumine this field, for movements away from equilibrium, departures from previous trends, are characteristic of it.' In the model of aggressive price leadership which has been analysed, unit costs under total adaptation have been falling over time, in effect producing dynamic increasing returns. Whilst it is not assumed that other industries also have a structure of aggressive price leadership, it is taken, at least, that all industries are subject to dynamic increasing returns for some reason or other. With the addition of this fairly realistic assumption, it is possible to lift the partial equilibrium argument of section 4.8 and put it into what might be described as a 'general disequilibrium' setting.

Young's basic argument is a variant of Say's Law. Before distracting complications are added, it is instructive to consider the reasoning at a simple level. Imagine a barter economy in which a firm takes advantage of the division of labour, as a result of which greater output can now be produced with the same number of men. Because there is a greater supply of this good, say A, an increased demand has been generated, in effect, for the goods B, C, D, E etc. (produced in other industries) for which A can be exchanged. Suppose for the sake of argument that the producers of goods B, C and D try to take advantage of this increased demand by enlarging their supply in a labour-saving fashion. They too will then generate increased demand: mutually for each others goods; and globally for all other goods A, E, F, G etc. for which B, C and D are exchangeable. Provided increasing returns prevail generally, this process will continue, and as Young (1928, p. 533) put it: 'Change becomes progressive and propagates itself in a cumulative way.'

Now to some complications. A condition which must be satisfied in order that the process may continue is that an increase in the supply of any good should generate an increase in the demand for all other goods. Young thought this condition would be satisfied if the demand for each good was relatively elastic, the reasoning being that if a given percentage fall in supply price engendered a greater percentage increase in sales, the increased revenue, when distributed to factors, would generate increased demand for other goods. The fallacy in this argument, which Kaldor pointed out, is that the increased revenue is only gained by diverting expenditure from other goods, that is, by *decreasing* demand for them. Kaldor offers an alternative, more complex, argument which we develop in further detail in chapter 8. Briefly, it says that in disequilibrium situations (which he considers to be characteristic of decentralized market economies) excess supply and excess demand are absorbed by producers and merchants. In rather imperfectly competitive markets, an increased demand causes producers to deplete stocks, and they then undertake induced investment in the form of an increased value of goods in process and, if the excess demand continues, in the form of the purchase of new plant to expand capacity. In relatively competitive markets, excess supply is absorbed by merchants; and provided they have sufficent confidence in future prices to increase not just the volume but also the value of their stocks, they too will have undertaken induced investment. The addition to income of these induced investments generates an increase in effective demand which is the motor driving this process of cumulative expansion described by Young.

In section 4.8 the dynamic process of innovation finally stopped when the leader was supplying the whole market at a price he had set. At no stage was it considered how firms in the industry were interacting with firms in other industries. As firms in our price leadership model are subject to increasing returns, and as the analysis will follow Kaldor in assuming increasing returns for other industries, the expansionary process described by Young will be in operation. Smith himself was aware of the interaction of market expansion and cost reduction:

The increase of demand, besides, though in the beginning it may sometimes raise the price of goods, never fails to lower it in the long run. It encourages production and thereby increases the competition of producers, who, in order to undersell one another have recourse to new divisions of labour and new improvements of art, which might never otherwise have been thought of. (WN, p. 748)

In this general disequilibrium framework, some of the conclusions of the constant mark-up, stable demand case remain valid. The leader will still be totally dominant with respect to cost, output and gross profit. Price and the profit margin will fall over time. The leader may be subject to a classical falling rate of profit. Followers will be at a competitive disadvantage in the innovatory process and will shut down if the leader's price falls below their unit direct costs. The major difference is that, *prima facie*, concentration does not necessarily increase over time. Previously, capacity output was unbounded but demand was stable; hence the capacity of the leader would eventually satisfy total demand at some price. By contrast, demand is now continually expanding, and even though firms with recent vintages of plant must have *relatively* high market shares compared with other firms, these market shares could be small compared with the aggregate output of the industry.

One qualification should be made to this argument. No consideration has yet been given to what would happen when the lower bound on cost is approached. In order for an invention to be valuable when cost is very close to this bound, new plant must have enormously enlarged capacity. In this situation, which no advanced economy seems to have approached as yet, it may be that the tendency to concentration will reassert itself as technical leaders, being unable to achieve appreciable cost reductions, concentrate instead on substantial capacity extension.

4.10 CONCLUSION

Probably the most important conclusions of this chapter are contained under the headings of constant mark-up and stable demand, and constant mark-up and expanding demand. Results under the former are only important in so far as they carry through to the latter. The principal results are:

1   The leader may be subject to a classical falling rate of profit, even if gross profits are expanding over time.

90 *Growth and Accumulation at the Industry Level*

2. Followers are at a competitive disadvantage compared with the leader in the innovatory process.
3. There is no necessary tendency to concentration over time, unless the lower bound on cost is being approached.
4. There is no necessary tendency of any firm to an equilibrium position.
5. There is in principle no limit to the growth of aggregate output of the industry.

The advantage of this chapter's approach seems to be its emphasis on the adoption of new technologies.[10] In place of the uniformity of standard competitive models, market and technological advantages interact to perpetuate inequalities between firms, locking them into vicious or virtuous circles.

APPENDIX

A.4.1 Now $p(t) = p$, a constant for all t. From (4.1), $p = [1 + k_1(t)]c_1(t)$. From (4.2), $c_1(t) < c_1(t - h)$, whence $k_1(t - h) < k_1(t)$.

A.4.2 From (4.1), $p - c_1(t) = \pi_1(t)$, and from (4.2), $c_1(t) < c_1(t - h)$, whence $\pi_1(t) > \pi_1(t - h)$. From (4.2), $a_1(t) > a_1(t - h)$, whence $\Pi_1(t) > \Pi_1(t - h)$. Thus condition (4.5) is satisfied.

A.4.3 From (4.1), $p = c_i(t) + \pi_i(t) = c_1(t) + \pi_1(t)$. But from (4.4), $c_i(t) > c_1(t)$, whence $\pi_i(t) < \pi_1(t)$. From (4.4), $a_i(t) < a_1(t)$, whence $\Pi_i(t) < \Pi_1(t)$.

A.4.4 Leader's mark-up $k_1(t) = k$, a constant for all t under the assumptions of section 4.8. From (4.1), $p(t) = (1 + k)c_1(t)$. From (4.2), $c_1(t) < c_1(t - h)$, whence $p(t) < p(t - h)$, i.e. price is falling over time. Similarly, as $\pi_1(t) = kc_1(t)$, we have $\pi_1(t) < \pi_1(t - h)$, i.e. unit gross profit is falling over time.

A.4.5 For the leader, $p(t) = (1 + k)c_1(t)$, and the same price $p(t) = [1 + k_i(t)]c_i(t)$ for the ith follower. Subtracting, $(1 + k)c_1(t) = [1 + k_i(t)]c_i(t)$. But from (4.4), $c_i(t) > c_1(t)$, whence $k_i(t) < k$. By a similar argument to A.4.3, it follows that $\pi_i(t) < \pi_1(t)$ and $\Pi_i(t) < \Pi_1(t)$.

A.4.6 As $a_1(t) > a_1(t - h)$, but $\pi_1(t) < \pi_1(t - h)$. Therefore the relative size of $\Pi_1(t)$ and $\Pi_1(t - h)$ is unknown.

A.4.7 In the notation of Moore (1959), $C_2 = C_1[X_2/X_1]^{0.6}$, where C_1 and C_2 are the costs of two pieces of machinery with capacities of X_1 and X_2. Thus $C_2/X_2^{0.6} = C_1/X_1^{0.6}$. That is, $(C_2/X_2^{0.6})/(C_1/X_1^{0.6}) = 1$. Now

$$\frac{C_2}{X_2} \bigg/ \frac{C_1}{X_1} = \left(\frac{C_2}{X_2^{0.6}} \bigg/ \frac{C_1}{X_1^{0.6}}\right)\left(\frac{X_1}{X_2}\right)^{0.4}$$

The first term in brackets is unity and the second term is less than unity for $X_2 > X_1$. Therefore $(C_2/X_2) < (C_1/X_1)$ for $X_2 > X_1$. That is, cost per unit of capacity declines as capacity increases.

A.4.8 The costs of capital before and after innovation are $\kappa(t)a_1(t)$ and $\kappa(t+1)a_1(t+1)$. The general expression for the rate of profit is

$$\rho(t) = \frac{\pi_1(t)a_1(t)}{\kappa(t)a_1(t)}$$

or $\pi_1(t)/\kappa(t)$. If $\kappa(t+1) > \kappa(t)$ and from A.4.4 $\pi_1(t+1) < \pi_1(t)$, then $\rho(t+1) < \rho(t)$.

A.4.9 For the leader h_i periods ago, the basic relationships are

$$p(t - h_i) = c_1(t - h_i) + kc_1(t - h_i)$$
$$= c_1(t - h_i) + \pi_i(t - h_i)$$

and $\Pi_1(t - h_i) = a_1(t - h_i)\pi_1(t - h_i)$. For the ith follower, currently working with the same type of plant:

$$p(t) = c_i(t) + \pi_i(t)$$
$$= [1 + k_i(t)]c_1(t - h_i) \quad \text{by (4.3)}$$

But $k_i(t) < k$ from A.4.5, from which $k_i(t)c_1(t - h_i) < kc_1(t - h_i)$ or $\pi_i(t) < \pi_1(t - h_i)$. As $a_i(t) = a_1(t - h_i)$ from (4.3), it follows that $\Pi_i(t) < \Pi_1(t - h_i)$.

NOTES

1 As I emphasize in Reid (1979), this view is very much in sympathy with the one expressed by Phillip Andrews (1964) in *On Competition in Economic Theory*.
2 Partial adaptation is a term due to Wiles (1961, p. 8). It is roughly equivalent to behaviour in the short run.
3 In Adam Smith's analysis, as here, technical change is embodied in the capital structure, being caused by the division of labour. On this, see Hollander (1973, ch. 7). Of Smith, Hollander (1973, pp. 104-5) says: 'The bulk of his attention in dealing with details of speciali zation is upon sub-division of labour within the plant. For both invention and innovation are said to be dependent upon scale . . . Smith seems to have in mind increase in scale of plant when dealing specifically with the major conditions for technical advance.' It is precisely this type of reasoning that lies behind the technological assumptions of the text of this chapter.
4 This assumption may be subjected to some criticism, as it ignores the rate of return on what we call a 'valuable invention'. As will be seen, this may imply a classical falling rate of profit over time. The assumption is justified by its generic similarity to growth maximizing and profit satisficing behaviour. A quotation from Baumol (1962, p. 1085) makes this clear:

92 Growth and Accumulation at the Industry Level

'From the point of view of a long-run growth (or sales) maximizer, profit no longer acts as a constraint. Rather, it is an instrumental variable, a means whereby management works towards its goals. Specifically, profits are a means for obtaining capital needed to finance expansion plans.' Because it is assumed that gross profit in period $t + 1$ merely exceeds gross profit in period t, ignoring magnitudes, it is clear that a kind of satisficing behaviour is being assumed. See Reid (1987b, ch. 8) for an exact characterization of satisficing rules. Note that discounting is not introduced explicitly into the notation in the text of this chapter, or in the Appendix. The effect of discounting is of course to make remote values carry less weight. The reader can if he wishes regard value formulae in this chapter as expressed in discounted present values as appropriate. Alternatively, or in addition, he can ignore discounting as an adjustment that merely increases notation and alters formulae in a purely formal sense without making any difference to the qualitative conclusions. See Vickers (1985, p. 15) in his treatment of patent races, and Baumol (1982, p. 13) in his discussion of the notation used to expound intertemporal unsustainability.

5 A term due to Wiles (1961, p. 8).

6 Propositions numbered A.4.1 to A.4.9 are contained in the appendix to chapter 4.

7 The original stimulus to adopt this assumption was a study by Tucker (1964) on the development of brand loyalty. The first two conclusions of his study were (p. 35): '(1) Some consumers will become brand loyal even when there is no discriminable difference between brands other than the brand itself. (2) The brand loyalty established under such conditions is not trivial, although it may be based on what are apparently trivial and superficial differences.' On the other hand, some consumers were conspicuously non-loyal, and exploratory in their purchases. It is convenient to extend these ideas to purchasers of intermediate goods. Provided the exploratory behaviour of non-loyal customers is fairly evenly spread over purchases from all vintages, and the brand-loyal customers tend to buy goods produced by the most recent vintages, the priority pattern will tend to be established.

8 It has been pointed out by several writers, most notably Pearce and Gabor (1952), that profit maximizing behaviour will not in general maximize the rate of return on capital. In the case of the marginal analysis in competitive markets, firms will tend to increase output beyond the point at which the rate of return would be maximized. To an extent, therefore, it is not surprising that in the present analysis, where the firm seeks merely to *improve* profits in successive periods, the rate of profit might actually fall.

9 In a patent race model, Vickers (1985) shows that if the low-cost firm wins the current race, it will always win. This increasing dominance property reinforces the sort of conclusion reached here.

10 There are, naturally, limitations as well. Exit, rather than entry, possibilities have been emphasized. The technical improvement of existing goods, rather than the development of new goods, is emphasized. The possibility of 'leapfrogging' by rivals, to break the dominance of the leader, is excluded. These are all important issues which are integral to the Smithian view but have had to be excluded for analytical simplicity.

5
The Division of Labour and Technical Change

5.1 INTRODUCTION

The concept of the division of labour is introduced so early in *The Wealth of Nations* that even the most superficial acquaintance with the work is likely to communicate the idea to the reader. Adam Smith was by no means the only writer to have grasped the significance of the division of labour. There were others before, such as Sir William Petty,[1] Adam Ferguson and Anne Turgot; and even more afterwards, including David Ricardo and John Stuart Mill. But there can be little doubt that, of them all, Smith is most notably remembered for his analysis of the division of labour, possibly in large part because it gives rise to a form of technical change which can propel a process of cumulative growth.

This chapter aims to give a more detailed treatment of the division of labour than is generally available.[2] Of course, Adam Smith's original treatment, in terms of advantages arising from increased dexterity, time-saving and inventiveness, is taken as the point of departure, but much more requires to be said. A new advantage from the division of labour, mentioned by Smith in his *Lectures on Rhetoric and Belles Lettres* but not in *The Wealth of Nations*, is today assuming greater importance. It is what Arrow (1979) calls specialization in know-how, and Casson (1988) the division of thought,[3] and it requires further discussion both here and in chapter 9. It is especially relevant to contemporary developments in advanced economies, associated with the expansion of the tertiary sector (providing services rather than manufactured goods).

The division of labour within the firm requires more precise analysis than is usual. In chapter 4 it was seen to play the role of providing dynamic increasing

94 *The Division of Labour and Technical Change*

returns for the firm, in the sense that capacity unit variable costs for the firm lay along a flattened L-shaped curve over time. There, we also anticipated generalizations of the division of labour to specialization between firms, and ultimately between industries. More recently, the ultimate generalization has been taken to the *international* division of labour.[4] The basis for such generalization must now be examined in more detail. Finally, perhaps the crucial point, we now wish to provide a more detailed underpinning for the assumption implicit in much of the discussion in earlier chapters, namely that the division of labour leads to endogenous technical change. The argument is essentially Allyn Young's, though he did not give it formal expression. Recent writers amplifying his approach, such as Lauchlin Currie (1981), have also found it difficult to provide a formal treatment. As a principal purpose of this work is to advance formal methods of analysis as applied to classical economic growth, the development of an appropriate formalization is crucial. The main contribution of this chapter is to show how this can be done using an appropriately specified production function. This introduces a device which is central to the modelling of growth in subsequent chapters, especially in chapters 6, 7 and 8.

5.2 THE DIVISION OF LABOUR

Modern theoretical treatments in the neoclassical tradition of the division of labour are not extensive, though this should not lead one to agree with Professor Stigler (1976) that Smith's analysis of the division of labour is one of his 'failures'. Stigler's point would be that Smith's analysis must be adjudged a failure on this topic because it has not, in his view, led to a theory, hypothesis or proposition which is now part of contemporary economic analysis. It is not, Stigler (1976, p. 1201) would have it, 'a part of the living economics of successors'. Yet Stigler's attitude is ambivalent, if not schizophrenic, for he himself in Stigler (1951) has made one of the best known contributions to advancing the theory of the division of labour! We shall deal with it shortly. Stigler (1976, p. 1211) does not deny 'the ubiquity of the division of labour' concept (in terms of what he calls a test of 'congruence' with reality), or its specific theoretical implications (e.g. for the analysis of protectionism). In view of all this one might respectfully ask whether failure in Stigler's sense is an awfully damning thing.

As against Stigler one could argue that the division of labour concept has proved sufficiently powerful in its extant form not to require substantial modification, even up to this day. This would be no criticism of the theory at all, but more a reflection of its durability and robustness. Further, failure to develop it in the dominant neoclassical framework, which has been established for over a century now, should perhaps be no surprise, for the division of labour analysis is a part of classical economics. Given the eclipse of classical analysis of the non-Marxian variety, barring its mutation to a fiercely radical form of libertarianism which many find intellectually, ethically and politically unpalatable, it might simply be that insufficient effort has been devoted by the ablest of contemporary theorists to ways of advancing the theory. The classical tradition has of course been kept alive and vigorous, largely outside the Western universities, by writers in the Marxist tradition, who would seek to ignore or conveniently forget the Smithian origins of so much of the sounder bits of economic analysis they use. There is a vast radical-left literature on the division of labour, with Braverman (1974) and Marglin (1975) being perhaps the most influential, and a newly emerging and extensive literature from the same camp designed to extend the analysis to the 'new international division of labour', of which Fröbel, Heinrichs and Kreye (1980) is representative.

In fact, shortly after Stigler (1976) rated Smith's analysis of the division of labour as a failure, Ippolito (1977) provided a detailed (and arguably prolix) modern theoretical treatment of the topic with testable empirical implications. At a deeper level, shortly after came Arrow's (1979) paper on the division of labour as a kind of specialization in knowing how to do things. But perhaps most important is the recent work of Casson (1986, 1988), which is informed by a thorough knowledge of the literature on the division of labour and provides perhaps the most significant theoretical extension of the concept since *The Wealth of Nations*.

However, let us start at the beginning, with Adam Smith and his pin factory. In almost all respects, Smith had precursors, and this is as true of his analysis of the division of labour[5] as of many other major themes. However, it is proper to take Smith as the starting point because his statement of the productivity advantages of the division of labour has been far more influential than that of any other writer before or since. Indeed his pin factory example in *The Wealth of Nations* must be one of the most extensively quoted prose extracts in the English language. Rather than refer to *The Wealth of Nations* first, we turn to the more detailed treatment in the *Lectures on Jurisprudence*. For example, in LJ(A) (pp. 341-3) it is observed that if one man performed all tasks in pin-making, from mining ore to sharpening the point of the pin, perhaps only one pin a year would be made. This would suggest a value in his day of £6, this being the annual remuneration of a labourer. However, were pin-making to be performed by many workers each specializing in a different task,[6] a total of 36,000 pins would be made by this workforce per day, attributing 2000 to each worker. Whilst admitting that he has produced a 'frivolous example', Smith suggests 'the case is the same in all other mechanicall arts.' This increase in productivity caused by the division of labour encourages the division of work by trade, and such specialization further raises productivity and lowers skill, this being most pronounced in the advanced economies. The productivity increase is attributed to three circumstances: firstly, the improved dexterity arising from constant repetition of a standardized task; secondly, the time saved from confining work to a single task, rather than alternating between several, with time and productivity lost at each alternation; and thirdly, the inventions that are suggested by close concentration on a limited task.[7] This analysis of the division of labour in the *Lectures on Jurisprudence* provided the basis for the more elegant treatment in *The Wealth of Nations* that is now so well known, with its memorable statements[8] like: 'It is the great multiplication of the productions of all the different arts, in consequence of the division of labour, which occasions, in a well-governed society, that universal opulence which extends itself to the lowest ranks of the people' (WN, p. 22). In Smith, the emergence of the division of labour is ascribed to the propensity to truck, barter and exchange (WN, p. 25), its limits being determined by the extent of the market (WN, p. 31). Whereas modern treatments we shall come to shortly (like Casson 1986, 1988) would put the division of labour into an allocative framework, there being essentially a price attached to the division of labour which enables an optimum to be determined, Smith himself emphasized, as we have seen in chapter 2, the importance of accumulation over allocation. The Smithian division of labour is the main force behind economic growth, and its allocative importance is not great. Indeed, this is emphasized by Smith's treatment in *The Wealth of Nations* of the advance of the division of labour before considering the emergence of an allocative market mechanism, though to him the complete division of labour, entailing specialization both by employment and by manufacturing process, could only occur in commercial society.[9] Rosenberg (1976) would add another advantage of the division of labour to Smith's dexterity, time-saving and invention, namely motivation. In Smith's *Lectures on Rhetoric and Belles Lettres* it is remarked that there are disadvantages in the duties of a judge, general and legislator being undertaken by one person. They hinge on the poor incentive to perform all of these duties well if a person is evaluated on but one of his duties. If a man were both a judge and a general, but his standing in society were determined by his military activities, there would be no incentive for him to perform his judicial activities carefully. But more than this, in a case like the judiciary, to have but a few persons who are *exclusively* involved in judging under an advanced division of labour, rather than many who are *partly* involved, establishes more clearly who is responsible (or in bad judgements, at fault) and whether individual effort by a judge is promoting the benefits of society. Individual incentives can be impaired if responsibility is seen to lie with a social group rather than with a single person, for it is hard to apportion credit or blame in a group. Given the great importance of establishing an effective system of justice for the functioning of a civilized, commercial society, including the effective operation of its markets, the division of labour *by function* as applied to crucial activities like distributing justice, leading armies and formulating legislation is particularly important. Notice again that it has no necessary link to the market. Indeed, in the case of justice, free markets may favour the wealthy litigants and encourage judicial corruption. For that reason, the administration of justice is one of the necessary 'coercive' activities of the state, and is not market mediated.

This fourth advantage of the division of labour is related to the view of Arrow (1979, p. 154) that 'division of labour [is] primarily specialization in knowing how to do things.' Whilst Smith identified advantages of the division of labour, of which the motivational one mentioned above may be added to his better-known list of three other advantages, Arrow has pointed to some unrecognized drawbacks of the division of labour. As our earlier remarks on the absence of any necessary connection between the division of labour and the market may have suggested, cooperation rather than competition is the essence of the division of labour. Arrow would argue that the division of labour essentially raises the value of cooperation (i.e. specialization unambiguously confers group gains). However, there is a cost in achieving this cooperation, and conflict may not always be avoided. In order to reap the benefits of the division of labour by appropriate cooperation there must be communication between the economic agents involved. Markets provide one means of communicating, as do institutions (e.g. the firm) within which the division of labour takes place. In neither case is communication costless.[10] Smith himself gave no consideration to this point, but it is important. It implies, for example, that coherent groups will be formed amongst economic agents who can communicate with little cost, perhaps because of similar economic circumstances. This can lay the basis for conflict if the costs of communicating between groups are high. Thus within a firm, the employees may share common circumstances and can communicate readily, and the bosses may similarly find communication amongst themselves relatively inexpensive. But a higher cost of communication between bosses and worker may consolidate groupings which were initially quite fluid. For example, one can regard the boss/worker distinction as arising from a process of rational decision-making in which an economic agent compares the expected utility of the uncertain residual he gets as a boss with the utility he gets (with certainty) from an employee's wage. Whether one is a boss or a worker is then a matter of rational choice: the role adopted is, in this sense, voluntary.

What Arrow's critique suggests is that once a choice such as this has been made, it becomes in a sense less voluntary, for difficulties of communication *between* bosses and workers, and ease of communication *within* each of these groups, buttresses the role distinctions. Of course a role distinction in itself is an aspect of the division of labour and facilitates productivity gains. But also, as we know when boss/worker distinctions become very sharp, it can lead to conflict, with results like strikes or lock-outs. Differential ease of communication when allied to self-interested behaviour can lead to exploitation and mistrust. Messages from a person or group with a perceived informational advantage may be ignored, even though more information might appear superior to no more information, simply because those with an informational disadvantage fear manipulation. Arrow (1979, p. 163) suggests that one way of mitigating this is through the adoption of an ethical code: 'The code of professional ethics is a survival mechanism, a natural social arrangement for improving the benefits of the division of labour by preventing them from getting lost in a welter of exploitation and distrust.' The basis of an ethical code must be justice, but even this can be difficult to agree upon in a society characterized by the advanced division of labour. Even if individuals were not self-seeking, the division of labour or specialization would put economic agents into a variety of environments and bring them through different life experiences. Background differences of this sort would lead to different perceptions of what is just. Given the inexorable process of the division of labour, driven by the potential for cooperative gain, agreement on justice seems unlikely; and conflict, which reflects the activities of certain informationally efficient groupings, seems inevitable. Adam Smith himself was aware of the potential for conflict outside the allocative sphere,[11] but this was more a matter of observation than economic theory. What we have shown is that an analytical basis can now be provided, based upon an extension of Smith's division of labour itself, for suggesting that conflict is in a sense *inevitable*, given positive, and differential, information costs.

Arrow's suggestion that the division of labour is a cooperative activity which has a cost may be analysed further in an approach due to Casson (1986), though there is no evidence that Casson has been directly influenced by Arrow. The key to Arrow's argument is the difficulty in communicating as the division of labour advances, and in Casson (1986) this argument takes the form that coordination costs rise with increases in the division of labour. The artisan or craftsman performs many tasks naturally, and inexpensively coordinates these tasks himself. But he does not work particularly productively. The division of labour disturbs this natural form of coordination to increase productivity, but in doing so increases the costs of coordination. This task is no longer a natural part of work, but is an activity extrinsic to production involving capabilities of supervision, direction and monitoring. These are relatively costly. Further, as the scale of operation increases through the more extensive division of labour, these coordination activities themselves may become the subject of the division of labour,[12] with specialist individuals or teams having exclusive responsibility for just one aspect of coordination like monitoring. As Casson (1986, p. 70) indicates, the division of labour applied to coordinating activities tends to create new jobs requiring high levels of skill. On the one hand there are professional skills like accountancy, production management and actuarial analysis, which require many years of training to acquire. On the other hand there are less tangible but high-level skills, such as the capacity to make sound business judgements and to improvise. Though Casson does not make this point himself, his earlier work,[13] where he defined entrepreneurship as 'identifying and making judgemental decisions', suggests that entrepreneurship itself may be regarded as an aspect of the advanced division of labour applied to coordinating activities. As we shall observe in chapter 9, these aspects of the division of labour encouraged the emergence of post-industrialism, with 'brain-intensive' rather than capital- or labour-intensive activities being the most economically significant (see note 2 in chapter 9). Adam Smith himself had no theory of entrepreneurship,[14] and indeed was somewhat distrustful of the activities of the 'projector'. Although he must certainly have been aware of the French literature on entrepreneurship, it seems likely that his practical observation that the capitalist and the manager-entrepreneur were often one and the same led him to regard the distinction as unfruitful. Of course, as the division of labour in coordinating activities has advanced, the explicit recognition of the entrepreneurial function has become crucial.

If, following Casson (1986), we look at the determination of the division of labour as an aspect of optimization by the firm, a trade-off is recognized between reducing manual labour by the greater division of labour and hiring additional inputs of coordinating services. An isoquant, everywhere convex to the origin, can be constructed between axes of manual employment and coordination services. Given appropriate prices for manual labour and coordination services, an *optimum* division of labour can be determined. When it is positive, it implies that the marginal rate of substitution between manual labour and coordinating services is equal to the relative price of manual labour to coordination services. Casson's theory is in fact but part of a larger theory designed to explain the new international division of labour.[15] There is actually a four-stage optimization process: firstly, to minimize production costs, given output and locations; secondly, to minimize location costs; thirdly, to minimize production costs with production unit outputs and the number of production units as the decision variables; and fourthly, to maximize industry profit by the choice of output. In the pure monopoly case, profit is maximized with marginal revenue set equal to marginal cost, which in this case is the minimum average cost of a production unit, determined by the previous three optimizations. In the perfectly competitive case, free entry implies that profit is zero. Price is equal to average cost for each production unit. As compared with the pure monopoly case, there is a lower price, a higher output, a greater number of production units and a greater output per unit. Attractive as the idea is of an *optimal* division of labour, Casson's analysis is ultimately severely limited in that it does not admit of economies of scale. Indeed, his isoquant map is homothetic, implying that the optimal proportion of manual employment to coordination services is independent of the scale of output.

Implied in Smith's analysis is the notion that the division of labour leads to *increasing returns* to scale. As Groenewegen (1977) has argued, after Smith, the theoretical significance of this feature of the division of labour was not overlooked. Senior, Mill and pre-eminently Marshall emphasized the significance of the division of labour for increasing returns in the production of manufactures. In more recent times this source of increasing returns has been made the cornerstone of the disequilibrium growth analyses of Young and Kaldor. However, from the 1870s until the present day, the difficulties that increasing returns raise for neoclassical marginal analysis have been so great that they have tended to be ignored. A welcome sign of change in this respect is the newly emerging literature on international trade, product differentiation and increasing returns, of which Jones and Kenen (1984) provide a convenient summary. We shall be using some elements of this new theory in chapter 8. For the moment, the main point to emphasize would be that the implications of the division of labour for increasing returns should not be ignored.

Before his bicentennial recantation on the significance of the division of labour, Stigler (1951, p. 185) felt that Smith's analysis was 'the core of a theory of the functions of firm and industry'. Starting with Smith, Stigler developed an analysis of increasing returns which laid the basis for a whole new influential theory of vertical integration, which has been particularly important to the development of the theory of the multinational enterprise. The starting point of Stigler's analysis was what he thought to be a conundrum. If the division of labour implies increasing returns, then the lower unit costs which can be achieved by increasing output will encourage combination and aggressive tactics to force out rivals. It will foster monopolization if the market extent is limited and each firm is motivated to achieve the maximum benefits of the division of labour. But if industries are characteristically competitive, rather than monopolized, Smith's analysis is false. So runs the argument. We have seen already in chapter 4, with our analysis of industries, that Stigler's conundrum is purely artificial. If increasing returns are pervasive, competition is directed not only at rivals' market shares but also at acquiring parts of *expanding* markets. In practice such expanding markets include entirely *new* markets, and new entry is another counteracting factor to increasing concentration. One cannot therefore accept Stigler's sharp dichotomization into monopoly or atomistic competition as having validity. Indeed, as his analysis proceeds, we see it very much relies on the idea that firms coordinate mixtures of activities,[16] each having different implications for economies of scale. Thus the total average cost curve is defined as the vertical summation of average cost curves for each of the firm's activities. The question that naturally arises is why firms do not take advantage of those activities which enjoy increasing returns. The answer is that this requires them also to increase the use of activities which are subject to decreasing returns, which can cause *total* average cost to increase. One reaction by a firm to this technological configuration might be to restrict the use of increasing cost activities by buying in from other firms, which are working at lower points on their relevant average cost curves, the necessary additional materials or services. It is argued that activities can be rival or complementary. Rivalry implies that the costs of other activities are pushed up as the output of a given activity is increased. Stigler argues, from somewhat narrow and *ad hoc* evidence, that activities tend to be rivalrous, and that therefore firms will tend to increase their output when an activity is abandoned (i.e. vertical *dis*integration will occur). This led Stigler to suggest what he called Smith's Theorem: that growing industries would be characterized by vertical disintegration and declining industries by vertical integration. By appeal to a variety of economic statistics, of which the most detailed were from cotton textiles machinery manufactures, Stigler concluded that Smith's Theorem was supported by the evidence.

Given the importance of the theory of vertical integration, Stigler's (1951) analysis is a crucial landmark. However, its focus seems far too narrow compared with, for example, the work of Williamson (1971). Given this, one would doubt even the logical validity of what he would call Smith's Theorem. One would want to consider, *inter alia*, how contracts could be written to take account of rivalry and complementary activities, how risk-bearing should be allocated, and how information could be gathered to achieve scale economies without loss of commercial advantage through unwitting dissemination of this information. On an empirical level, it is far from clear that vertical disintegration accompanies expansion. Indeed, in the early 1980s a common feature of the slowdown, and frequently decline, in manufactures in advanced Western economies was the externalization of activities in the face of tighter buyers' markets. This often took the form of vertical disintegration by externalizing service activities like accounting, marketing and distribution.[17] The reasons for this are not yet well understood, but clearly it is the major issue of structural change in advanced economies, where deindustrialization appears to be inevitably followed by tertiarization (i.e. the growth of the service sector). Clearly the phenomenon is at root a consequence of the advanced division of labour. Stigler's analysis is therefore no more than a beginning, but it does illustrate that the division of labour can be the object of rigorous economic analysis rather than merely a clothes-horse on which to hang the garments of doctrinaire propaganda.

Perhaps the most ambitious attempt to put Smith's analysis of the division of labour in technical garb is due to Ippolito (1977), though it is our observation that this treatment, perhaps because of its prolixity, has not been influential. Its purpose is to make precise the idea that specialization within the firm increases with the rate of output. Ippolito faced the difficulty that if the nature of the product, the state of technological advance, factor proportions, and much else besides change over time and over output rates, then it is not clear what meaning one attaches to an innocent looking term like 'progressive specialization'. The basic building block of Ippolito's analysis is an *activity*, which is precisely defined as a distinct and non-repetitive series of actions that takes a given number of time units to perform initially. The role of the entrepreneur is to allocate these activities of the various labour inputs available to the firm to produce a certain output. It is assumed that such an input either performs all, or none, of the repetitions for a particular activity. Then it is shown that, under this latter restriction, labour specialization within the firm will rise with output. Formally, Ippolito proposes a relationship like

$$Z = Z(n, t, s, r) \qquad (5.1)$$

where Z is the degree of the division of labour in the firm, n is the average number of activities employed per employed labour input, t is an index of time concentration within job allocations, s is an index of similarity of activities, and r is an index of labour productivity. If the output rate of the firm is denoted x, then what Ippolito calls Smith's Theorem may be written

$$\partial Z/\partial x > 0 \qquad (5.2)$$

which says that the division of labour within the firm rises with the firm's output level. The following plausible qualitative restrictions are assumed:

$$\begin{array}{l} \partial Z/\partial n, \ \partial Z/\partial r < 0 \\ \partial Z/\partial t, \ \partial Z/\partial s > 0 \end{array} \qquad (5.3)$$

Then the following restrictions will imply Smith's Theorem

$$\begin{array}{l} \partial n/\partial x < 0 \\ \partial t/\partial x, \ \partial s/\partial x > 0 \end{array} \qquad (5.4)$$

by taking the partial derivative of $Z(.)$ as in (5.1) with respect to x, assuming labour productivity given. What Ippolito shows is that, at higher output rates, labour will: perform fewer activities (implying more repetition); increase the concentration of productive time; and engage in job allocations with more similar activities. These are the restrictions above; hence Smith's Theorem holds as specified in (5.2). It is then suggested that the proven restriction $\partial Z/\partial x > 0$ amounts to the proposition that the division of labour is limited by the extent of the market. This is not correct, for the causality in $\partial Z/\partial x > 0$ is not clear. The *production* of x and the *demand* for x need to be distinguished. If the demand for x is x' then this will specify the extent of the division of labour Z' that is possible. The increasing nature of the relationship between Z and x is really something different. It is, however, important. As we shall show, it is a necessary component in a Smithian model of cumulative growth.

Finally, if a certain amount of human capital is applied to each activity in the firm, and labour skills are not firm specific, Ippolito's theory predicts that, *ceteris paribus*, the average wage rate in the firm varies inversely with the output. As output increases, the firm raises the specialization of labour, with job allocations including fewer activities and higher repetitions. The lower wage can be regarded as a lower rental on a smaller stock of human capital. This is closely related to the deskilling result which is a feature of the aggregate model in chapter 7. The tendency of more specialized labour to receive a lower wage rate is also well documented in an empirical sense. Ippolito presents his own test using monthly data on US shipping between 1941 and 1945. The monthly change in the average real wage rate in shipbuilding was regressed on the monthly change in the shipbuilding firms' average output rate and other variables. The expected negative sign on the output change variable was confirmed with a statistically significant coefficient. This is consistent with the theoretical prediction that firms reduce their investment in human capital at higher rates of output. A cumulative output variable was found to be positively correlated with the change in wages, with a statistically significant coefficient, confirming the prediction that learning effects induced by the progressive division of labour would raise productivity and hence the real wage. The latter is essentially a disequilibrium effect, and assumes no substitution of men by machines over the period in question. The positive influence of past output on wage rate changes, together with the negative relationship between output *changes* and wage changes, suggest that although skill requirements declined, initially lowering the real wage, this was followed by subsequent wage rises in line with productivity increases caused by learning.

5.3 ENDOGENOUS TECHNICAL CHANGE

Growth economists conventionally make the distinction between *exogenous*

104 *The Division of Labour and Technical Change*

and *endogenous* technical change. We have already encountered exogenous technical change in the formulation introduced in (3.50). There, the production function was written as

$$Y = f(K, N, \epsilon) \tag{5.5}$$

where Y is output, K is capital, N is labour and ϵ is a random variable or disturbance term. A particularly simple version of this would make the random variable appear in an additive form:

$$Y = F(K, N) + \epsilon \tag{5.6}$$

Now ϵ represents the effects of technical change on output. In a Schumpeterian framework, ϵ is a random shock to the system caused by the entrepreneur conceiving of innovative ways of combining[18] qualitatively invariant factors of production K and N. This sort of technical change provides no account of how different values of ϵ arise; exogenous forces (inspiration, leadership perhaps) are at work. By contrast the formulation in (3.42) is an (admittedly simple) example of endogenous technical change. The production function used to illustrate this was

$$Y = Y(K, N, \bar{T}, M(Y)) \tag{5.7}$$

where Y is output, K is capital, N is labour, T is land (assumed fixed at $\bar{T}$) and $M(.)$ is a technical progress term, which is determined not exogenously but rather endogenously by the level of output. The endogeneity does not end here, for this relationship is but part of a larger system, in this case equations (3.39) to (3.45). These link together the labour market, technology of production, division of labour, profitability and accumulation relationships. The system is one of simultaneous determination, and one of the variables being endogenously determined in this way, rather than exogenously assigned, is the technical progress term $M(.)$. So much then for the distinction between exogenous and endogenous theories of technical change.

Now the examples we have used so far in this section have used the device of 'aggregation by analogy'. That is to say, by analogy with behaviour at the microeconomic (in this case, firm-level) behaviour, one specifies a similar aggregate relationship. Thus underlying (5.6) and (5.7) are assumed patterns of behaviour at the level of the firm. The first says that technical change in the firm is exogenous and may be represented by a random variable; and the second says that technical change in the firm is endogenous and may be represented by a term which is dependent on output or, assuming the necessary demand, sales in a volume sense. There are a variety of ways in which this endogeneity may be modelled at the level of the firm. Arrow (1962), in perhaps the most famous theory of endogenous technical change, assumed that there were productivity increases due to learning which depended upon experience with a production process. His index of experience was cumulative gross investment. Kaldor (1957) specified a 'technical progress function' in which the annual growth rate of productivity per worker was a function of investment per worker. In Weizsäcker (1973) a distinction was made between using resources for production *per se* and using resources for productivity enhancement. The latter is an aspect of the division of labour, and Weizsäcker proved there was an inverse relationship between the division of labour, at the margin, and the length of the period of production (for enhancement of productivity).[19]

Our own approach is formally closest to Kaldor, for his technical progress function can be shown to imply a production function with a lagged dependent variable,[20] which is also a feature of a time-phased version of (5.7). Thus

$$Y = Y(K, N, \bar{T}, M(Y_{-1})) \quad (5.8)$$

where all variables are contemporaneous except the lagged dependent variable Y_{-1}, which denotes the previous period's output. Assuming $M' > 0$, this says that current technical change due to the division of labour depends upon the previous period's production. If the division of labour is partly an advantage of the division of thought or know-how, then this hypothesis can be seen to be related to Arrow's. One might also mention in the same context Ippolito's (1977) analysis of the human capital aspect of division of labour within the firm, where there is 'learning by repetition'.

Allyn Young (1928), in his famous analysis of increasing returns, really took for granted the endogeneity of technical progress within the firm caused by the division of labour. This implies increasing returns at the level of the firm. It has been up to later analysts to inquire in a more detailed way into how this mechanism works within the firm, for on this level Young himself found Adam Smith's account adequate as it stood. However, Young also conceived of the endogeneity of technical change in a much broader sense. We have already come across it in our discussion of cumulative growth in section 4.9. Young's emphasis was on the extension of the division of labour to specialization among firms, and by extension among industries. Part of the endogeneity of technical change is then due to forces which are external to specific firms and industries. Essentially the efficiency gains from the division of labour in one sector release resources which, when reallocated amongst other sectors, create further demands which permit a further extension of the division of labour, greater efficiency in turn, and so on. Carried to its logical conclusion this suggests an international division of labour, implying specialization among countries, notably in intermediate goods. As Casson (1986, p. 67) indicates, the argument concerning gains from trade may be applied to intermediate goods as well as to final goods. Under the international division of labour it is different intermediate products, rather than different industries, that become concentrated in different countries. However, even though comparative advantage should in principle be reflected in those intermediate products which a country exports, the standard Hecksher-Ohlin model of international trade is not well equipped to handle this. In view of these deficiencies,[21] Casson suggests using a variant of a model of location as the basis for his analysis of the gains from trade. Casson (1986, p. 66) categorizes the deficiencies as follows:

> It ignores changes in the division of labour within an industry other than those reflected in capital–labour substitution. It also has little to say about the existence of complementary intermediate products created by the intra-industry division of labour . . . It fails to take account of the fact that as technical progress generates a more sophisticated division of labour, so the number of intermediate products increases, and the nature of the intermediate products changes too.

We shall return to the international division of labour in chapter 9. Suffice it to say for now that it is an extension of the analysis of endogenous technical change which is the centrepiece of this section. If standard neoclassical theory does not readily embrace it, so much the worse for this brand of theory. The intrinsic empirical significance of the international division of labour cannot be denied.

5.4 TECHNICAL CHANGE AND THE PRODUCTION FUNCTION

We saw in chapter 3 how Barkai (1969) regarded the level of technique as dependent on the extent of the market, as gauged by the level of social product, and this approach was also utilized in our analysis there of growth paths and the stationary state. This systematic, endogenous effect upon productivity is one we prefer as a representation of the consequences of the division of labour for productivity increases. In the classical approach which this book espouses, the modelling of technical change in this way appears superior, for example, to the 'random shock' theory as embodied in (3.50) or (5.5). Our account does not involve assigning technical change to a mysterious exogenous – and unexplained – stochastic variable. Rather we have an explanation or account of the way in which technical change, some of it due to organizational innovation, has a systematic and endogenous effect on productivity.

Chapter 4 looked at technical change at the industry or sectoral level, but without any detailed consideration of how it was brought about. In this chapter, we have emphasized its dependence on the division of labour. For the purposes of simplicity, and certainly very much in the classical tradition of favouring aggregate analysis, we shall subsequently emphasize the consequences of technical change caused by the division of labour on an *aggregate production function*, at least until chapter 8 when sectoral considerations are reintroduced.

We have already encountered a device that will be used subsequently to model the division of labour in an aggregate model. The aggregate production function[22] was written in (3.42) as

$$Y = Y(K, N, T, M) \quad (5.9)$$

with Y being social product; K, N and T capital, labour and land inputs; and M a proxy for 'market extent'. The last was assumed to be an increasing function of social product: $M = M(Y)$ with $M' > 0$. All marginal products were assumed positive: $Y_K, Y_N, Y_T, Y_M > 0$.

What this representation deliberately suppressed, because of its use in an equilibrium model, was the time phasing of production. Inputs must be coordinated prior to the appearance of output; and the beneficial effects of the division of labour depend upon there having previously been established a market of a certain extent. Thus a time-phased version of the above might be written as

$$Y = Y(K_{-1}, N_{-1}, \bar{T}, M(Y_{-1})) \quad (5.10)$$

where Y means Y_t and K_{-1} means K_{t-1}, and similarly for other variables. Ultimate land scarcity has been imposed on the model by setting T at $\bar{T}$, a constant, and the 'market extent' proxy has been written $M = M(Y_{-1})$ with $\partial M / \partial Y_{-1} > 0$. Thus the greater the social product last year (i.e. the greater the extent of the market in period $t - 1$), the greater the opportunity for extending the division of labour, with its consequential effect on increasing productivity. Formally,

$$\partial Y / \partial Y_{-1} = \frac{\partial Y}{\partial M} \frac{\partial M}{\partial Y_{-1}} > 0 \quad (5.11)$$

This is probably the simplest way of representing formally the 'cumulative causation' argument first put forward by Allyn Young (1928), and subsequently re-emphasized in modern times by economists such as Kaldor (1985) and Lauchlin Currie (1981). We shall leave for subsequent chapters the various ways in which this device can be incorporated into complete models of classical growth in the Smithian tradition. It may be useful, by way of introduction to the methods used, to illustrate by a specific numerical example how the consequences of the division of labour may be traced out.

Consider the production function

$$Y = AK_{-1}^{\alpha} N_{-1}^{1-\alpha} M(Y_{-1}) \tag{5.12}$$

with A a positive constant and $M' > 0$. For simplicity, set $A \equiv 1$ and $\alpha = 0.6$, and assign $M(Y_{-1})$ the specific form of $Y_{-1}^{0.5}$. Then (5.12) becomes

$$Y = K_{-1}^{0.6} N_{-1}^{0.4} Y_{-1}^{0.5} \tag{5.13}$$

Table 5.1 provides a numerical example of the evolution of social product Y according to this simple model. Necessarily the model is incomplete: we defer until later the way in which the aggregate production function can be linked to a classical labour market. Capital, which here may be thought of as composed of fixed K^f and circulating K^c capital, Eltis (1984, p. 96), is rising. The workforce is also growing. If each period is thought of as a decade, the workforce has somewhat more than doubled over a century. Figures in the columns for capital K_{-1} and labour N_{-1} have been assigned plausible values, given by the rest of an (unspecified) model. Social product (Y and Y_{-1} in the current and previous decades, respectively) has been computed from a base value of $Y_0 = 100.00$ at the start of the century. Subsequent values of social product have been computed using (5.13). It will be observed that the division of labour caused by the extent of the market function $M(Y)$ has led to cumulative growth in social product. Actually, had capital and labour remained unchanged at the initial values of 40 and 150, a process of cumulative growth would have still been observed, as may readily be numerically confirmed.[23]

In table 5.1 we have also given capital per head K/N and social product per head Y/N figures, for purposes of illustration. Over the century, capital per head falls slowly and then starts to rise again over the last four decades. How-

Table 5.1 Numerical example of cumulative growth in social product

Period t	Capital K^f_{-1}	K^c_{-1}	K_{-1}	Labour N_{-1}	Capital per head K_{-1}/N_{-1}	Social product per head Y_{-1}/N_{-1}	Social product Y_{-1}	Y
1	19	21	40	150	0.2666	0.6666	100.0000	678.6916
2	21	20	41	163	0.2515	4.1638	678.6916	1,855.1610
3	23	20	43	185	0.2324	10.0279	1,855.1610	3,320.0899
4	25	21	46	204	0.2255	15.7848	3,220.0899	4,809.2980
5	27	22	49	225	0.2177	21.3747	4,809.2980	6,252.1803
6	30	23	53	253	0.2095	24.7121	6,252.1803	7,831.2210
7	34	24	58	272	0.2132	28.7913	7,831.2210	9,523.5551
8	39	27	66	295	0.2237	32.2832	9,523.5551	11,723.4306
9	47	31	78	325	0.2400	36.0721	11,723.4306	14,946.4297
10	58	34	92	340	0.2706	43.9601	14,946.4297	18,972.5957

ever, there is no marked percentage change in this figure throughout this time. It is convenient to think of the composition of the capital variable changing over the century, with circulating capital becoming less important relative to fixed capital as the economy expands cumulatively. Initially, on the figures presented, the consequences of changing the organization of production from predominantly outwork to factory work is to economize on circulating capital, as it is no longer necessary for every workman to carry his own stocks.[24] However, the requirements for fixed capital proceed steadily. As the century progresses and the scale of operation of factories increases, greatly extending the extent of markets, the relative amount of fixed capital compared with circulating capital rises, the overall effect being to cause capital per head to rise. Over this period social product per head rises very markedly – over seventyfold by the end of the century. This is largely driven by the 'market extent' function $M(Y) = Y^{0.5}$. It is, that is to say, largely a consequence of the division of labour. It is achieved, as we have seen, with very little change in 'capital intensity'. However, the *composition* of capital might be experiencing a more significant shift to fixed, rather than circulating, capital varieties.

We saw in chapter 1 how each societal stage can be represented by a growth trajectory. The figures in table 5.1 suggest a conclusion to this growth process, but as it is no more than a numerical example one cannot regard it as confirming this rigorously. As note 23 to this chapter suggests, this can be done for a simplified variant. It would now be of interest to construct a growth trajectory explicitly which did not depend on the selection of specific numbers.

Let us take as our starting point a variant of the aggregate production function (5.10), which we write as

$$Y = F(K, N, M) \qquad F_K, F_N, F_M > 0; F_{MM} < 0 \qquad (5.14)$$

As in the example of note 23 to this chapter, we set K and N, the capital[25] and workforce variables, at constant values:

$$K = \bar{K} \quad \text{and} \quad N = \bar{N} \qquad (5.15)$$

The 'marginal product' of the division of labour or technical change term in the production function is positive and decreasing ($F_M > 0$, $F_{MM} < 0$). Finally, we assume that the greater is the extent of the market, the greater is the scope for technical change due to the division of labour, but that this effect increases at a decreasing rate:

$$M = M(Y_{-1}) \qquad M' > 0, M'' < 0 \qquad (5.16)$$

Substituting (5.15) and (5.16) in (5.14) gives

$$Y = F(\bar{K}, \bar{N}, M(Y_{-1}))$$

110 *The Division of Labour and Technical Change*

This composition of functions in Y_{-1} will be rewritten as

$$Y = \xi(Y_{-1}) \tag{5.17}$$

Equation (5.17) provides an explicit example of the sort of growth trajectory given for a particular societal stage in chapter 1. It has this form because of the specific type of endogenous technical change we have postulated. The qualitative properties of $\xi(.)$ are readily examined. Differentiating we get

$$\frac{dY}{dY_{-1}} = F_M M' > 0$$

$$\frac{d^2 Y}{dY_{-1}^2} = F_{MM} M'^2 + F_M M'' < 0$$

Thus

$$\xi' \equiv \frac{dY}{dY_{-1}} > 0 \quad \text{i.e. } \xi \text{ positively sloped}$$

$$\xi'' \equiv \frac{d^2 Y}{dY_{-1}^2} < 0 \quad \text{i.e. } \xi \text{ strictly concave}$$

Now in terms of the analysis of chapter 1, the commencement of a new societal stage requires the existence of a stable equilibrium that is converted into an unstable equilibrium. Considering the change from stage I to stage II and denoting equilibrium social product by Y_I^*, we require technically that

$$0 < \xi_I'(Y_I^*) < 1 \quad \text{and} \quad \xi_{II}'(Y_I^*) > 1$$

where Y_I^* is shared as the terminal point of one society and the starting point of another. This is illustrated in figure 5.1, which is an abbreviated version of the phase diagram first presented in figure 1.1. The logic of the argument starts with the conclusion of stage I along the ξ_I function at a level of social product given by Y_I^*. Now $\xi_{II}'' > 0$, strict concavity of ξ_{II}, and $\xi_{II}'(Y_I^*) > 1$ guarantee the existence of a new equilibrium $Y_{II}^* > Y_I^*$ such that $0 < \xi_{II}'(Y_{II}^*) < 1$. That is, the existence of an initial unstable point at Y_I^* *ensures* the existence of a stable equilibrium point at a *higher* value of social product. This logic applies to all potential equilibrium points, and hence provides the basis for a sequential or stadial view of societal evolution. The main requirement is the emergence of an unstable equilibrium and an initial impetus in the right direction

The Division of Labour and Technical Change 111

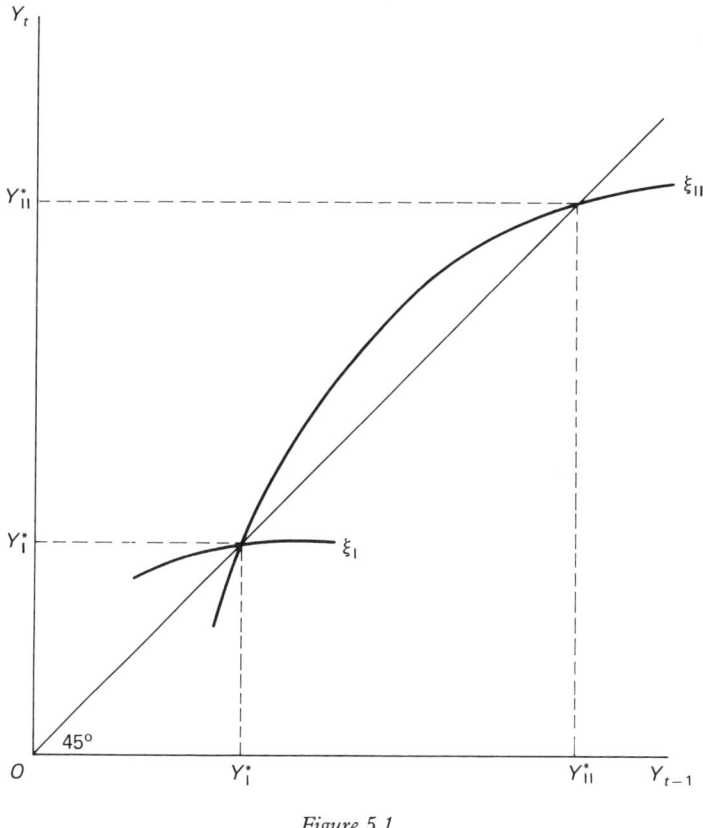

Figure 5.1

when a new societal order is emerging.

Of course, one would require different theories for different stages of society. Indeed, the theory we have given is itself quite partial and is intended to do no more than illustrate how, in principle, appropriate growth trajectories can be rigorously derived. Nevertheless, we feel the approach is suggestive. Endogenous technical change caused by the division of labour is pervasive. It is a powerful engine of growth, and one that is not confined to stages of society in which exchange is necessarily market mediated. It could, therefore, provide the starting point for theories of a number of stages of society, including the post-industrial.

112 *The Division of Labour and Technical Change*

5.5 CONCLUSION

The general position developed in this chapter is easily summarized. The division of labour was shown to be pervasive in its effects, from firms to industries to countries. It is the basis for endogenous technical change, being dependent on the extent of markets, and generally leads to increasing returns. This effect alone can provide the basis for cumulative growth in an economy.

Hicks (1960, p. 128) and Eltis (1973, p. 251) have both paid respects to the work of Adam Smith and Allyn Young on increasing returns and growth. They admit that increasing returns are empirically important and that theory should be modified and developed to embrace them. However, the difficulty is that much of the relevant theory is concerned with steady growth, which is generally incompatible with increasing returns. Further, such steady growth is typically also *equilibrium* growth. Solow (1988), in a recent survey of growth theory, has suggested that the time has come to look beyond steady equilibrium growth models. This too would be the conclusion of this chapter.

NOTES

1 See, for example, Rashid (1986).
2 Two recent contributions, which are quite extensive but cover different ground, are Casson (1986) and Casson (1988).
3 Casson's inspiration for this is the work of Charles Babbage (1832) on organizing the production of mathematical tables.
4 See Fröbel, Heinrichs and Kreye (1980) for a Marxist analysis, and Casson (1986, 1988) for an eclectic approach.
5 See Rashid (1986) for a discussion of precursors like William Petty, Bernard Mandeville, Joseph Harris and Josiah Tucker. The importance of Francis Hutcheson's *System of Moral Philosophy* (1755) is not to be neglected either.
6 Smith suggests eighteen tasks, each performed by one man. Possibly this was prompted by the article on *Épingle* in the *Encyclopédie* of 1755, which gives a detailed description of eighteen successive operations in pin-making.
7 See the treatments in WN (pp. 17–21), LJ(A) (pp. 345–7) and LJ(B) (pp. 491–2).
8 This is close to a previous statement in the 'Early draft of part of *The Wealth of Nations*' contained in LJ, (p. 564).
9 See Skinner (1979, ch. 6) for fuller treatment of this point.
10 This is the basis of so-called transactional economics, which was started by Coase (1937) and has had its most recent influential statement by Williamson (1985). Coase's point was that using markets or using organizations both involved costs. Which of the two one uses depends on relative costs.
11 See Skinner (1979, ch. 7) and especially Dasgupta (1983, 1985).
12 Essentially because of 'bounded rationality' used here in the sense of Herbert Simon (1957) to denote limited cognitive ability in handling very complex environments.
13 In Casson (1982, p. 337).
14 Or perhaps more accurately, as Kirzner (1979, ch. 3) suggests, the entrepreneurial and capitalistic roles are inseparable in Smith. This reflected the pattern in the economy of his day in Britain at least, though not in France.

The Division of Labour and Technical Change   113

15 We shall return to this in chapter 9.
16 Here, 'activity' does not imply the narrower sense of the word used in linear programming.
17 See Rajan (1987) for detailed evidence on this in the UK economy. He has estimated that about half of the new jobs created in the tertiary sector between 1985 and 1990 will be a result of redistributing activities which formerly took place elsewhere, notably in manufacturing.
18 It will be observed that a formulation such as (5.6) is used in the theory of the 'frontier production function'. Reducing X-inefficiency brings output closer to the frontier. One way to do this is by a more effective division of labour (e.g. to reduce 'sauntering': WN, p. 14).
19 Essentially, this is a formalization of an earlier insight by Young (1928, p. 539).
20 See Cigno (1975).
21 In view of these deficiencies, Casson suggests using a variant of a model of location as the basis for his analysis of the gains from trade.
22 See Spengler (1959, part 2) for one of the many post-war introductions of an aggregate production function into Smithian analysis.
23 In this case, the 'equation of motion' of the system is $Y = 67.8691\sqrt{Y_{-1}}$. Table 5.1 suggests the cumulative process will slow down in the general case. One would need more information to confirm this. In the special case of this note this is certainly true. For Y^*, the equilibrium value, we get $Y^* = 67.8691\sqrt{Y^*}$, whence $Y^* = 4606.2147$. Convergence to within unity of Y^* occurs after fifteen periods.
24 This account is stylized, and used for no further purpose than illustration. Groenewegen (1977) provides a more detailed analysis.
25 Here we emphasize the fixed capital variety.

6
Fluctuations and Growth at the Aggregate Level

6.1 INTRODUCTION

The emphasis in this book is on a particular type of economic analysis, the classical. However, it is not the only way of approaching the modelling of economic reality. Another alternative was explored by Hicks (1937), in his famous exercise in comparative modelling 'Mr Keynes and the classics: a suggested interpretation'. Alas, he undertook to compare what were not really comparable: the *short-period* analysis of Keynes, and the *long-period* analysis of the classical economists. Admittedly Hicks was concerned, as the title to his article suggested, with the stylized 'classics' rather than any historically recognizable classical economists, and in undertaking his comparison a great deal of creativity in interpreting both Keynes and the 'classics' was involved.[1] Given the enormous influence of the Keynesian school, it remains true today that one of the obvious comparisons one should make with any coherent body of economic analysis is with its Keynesian alternative.

The purpose of this chapter is to make a comparison between Keynesian and classical models in a time frame which is longer than the Keynesian short period. This naturally leads into possibilities of growth and fluctuations. A simple, aggregate model of growth and fluctuations is developed, inspired by Adam Smith's analysis of the division of labour. This is contrasted with a parallel Keynesian model. The latter is a variant due to Pasinetti (1974), and may be regarded as a generalization of the models of Samuelson (1939) and Hicks (1950). A comparison of the properties of the models is undertaken in terms of the existence and stability of equilibria using techniques attributable to Duesenberry (1958). Whilst the Keynesian model may or may not exhibit

116 *Fluctuations and Growth at the Aggregate Level*

fluctuations, and may or may not be characterized by a damped path of output over time, the classical model exhibits a time path of cumulative growth of the sort that has been discussed, but never formally modelled, by writers such as Allyn Young (1928), Gunnar Myrdal (1957), Lauchlin Currie (1981) and Nicholas Kaldor (1972, 1985).

An important difference between the models is in terms of their reactions to an increase in thrift. In the classical model the growth rates of capital and social product rise in the face of increased thriftiness, essentially because enlarged savings lead to increased investment, and this in turn enlarges markets leading to a greater social product. By contrast, the Keynesian model predicts that increased thrift will lower the rates of growth of capital and social product. Increased thrift reduces the value of the multiplier and leads to a decrease in effective demand. The accelerator effect, which is dependent on changes in demand, will consequently lead to a diminution in investment, resulting in a lower rate of growth of the capital stock. Beyond the short period, the Paradox of Thrift still holds sway.

6.2 BEYOND THE SHORT PERIOD

Much of the literature which contrasts Keynes and the classics, as in Hicks (1937), does so in a short-period framework. This is, of course, to take Keynesianism on its own terms, and to try to compare it with a short-period variant of the classical construction. However, this is not a procedure that presents classical analysis in a particularly favourable light, because it rules out of consideration many issues that were central to the classical writers. Growth, accumulation and technical change are amongst the matters that one neglects by taking only a short-period view of the classics. There are many versions of the classical schema to which one could turn in making longer-period comparisons of Keynes with the classics, but there is no doubt that Keynes's own choice, Pigou's *Theory of Unemployment* (1933), is not appropriate. Here we have chosen to develop our own simple formal model for comparative purposes, inspired by the writings of Adam Smith. Even so, one faces certain problems of representation, for different writers have viewed Smith's analysis of growth and accumulation in different ways.[2] Some emphasize his 'cheerful' view, concentrating on the possibility of progressive growth. Others direct attention at his 'dull' view, concentrating on the approach to the stationary state. Here, the particular stylization adopted exemplifies Smith's 'cheerful' view.

Turning now to Keynes and Keynesianism, one is again presented with a variety of choices. Keynes himself in his *General Theory* (1936) did move out of his short-period analysis to write no more than 'Notes on the trade cycle' in his twenty-second chapter. This particular part of the *General Theory* has been largely neglected, perhaps because Keynes's view on the trade cycle was that it was caused by rapid changes in expectations. His analysis in that chapter thus drops the 'given expectations' to which his reader was encouraged to become accustomed in the main body of the work.[3] Expressed briefly, Keynes argued that the downswing of the cycle was initiated by a collapse in the marginal efficiency of capital schedule. This schedule is expressed in terms of prospective rather than actual yields, and once expectations become pessimistic these prospective yields fall rapidly – too rapidly to be offset by a sufficiently sharp fall in the rate of interest. Keynes (1936, p. 316) talked of 'an over-optimistic and over-bought market' leading to collapse 'with sudden and even catastrophic force'. Keynes was here, as in so many other respects, very Marshallian, for his old teacher too had stressed the role of business confidence in generating cycles.

However, most Keynesians have chosen to look beyond the short period in a different fashion, ignoring the original emphasis of Keynes on expectations. Their approach might conveniently be summarized as being Kaleckian, in the sense that like Kalecki (1933) they have sought the source of cycles in some sort of lagged response.[4] In Kalecki's original work, this took the form of an order–delivery lag, but the possibilities are many and varied. The finest flower of such cyclical models is undoubtedly that of Hicks (1950). Harrod (1948) had attempted to look at progressive equilibrium in a Keynesian framework, and had found that his economy was subject to knife-edge instability. Hicks was dissatisfied with this result and developed a thorough analysis of a multiplier-accelerator business cycle model. In it, equilibrium output had an upward trend and fluctuations were constrained from above by a full employment ceiling and from below by both the eventual need for replacement investment and the inexorable path of autonomous investment. For comparative purposes we have chosen a variant of the multiplier-accelerator model due to Pasinetti (1974). Whilst having no analysis of constrained cycles, it is more general than the models of Hicks (1950) and Samuelson (1939) with respect to the formulation of the acceleration principle.

6.3 KEYNES AND THE CLASSICS

As we have already remarked in chapter 2, recent reappraisals of the classical economists have brought back into contemporary discussions of both theory and policy a concern for accumulation as opposed to allocation. Particularly influential in achieving this have been the writings of the so-called modern classical school, of which Walsh and Gram (1980) provide a paradigm example. As we saw in chapter 2, this work explores important aspects of the classical writers, most notably the duality between surplus in the quantity relations and a uniform rate of profit in the price relations, in the context of a sectoral general equilibrium model. This is ideally suited to making comparisons between the classical and neoclassical theories of general equilibrium. However, it is less well suited to making comparisons between classical and Keynesian theories of growth and fluctuations. It is with the latter type of comparison that this chapter is concerned.

Inevitably the point of departure in constructing an appropriate classical 'comparison model' is Adam Smith. And this being so, we should, as Arrow (1979) has affirmed, 'take the concept of the division of labour to be a basic structural aspect of the economic world'. The division of labour is intrinsically a dynamic process, and is therefore not easily incorporated into general equilibrium models of either the classical or the neoclassical variety. It creates the possibility of dynamic increasing returns. The division of labour, through productivity gains, extends markets; and extended markets provide further scope for the division of labour. Thus the possibility for enlarging social product this year is dependent on the extent to which it was enlarged last year, for last year's enlarged market was a prerequisite to the division of labour. A relationship such as this can be represented formally by a production function with a lagged dependent variable. The introduction of such a variable amounts to saying that technical change is endogenous. This is the approach to be taken here.

By contrast, Keynesian analysis typically has no theory of technical change, and the production function often does not appear explicitly. Instead, an accelerator relationship is derived from a particular type of technology (e.g. fixed coefficients). This, when linked to a stable consumption relationship, leads to the specification of a Harrod-Domar type of model, or, if some sort of lag structure is introduced, a multiplier-accelerator type of model. It is the latter which will concern us here.

6.4 TWO MODELS OF FLUCTUATIONS AND GROWTH

The particular representation of the Keynesian model we will adopt is that generalization of the multiplier-accelerator model due to Pasinetti (1974, ch. III). It is defined as follows:

$$K_t \equiv K_{t-1} + I_t \qquad (6.1)$$

$$Y_t \equiv C_t + I_t \qquad (6.2)$$

$$C_t = cY_{t-1} \qquad 0 < c < 1 \qquad (6.3)$$

$$I_t = dY_{t-1} - fK_{t-1} \qquad f, d > 0 \qquad (6.4)$$

where I is the total net investment, K is capital stock at the end of period t, C is total consumption, Y is total effective demand or total net income, and c is the marginal propensity to consume. All variables in this, as in the next, model are defined in terms of deviations from stationary state magnitudes. Relationship (6.4) gives expression to the capital stock adjustment principle, and the term d can be regarded as the product of f and a parameter representing the desired capital–output ratio.

The parallel classical model which will be used for comparative purposes explicitly incorporates two phenomena central to Adam Smith's analysis of growth: the extent of the market; and the division of labour Reid (1985b). The extent of the market is measured by real output[5] or social product Y. The extent of the market determines the division of labour D, which may be expressed $D = D(Y)$, $D' > 0$. Further, via the aggregate production function, the division of labour determines the extent of the market, which may be expressed $Y = Y(K,D)$, Y_K, $Y_D > 0$, where K is fixed capital. Here adjustments in the classical labour market are assumed to be sufficiently slow, compared with the other variables under consideration, that the workforce can be assumed a given constant which can be absorbed into the functional form $Y(.)$. In chapter 7, where stationary states of a classical growth process are emphasized, the labour market will be explicitly modelled. The aggregate schedule of propensity to save is given by $S = S(Y)$, $S' > 0$, and the model is completed by Say's Identity, $I \equiv S$, and the definition of net investment as current capital stock less the previous period's capital stock. Now the parallel comparison model of Pasinetti is set up in linear deviation form, so the above formulation will be treated likewise. It is defined by the following relationships:

$$I_t \equiv K_t - K_{t-1} \qquad (6.5)$$

$$I_t \equiv S_t \qquad (6.6)$$

$$S_t = sY_t \qquad 0 < s < 1 \qquad (6.7)$$

$$Y_t = \alpha K_{t-1} + \beta D_t \qquad \alpha, \beta > 0$$

$$D_t = \gamma Y_{t-1} \qquad \gamma > 0$$

The last two relationships say: (a) that social product Y (cf. the Keynesian effective demand) depends on capital and the division of labour D; and (b) that the division of labour which is possible this year depends on the extent of the market (i.e. the magnitude of social product) last year. The symbol s of (6.7) will be identified as the classical model's thriftiness parameter (cf. the marginal propensity to save $1 - c$ of the Keynesian model). The variable D is really just a *Hilfskonstruktion*, and can be eliminated from the system by combining the last two equations as

$$Y_t = \alpha K_{t-1} + \gamma \beta Y_{t-1} \tag{6.8}$$

As we shall see in chapter 7, the term β in (6.8) can be treated as a parameter representing the propensity to the division of labour.

To conclude, equations (6.1) to (6.4) of the Keynesian model can be contrasted with equations (6.5) to (6.8) of the classical model. Each is a determinate four-equation model in the four variables Y, C, I and K.

6.5 EXISTENCE AND STABILITY OF EQUILIBRIUM

A simple and effective device for exploring the properties of the equilibria of a Keynesian model such as that in the previous section was first developed by Duesenberry (1958) and later imitated by Pasinetti (1974). It involved deriving from the equations of the model a pair of simultaneous equations, with the growth rates of capital and income as the dependent variables and the capital–output ratio as the independent variable. The procedure is not general but, as we shall now demonstrate, it turns out that it can also be applied to the classical model specified by (6.5) to (6.8). Setting the investment variables in (6.5) and (6.6) equal gives

$$\begin{aligned} S_t &= K_t - K_{t-1} \\ &= sY_t \quad \text{using (6.7)} \\ &= s\alpha K_{t-1} + s\beta\gamma Y_{t-1} \quad \text{using (6.8)} \end{aligned}$$

Thus

$$\frac{K_t - K_{t-1}}{K_{t-1}} = s\alpha + s\beta\gamma \frac{Y_{t-1}}{K_{t-1}}$$

or

$$\dot{k} = s\alpha + s\beta\gamma Z \tag{6.9}$$

where $\dot{k}$, usually used to denote the continuous time derivative of the capital stock variable, is used here as a shorthand for the growth rate of capital. Z denotes the output–capital ratio. From (6.8) we get

$$Y_t - Y_{t-1} = \alpha K_{t-1} + (\beta\gamma - 1)Y_{t-1}$$

which implies

$$\frac{Y_t - Y_{t-1}}{Y_{t-1}} = \alpha \frac{K_{t-1}}{Y_{t-1}} + (\beta\gamma - 1)$$

or

$$\dot{y} = \frac{\alpha}{Z} + (\beta\gamma - 1) \qquad (6.10)$$

where $\dot{y}$ denotes the growth rate of social product. The latter's functional form is readily investigated. We have $d\dot{y}/dZ = -\alpha/Z^2 < 0$ and $d^2\dot{y}/dZ^2 = 2\alpha/Z^3 > 0$. Also, $\dot{y} \to \infty$ as $Z \to 0$, and $Z = (1 - \beta\gamma)^{-1}\alpha$ when $\dot{y} = 0$. Finally, $\dot{y} \to (\beta\gamma - 1)$ as $Z \to \infty$. Put simply, the relationship of $\dot{y}$ to Z is that of one branch of a hyperbola defined in the first (or first and fourth) quadrants. The form of (6.9) is obvious. The functions (6.9) and (6.10) are graphed in figure 6.1.[6]

By a similar set of manipulations to those performed for the classical model, the Keynesian model can be shown to lead to the following functional relationships:

$$\dot{y} = (d + c - 1) - f\kappa \qquad (6.11)$$

$$\dot{k} = -f + \frac{d}{\kappa} \qquad (6.12)$$

where κ is the capital–output ratio (i.e. $\kappa = 1/Z$). These relationships are graphed in figure 6.2. For a marginal propensity to consume c, the $\dot{y}$ equation of the Keynesian model is a straight line intersecting the $\dot{k}$ equation in A and B. Notice that in the way we have developed the models the $\dot{y}$ relationship is a linear function and the $\dot{k}$ relationship a hyperbola for the Keynesian model, and vice versa for the classical model.

Let us first inquire whether equilibrium solutions exist for each model. Equilibrium is attained when, at a positive capital–output (or output–capital) ratio, the rate of growth of capital is equal to the rate of growth of income. The equilibrium possibilities are more varied for the Keynesian model. Given a marginal propensity to consume c, equilibria occur at A and B, and for a lower marginal propensity to consume c' they become A' and B'. Thus multiple equilibria are possible in the Keynesian case. They may be distinguished on stability grounds, and Pasinetti (1974, p. 58) shows that points such as A and A' are stable whilst those such as B and B' are unstable. The further complication arises in the Keynesian case that no real equilibria may exist should the marginal propensity to consume be sufficiently low. When it assumes the value c'', as in figure 6.2, the $\dot{y}''$ curve lies everywhere below the $\dot{k}$ curve. Duesenberry (1958, p. 207) regarded such a situation as characteristic of a long

122 *Fluctuations and Growth at the Aggregate Level*

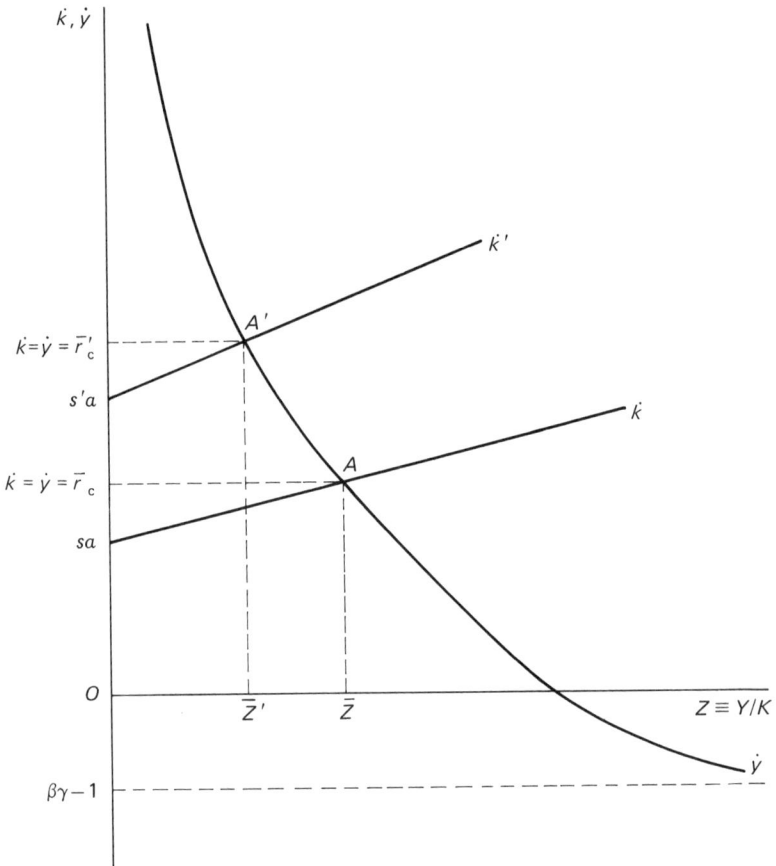

Figure 6.1 The classical case

depression in which income growth became negative until sufficient disinvestment had taken place to provide a stimulus to income growth. At a deeper level, Pasinetti (1974) perceived that a solution such as this implied disequilibrium cyclical behaviour.

The characteristics of equilibrium for the classical model are, by contrast, simple and unambiguous. As figure 6.1 suggests, the equilibrium point A exists and is necessarily unique, for the branch of $\dot{y}$ in the third quadrant is inadmissible. Furthermore, points such as A and A' are stable equilibria. Consider a point due east of A. The rate of growth of capital exceeds the rate of growth of income, and hence the output–capital ratio Z falls. Similarly, for a

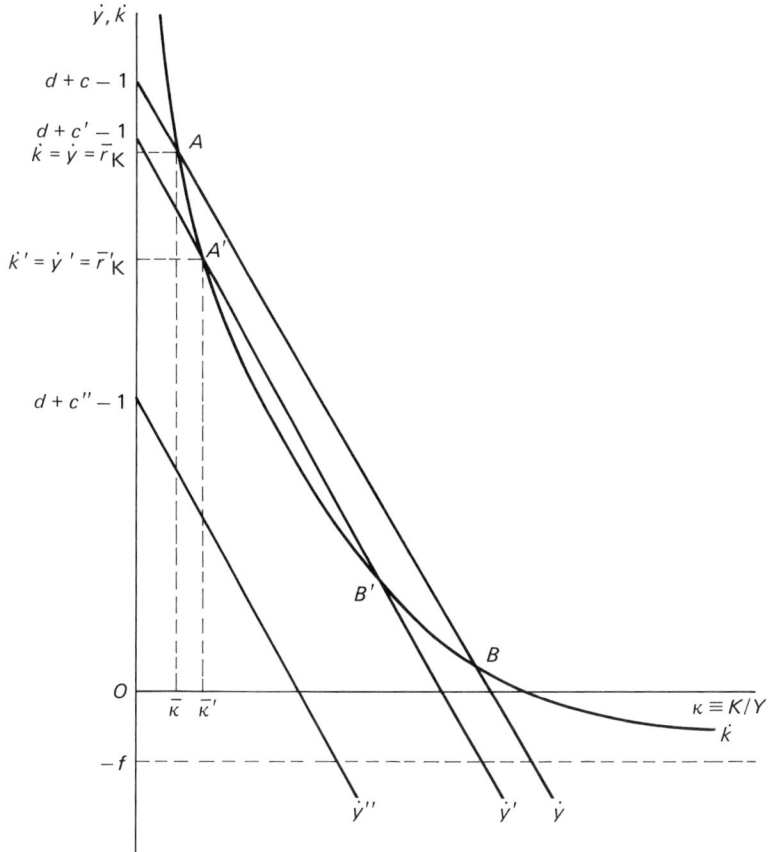

Figure 6.2 The Keynesian case

point due west of A, we have $\dot{y} > \dot{k}$, implying a rising output–capital ratio. Thus, given the thriftiness parameter s, the (stable) equilibrium value of the output–capital ratio is $\bar{Z}$, with income and capital growing at the same rate $\bar{r}_c$ (where the subscript refers to 'classical' rather than to 'consumption').

Pasinetti provides a very detailed account of the solution to the Keynesian model. Briefly, two conditions must be satisfied. Firstly, to ensure any possibility of growth it is necessary that $d > 1 - c$, which is to say that the marginal propensity to invest must exceed the marginal propensity to save. Secondly, $f < d + c + 1$ has to be imposed. It seems likely to be fulfilled, but this cannot be guaranteed. From the roots of the auxiliary equation to the reduced equation

124 *Fluctuations and Growth at the Aggregate Level*

for (6.1) to (6.4) it can be deduced that four solution paths for income emerge: exponential growth, exponential decline, explosive cyclical growth, or damped cyclical growth. In principle this same range of solution paths should emerge from the classical model, but it so happens that in this case there are restrictions which limit the possible solution paths. The classical model, given by (6.5) to (6.8), can be expressed as a homogeneous, linear, second-order difference equation, as can the Keynesian. Details of the properties of this equation in the classical case are explored fully in the appendix to this chapter. The essential result is that the classical model will not be subject to oscillatory behaviour for the qualitative restrictions on the parameters of the model. It is thus unlike the Keynesian case, where it is not possible to exclude cyclical behaviour; and indeed some economists would regard this as one of the prime characteristics of the Keynesian case.

The algebra of the appendix to this chapter confirms what one would expect from a comparison of figures 6.1 and 6.2. The complex roots case considered in Pasinetti's Keynesian model arises from the possibility that the $\dot{k}$ and $\dot{y}$ curves may not intersect (as when the marginal propensity to consume is c'', with a corresponding $\dot{y}''$ curve). In the classical model this is not possible, for the $\dot{k}$ curve must always cut the $\dot{y}$ curve in the positive quadrant given the parameter restrictions of the model. Another point suggested by figure 6.1 is that the classical model implies steady growth at a rate $\bar{r}_c$. This sort of solution is possible in the Keynesian model, as represented by a point such as A in figure 6.2. However, steady decline is also possible, as represented by a point such as B in figure 6.2. For growth rates less than that value at which $\dot{k}$ and $\dot{y}$ intersect there is, in this case, a systematic tendency for the growth rate to fall. By contrast the classical model can only produce steady growth, as the appendix confirms.

Economists who regard their work as building directly on the writings of Adam Smith, such as Young (1928) and Kaldor (1972), have emphasized the cumulative nature of the classical growth process. Young (1928, p. 533) spoke of a growth process in which 'change becomes progressive and propagates itself in a cumulative way'. Kaldor (1972, p. 1250), building in turn on the work of Young, developed a theory of 'endogenous self-sustained growth'. These characteristics are exactly those of the classical model described here.

6.6 COMPARATIVE DYNAMICS

Finally, let us look at one very important case of comparative dynamics. What are the consequences for the growth rates of capital and income, in each model, of what would be described in classical terminology as 'an increase in thriftiness' and in Keynesian terminology as 'a decrease in the marginal propensity to consume'?

Setting $\bar{r}_c = \dot{y} = \dot{k}$ for the classical model in (6.9) and (6.10) and differentiating gives

$$\partial \bar{r}_c / \partial s = \alpha + \beta \gamma Z > 0$$

$$\partial Z / \partial s = -(\alpha + \beta \gamma Z)/(s\beta\gamma + \alpha Z^{-2}) < 0$$

That is, increasing thrift lowers the output–capital ratio and raises the rate of growth of social product. Expressed geometrically, in the classical model a rise in thriftiness, reflected by an increase in s to s', will increase the intercept on the ordinate of the $\dot{k}$ equation given by (6.9), and will also increase the slope of this function. The $\dot{y}$ function given by (6.10) is unaffected. The unambiguous consequence, illustrated in figure 6.1, is that the equilibrium growth rates of capital and social product rise from $\bar{r}_c$ to $\bar{r}_c'$ and the output–capital ratio falls to $\bar{Z}'$. For the Keynesian model, the consequence of a downward shift of the marginal propensity to consume from c to c' is a parallel shift downward of the $\dot{y}$ curve to $\dot{y}'$. In figure 6.2, the symbol $\bar{r}_K$ denotes an equal income and capital growth rate for the Keynesian model (with the subscript K denoting 'Keynesian' rather than 'capital'). The change of c to c', reflecting an increase in thrift, leads to a reduction in the equilibrium rates of growth of income and capital (from $\bar{r}_K$ to $\bar{r}_K'$) and an increase in the capital–output ratio (from $\bar{\kappa}$ to $\bar{\kappa}'$), which is to say a decrease in the output–capital ratio Z. In both cases increased thrift will reduce the output–capital ratio. However, in a classical world capital and income grow faster, whereas in a Keynesian world they grow slower. This neatly demonstrates the difference between classical and Keynesian theories in a growth context.

In the Keynesian case, an increase in thrift decreases effective demand through the multiplier. Then the accelerator effect, driven by this decreased demand, leads to diminished investment and thus to a slower rate of growth of the capital stock. In the classical case, thriftiness enlarges savings and therefore investment, thus leading to capital accumulation. The consequential increase in output provides further scope for the division of labour, and thus greater output, further savings, and so on. The principal difference between the two approaches of course lies in the endogenous technical change which is inherent in the classical model. Technical change – through the division of labour – and market expansion are mutually reinforcing.

6.7 CONCLUSION

In this chapter we have chosen to compare two stylized models, the one

Keynesian and other classical. Both are determinate four-equation models in the variables Y, C, I and K. Both lead to reduced equations which are second order, linear and homogeneous. Despite other similarities (e.g. the definition of investment, the equality of savings and investment) the models exhibit markedly different qualitative characteristics. A unique stable equilibrium is characteristic of the classical model, whereas the Keynesian exhibits multiple equilibria which must be distinguished on stability grounds. The solution paths of the Keynesian model are various, and include explosive cases. No meaningful parameter restrictions can reduce this variety of cases. In the classical model, meaningful parameter restrictions lead to the conclusion that a steady rate of growth will be achieved. Finally it was shown that increased thriftiness would raise the growth rates of capital and income in the classical case, but lower them in the Keynesian case. The latter effect can be ascribed to the neglect of any form of technical change in the Keynesian case, as compared with the inclusion of a simple form of technical change in the classical case – that caused by the fundamental process of the division of labour.

It is worth concluding by noting that the division of labour involves an important, but circumscribed, view of technical change. In the way that it has been modelled here, this form of technical change has had pacific consequences. However, when more fundamental types of technical change become possible, due perhaps to the discovery of entirely new scientific principles (e.g. laser or semiconductor technology), the consequences may be more disruptive. Even if the flow of inventive activity is fairly steady, there is evidence that innovatory investment is more intermittent. The prerequisites for such investment are complex. Certainly the appropriate scientific knowledge must be available, but in addition the many technological skills required to implement that knowledge must have been developed. Finally, a propitious economic environment must exist, which, in a capitalist economy, must include an adequate supply of entrepreneurial ability. Such situations are hard to model formally, and it is clear that some sort of threshold mechanism must be contemplated. That is to say, not until certain variables in the model have attained critical values will innovatory investment take place. These critical values might best be expressed in probabilistic terms. Proceeding along these lines, no doubt the consequence of technical change will be to impose a cyclical pattern on the path of steady expansion which characterized the classical model. In the Keynesian model these bursts of innovatory investment will be a further source of instability in a model which already generates cycles in an endogenous sense through its lag structure.

The advantage of the approach developed in this chapter, which can be regarded as a form of 'comparative modelling', is that it abstracts from certain features which might be regarded as common to both models (e.g. intermittent innovatory investment) and concentrates on properties which are intrinsic to either the classical or the Keynesian view. By adopting this approach it has proved possible to highlight the qualitative differences between the models when one moves beyond the short period.

APPENDIX

Write (6.8) as

$$K_{t-1} = \frac{1}{\alpha} Y_t - \frac{\beta \gamma Y_{t-1}}{\alpha}$$

When substituted into $sY_t = K_t - K_{t-1}$ from (6.5), (6.6) and (6.7), this gives

$$Y_t - (\beta\gamma + \alpha s + 1)Y_{t-1} + \beta\gamma Y_{t-2} = 0 \qquad (6.13)$$

Without yet appealing to parameter restrictions, the solution to (6.13) may be expressed by[7]

$Y_t = A_1 \lambda_1^t + A_2 \lambda_2^t$ (distinct real roots)
$Y_t = A_3 \lambda^t + A_4 t \lambda^t$ (equal real roots)
$Y_t = \rho^t(A_5 \cos \omega t + A_6 \sin \omega t)$ (complex roots)

where A_1 to A_6, ρ and ω are constants, and λ_1, λ_2 are roots of the auxiliary equation

$$\lambda^2 + \lambda g + h = 0 \qquad (6.14)$$

In the particular case of (6.13), $g = -(\beta\gamma + \alpha s + 1)$, $h = \beta\gamma$. Irrespective of whether the roots are real (distinct or repeated) or complex, the necessary and sufficient condition for convergence to a stationary state is that every root be less than unity in absolute value. It should be noted that the discriminant $(\beta\gamma + \alpha s + 1)^2 - 4\beta\gamma$ of the quadratic auxiliary equation (6.14) is necessarily positive. For $(\beta\gamma - 1)^2 > 0$ with $\beta, \gamma > 0$ implies $(\beta^2\gamma^2 + 2\beta\gamma + 1) > 4\beta\gamma$, whence $(\beta\gamma + 1)^2 > 4\beta\gamma$. *A fortiori* the inequality $(\beta\gamma + \alpha s + 1)^2 > 4\beta\gamma$ with $\alpha, s > 0$ must hold, and hence the discriminant is positive. We can therefore rule out complex roots, and conclude that the model cannot exhibit oscillations as in the Keynesian case.

Our stability analysis can be directed at the necessarily real roots case. We note that $\lambda_1 + \lambda_2 = -g$ and $\lambda_1 \lambda_2 = h$ must hold as relationships between the roots and parameters of the auxiliary equation (6.14). So

$$\lambda_1 + \lambda_2 = (\beta\gamma + \alpha s + 1) \qquad (6.15)$$

$$\lambda_1 \lambda_2 = \beta\gamma \qquad (6.16)$$

128 Fluctuations and Growth at the Aggregate Level

for the classical model. Now $\beta\gamma > 0$, whence λ_1 and λ_2 must be of like sign. Further, $\lambda_1 + \lambda_2 > 0$, given known parameter restrictions. This implies that both roots must be positive and thus, as oscillations are already ruled out, that steady cumulative growth or decline will occur.

Technically, it is not possible for cumulative decline (i.e. dominant root less than unity) to occur. Suppose $\lambda_1, \lambda_2 < 1$. Then

$$(1 - \lambda_1)(1 - \lambda_2) = 1 - \lambda_1 - \lambda_2 + \lambda_1\lambda_2 > 0$$

which would imply, using (6.15) and (6.16), that $-\beta\gamma - \alpha s + \beta\gamma > 0$, i.e. $\alpha s < 0$, which is a contradiction. One can similarly rule out the case in which both roots are greater than unity – the ultra-explosive case. When the dominant root exceeds unity, but the other (subordinate) root is less than unity, then $(1 - \lambda_1)(1 - \lambda_2) = -\alpha s < 0$ or $\alpha s > 0$, which is an admissible restriction. Growth is steady (caused by the influence of the dominant root) but the subordinate root plays a part in limiting the growth rate of the system.[8]

NOTES

1. See Reid and Wolfe (1979) for further interpretation of this and other aspects of the work of J. R. Hicks.
2. For an analysis of this issue, see Reid (1983).
3. The significance of this 'given expectations' assumption is fully explored by Kregel (1976).
4. Bray (1977) has argued that Keynes was evidently unaware that a lagged linear system could oscillate. This emerged in Keynes's review of Tinbergen's econometric study for the League of Nations. Thus the only possible inspiration for Keynesian multiplier-accelerator models was from writers other than Keynes himself.
5. For a justification of this, see Barkai (1969) and Currie (1981).
6. It will be observed that the variable measured along the abscissa in figure 6.1 (namely the output–capital ratio $Z = Y/K$) is the reciprocal of the variable κ used by Pasinetti, as illustrated in figure 6.2. This facilitates the discussion of the comparative dynamics of the classical model in section 6.6, and of course makes no difference to the analytical conclusions reached.
7. See Goldberg (1958) for a full treatment.
8. Setting either root equal to unity, irrespective of whether the other is greater or less than unity, leads to an inadmissible restriction. For example, suppose $\lambda_1 = 1$. Then $\lambda_2 = \beta\gamma$ and thus $\beta\gamma + \alpha s + 1 = 1 + \beta\gamma$, implying that $\alpha s = 0$, which is inadmissible.

7
Bargaining Power and the Division of Labour

7.1 INTRODUCTION

This chapter develops an aggregate classical model[1] which introduces parameters for bargaining and the division of labour, and investigates the sensitivity of the model to variations in these parameters. The model is inspired by the writings of Adam Smith, rather than strictly representational of them; it aims to be 'the legacy of Adam Smith' rather than the reincarnation.

The division of labour gives rise to endogenous technical change and is introduced as a technical progress term in an aggregate production function. The functional distribution of income is determined exogenously by a bargaining process. The classical labour market is explicitly modelled, with labour supply increasing in the real wage rate, and labour demand decreasing in the real wage rate but increasing in a capital variable which is the sum of fixed and circulating capital. Local properties of the model are explored, using comparative statics methods, for the bargaining and division of labour parameters. Global properties are explored in a sensitivity analysis for a largely linearized version of the model using plausible parameter values. Thus important properties of the model are displayed. In particular, it indicates the hitherto unexplored formal possibility of distributional conflict: the ratio of the real wage rate to the rate of profit falls as the division of labour increases, as does the ratio of the wage bill to profit. This corresponds to the well-known deskilling phenomenon.

This is the dark side of our conclusions on the division of labour. The bright side is that increasing the division of labour increases income per head along with profit, which suggests that the distributional conflict can be ameliorated if

130 *Bargaining Power and the Division of Labour*

economic agents have access to multiple income sources (i.e. various combinations of wage, profit and rental incomes).

The bargaining parameter is the ratio of aggregate profit to total income and is exogenously determined by the institutions in which labour and capital are organized. It indicates that bargaining, at the aggregate level at least, is distributionally neutral in the sense that the ratio of the wage rate to the profit rate and of the wage bill to profit are both insensitive to the bargaining parameter. The advantages of increased bargaining power lie elsewhere. They are in the coordination of larger production teams (hence increasing the workforce), the increased scale of operation (hence increasing national income), and a higher level of technical change. Profit too rises, but not alone. Entrepreneurs must bring the workforce along with them when they increase the scale of operations, and both the wage rate and the wage bill rise. What we have therefore is a model which challenges conventional fears about the consequences of increased division of labour or shifts in the functional distribution of income which favour profit over other sources of income. Particularly if economic agents have access to multiple income sources (e.g. workers sharing in profit) the model suggests an outcome which Adam Smith himself would no doubt have described as 'cheerful'.

7.2 AN AGGREGATE CLASSICAL MODEL

The model possessing these properties will now be expounded. In outline its structure is as follows. Aggregate output depends upon an aggregate production function which is subject to technical progress attributable to the division of labour. The division of labour itself depends upon the level of output, or the extent of the market. The rate of profit depends upon the stock of capital (negatively) and the degree of the division of labour (positively). Distributive shares are not determined by marginal productivities – directly, anyway – but by an exogenously given bargaining process. There is market clearing in the classical labour market with the demand for the workforce depending on the capital stock (positively) and the real wage rate (negatively). On the supply side, the workforce increases with the real wage. Rent is a residual.

Now to technical details. The aggregate production function is

$$Y = F(K, N, T, D) \tag{7.1}$$

where Y is output (social product), K is capital,[2] N is labour, T is natural resources and D is a technical progress term of the sort introduced in section 6.4. Output is in value terms and may be thought of as social product. Labour is to be thought of as the workforce. Natural resources may be construed as 'land', broadly speaking. The technical progress term captures the effect of the division of labour. $F(.)$ is increasing in all its arguments.[3] Natural resources will be assumed to be given as

$$T = \bar{T} \tag{7.2}$$

The division of labour, which causes technical progress D, depends positively on the extent of the market:

$$D = D(Y) \quad D' > 0 \tag{7.3}$$

In (7.3) the extent of the market is measured by the scale of aggregate output. For an aggregate profit of Π, the rate of profits r is defined by[4]

$$r = \Pi/K \tag{7.4}$$

From (7.4) we can also write profit as $\Pi = rK$.[5] Moving on from the *definition* of the rate of profits, its *determination* is according to the function

$$r = r(D, K) \quad r_D > 0; r_K < 0 \tag{7.5}$$

Thus the tendency of the rate of profits to fall ($r_K < 0$) must be set against the tendency for it to be raised by technical progress ($r_D > 0$). Smith's analysis of the rate of profits (WN, p. 105) emphasizes that it is mutual competition amongst merchants which tends to lower the rate of profits in various trades, and that therefore 'when there is a like increase of stock in all the different trades carried on in the same society, the same competition must produce the same effect in them all.' A counterforce to this is the division of labour, for Smith argues (WN, p. 20) that 'men are more likely to discover easier and readier methods of attaining any object when the whole attention of their minds is directed towards that single object', and that such men 'soon find out easier and readier methods of performing their own particular work'. It is these 'easier and readier methods' which, other things being equal, tend to raise the rate of profits.

The functional share of profit in national income is

$$0 \leq \frac{\Pi}{Y} \leq 1$$

Bargaining over distributive shares is assumed to depend systematically on this ratio according to the implicit function

$$\beta\left(\frac{\Pi}{Y}\right) = 0 \tag{7.6}$$

We shall later assign a specific functional form to $\beta(.)$, but for the moment it suffices to say that it arises from some exogenously given bargaining process which in turn depends on institutional factors (e.g. the way the workforce is organized and the way firms write contracts).

Finally, we turn to the classical labour market. The demand for labour function $N^D(.)$ is given by:

$$N = N^D(K, w) \qquad N^D_K > 0; N^D_w < 0 \qquad (7.7)$$

where w is the real wage rate.[6] The supply of labour N^S is given by

$$N = N^S(w) \qquad N^S_w > 0 \qquad (7.8)$$

Labour is to be thought of as the workforce, and with market clearing we have labour supply equal to labour demand, $N^S = N^D$. The wage bill in aggregate W is of course

$$W = wN \qquad (7.9)$$

Finally, rent R is determined residually as

$$R = Y - W - \Pi \qquad (7.10)$$

From (7.10) the functional division of social product or national income into rent, wages and profit can be displayed as $Y = R + W + \Pi$.

Formally, we have a system of ten equations in ten variables: Y, K, N, T, D, Π, r, w, W and R. That is, the system is determinate.

7.3 A PARAMETERIZATION OF THE MODEL

From an analytical standpoint the general model of the previous section limits the scope for reaching qualitative conclusions. We therefore proceed by presenting a parameterized version, adopting in most cases (barring the production function) linear approximations to the functional relationships in (7.1) to (7.10). In this variant the model is as follows:

$$Y = K^\alpha N^{1-\alpha} + D \qquad 0 < \alpha < 1 \qquad (7.11)$$

$$D = kY \qquad 0 < k < 1 \qquad (7.12)$$

$$r = aD - cK \qquad a, c > 0 \qquad (7.13)$$

$$r = \Pi/K \qquad r > 0 \qquad (7.14)$$

$$b = \Pi/Y \qquad 0 < b < 1 \qquad (7.15)$$

$$N = dK - fw \qquad d, f > 0 \qquad (7.16)$$

$$N = gw \qquad g > 0 \qquad (7.17)$$

$$W = wN \tag{7.18}$$

$$R = Y - W - \Pi \tag{7.19}$$

Definitional relationships like those for the rate of profits (7.14), the wage bill (7.18), and rent (7.19) are as before. Natural resources are taken as given and are absorbed into the production function (7.11) by an appropriate normalization. The form of the production function is chosen out of convenience. In particular, as no marginal productivity theory of distribution is being assumed, there is no standard relationship between the parameter α and functional shares of national income. Technical advance simply shifts the production function upwards without capital or labour bias. Distribution is determined by bargaining, and the simple form chosen for the function (7.6) in the parameterized model is just $\beta(\Pi/Y) \equiv (\Pi/Y) - b = 0$, which exogenously determines the profit share of national income as a constant b, as in (7.15).

7.4 THE DIVISION OF LABOUR AND BARGAINING POWER

The two main issues to be explored for this parameterized version of the model are how equilibrium values of the variables are affected by variations in the *propensity to the division of labour k* and the *bargaining power b* of capital.

Referring to the appendix to this chapter for algebraic details, consider first the derivatives of variables with respect to the division of labour parameter k. We find that

$$\frac{\partial K}{\partial k}, \frac{\partial N}{\partial k}, \frac{\partial w}{\partial k} < 0 \tag{7.20}$$

Intuitively, the division of labour, which here is an organizational phenomenon, economizes on capital and labour inputs. The implied diminution in the workforce is associated, via the classical labour market, with a lower supply price (wage rate) of labour. An appropriate expression for equilibrium Y is given in the appendix, as is its derivative with respect to k. It is clear that whilst one can unambiguously assert that a very marked division of labour will lead to a very high equilibrium national income (i.e. $Y \to \infty$ as $k \to 1$) it turns out that for intermediate propensities to the division of labour the sign of $\partial Y/\partial k$ is indeterminate. We can only say that the larger is k, the more likely is $\partial Y/\partial k$ to be positive.

It should be observed that this ambiguity is to be contrasted with the conclusion reached if only the technological part of the model is examined. Temporarily using just (7.11) and (7.12), with K and N assumed given at values $\bar{K}$ and $\bar{N}$, results in

$$Y = (1-k)^{-1}\bar{K}^\alpha \bar{N}^{1-\alpha}$$

from which $\partial Y/\partial k > 0$, implying that an increased propensity to the division of labour unambiguously raises the equilibrium level of income. Indeed, as $k \to 1$ we have $Y \to \infty$, suggesting that the benefits from the division of labour are potentially without limit. An expanded output enlarges opportunities for the division of labour, raises productivity and expands output further. These effects are mutually reinforcing. But in this case, unrealistically, capital and labour are fixed. Making both endogenous as in our full system (7.11) to (7.19) opens up the possibility of using enhanced productivity to economize on the use of labour and capital at *the same time* as increasing output. Indeed, the appendix to this chapter shows that income per member of the workforce must unambiguously rise as the division of labour increases: $\partial(Y/N)/\partial k > 0$. Clearly inputs are being used more economically to produce an enlarged output. The result is important in that Smith and many since[7] have associated increases in income per head Y/N with increases in welfare. It suggests that welfare rises with the division of labour. This is to put aside for the moment the issues of distribution and alienation. Our model enables us rigorously to confirm properties which later commentators on Smith were able to suggest, but not to prove, like: 'The post-technological change equilibrium profit rate would be higher than the pre-technological change profit rate.' In the appendix we show $r > 0$ and $\partial r/\partial k > 0$, providing a rigorous proof of this conjecture, where here we are associating changes in the propensity to the division of labour with 'technological change'. This is to state something new which is neither in Smith nor in the writings of his later commentators. This new result arises because there is a distinction to be made between the induced or endogenous technical change which comes about in attaining the equilibrium rate of profits $r = b\lambda/(1-k)$, and the exogenous technological change which, as it were, alters the rate at which induced technological change can take place, this being associated with exogenous shifts in k. Such exogenous shifts ultimately reflect changes in workplace practices. In Smith, such changes occur *at the same time* as the new equilibrium is being moved to. Here we have a device for separating out such effects, and in doing so we are able to reach new conclusions.

We note from (7.20) that increasing values of k, reflecting an advancing level of specialization in the workplace, are associated with a lowered wage rate. This property is also a feature of the model used by Ippolito (1977) to investigate progressive specializations within the firm. There, the average wage rate falls as the firm's output rises, with job allocations at higher outputs having fewer activities which are repeated more often.

Our next task is to examine the consequences of increased bargaining power by the owners of capital. What is important about our model is that it shows that

$$\partial K/\partial b, \partial N/\partial b, \partial Y/\partial b > 0 \tag{7.21}$$

That is, as bargaining power increases, more capital *and* labour are used to produce more output. Further, the rate of profit *and* the wage rate are increased:

$$\partial w/\partial b, \partial r/\partial b > 0$$

Interestingly, here there is no capital/labour trade-off relationship when capital's bargaining increases, because more use is made of labour *and* capital in production, and higher wage *and* profits rates are attained. What is happening is that profit is rising relative to income by both an increase in capital employed and an increase in the rate of profit.

Through the classical labour market the demand for labour rises with the increase in capital employed, which increases the real wage rate and the size of the workforce. Thus the wage bill itself rises, despite capital's bargaining power being increased. We do not have a model of exploitation because increasing capital's power has a neutral effect on the ratio of the wage to profits rate and the ratio of the wage bill to total profit:

$$\frac{\partial}{\partial b}\left(\frac{w}{r}\right) = 0 \quad \text{and} \quad \frac{\partial}{\partial b}\left(\frac{W}{\Pi}\right) = 0 \tag{7.22}$$

Labour and capital share the benefits of increased output ($\partial Y/\partial b > 0$), with capital taking the initiative in bringing about the change. The lack of an asymmetric effect as between labour and capital is attributable to the fact that technical progress caused by the division of labour is neutral on these inputs. The additively separable assumption embodied in the production function (7.11) implies that enlarged markets bodily shift the production function with no favouring of capital or labour. The effect on rent is ambiguous, but what we can say – and will illustrate numerically below – is that as capital's bargaining power increases towards its upper limit, then because it brings labour along with it in enjoying the benefits of an increased national income, unearned or rentier income will ultimately suffer. Of course to Adam Smith the rentiers, whom he characterized as reaping where they had not sown, were not particularly deserving recipients of income anyway. Adam Smith's own criterion of welfare – income per head – provides no guidance here on what might be a desirable level of bargaining power of capital, for $\partial(Y/N)/\partial b = 0$. Indeed, distributional effects on welfare are deliberately ignored by him in the selection of a (Y/N) index of welfare. One might tentatively argue that in a broader welfare framework, there might be perceived benefits in the positive effect of

136 *Bargaining Power and the Division of Labour*

increasing capital's bargaining power on national income ($\partial Y/\partial b > 0$), for one way of reducing the potential for distributional conflict is simply to ensure that there is more national income to be shared out. Even if *relative* shares may not advantage a type of income flow, the prospect of an *absolute* increase in that income flow may diminish conflict.

7.5 SOME NUMERICAL EXAMPLES

So far we have only explored the model in terms of local, instantaneous rate of change effects. The purpose of this section is to look at the model globally for wide ranges of the key parameters: the propensity to the division of labour k; and capital's bargaining power b. Equilibrium values of the variables of the model are given for $k = 0.1$ to 0.9 in table 7.1 and for $b = 0.1$ to 0.9 in table 7.2.

Let us consider first the effects on equilibrium values of shifts in the propensity to the division of labour k. Table 7.1 provides the necessary information when the parameters of equations (7.11) to (7.19) have the following assigned values: $\alpha = 0.75, d = 1.9, f = 3.1, g = 4.2, c = 0.3, a = 3.8, b = 0.68$. We observe that national income is U-shaped in the propensity to the division of labour. The equilibrium real wage rate is decreasing in k, but national income per head is increasing in k. A distributional conflict might be suggested if one feels that labour's interest is to have a low propensity to the division of labour (less alienation) and a high wage rate, whereas capital's interest is to have a high division of labour (more alienation) with a low wage rate (deskilling) but a high rate of profits. However, if technical progress through the division of labour is both capital and labour saving, as in this model, the force of such an argument is greatly diminished. Perhaps closer to Adam Smith's welfare index is not national income, but national income per head. The former measure might have one undecided between a high or a low division of labour, as each offers different ways of attaining relatively higher incomes, but only through favouring one type of income recipient over another. The latter measure removes the indecision in that income per head unambiguously rises with the division of labour, which suggests clear potential welfare gain, provided considerations of distribution are not crucial. Now table 7.1 suggests that there *could* be critical distributional considerations. Take the case $k = 0.9$, for which we have a national income of 2.051, aggregate profit of 1.394, rent of 0.645, but a wage bill of only 1.144×10^{-2}. Deskilling has advanced so far that wage rates are low, the workforce is small and the wage bill is correspondingly small. The ratios of wage rate to profits rate and of wage bill to aggregate profit are also both small. A high propensity to the division of labour clearly favours rentier and capitalist incomes over wage income.[8] If interests within society suggested,

Table 7.1 Classical model parameterized by the propensity to the division of labour k

k	K	N	w	Y	Π	r	D	Y/N	W	R	w/r	W/Π
0.1	5.865	6.411	1.526	6.663	4.531	0.773	0.666	1.039	9.786	−7.654	1.976	2.160
0.2	1.295	1.415	0.337	1.655	1.125	0.869	0.331	1.169	0.477	5.267[a]	0.388	0.424
0.3	0.728	0.795	0.189	1.063	0.723	0.993	0.319	1.336	0.151	0.189	0.191	0.208
0.4	0.506	0.553	0.132	0.862	0.586	1.159	0.345	1.559	7.284[a]	0.203	0.114	0.124
0.5	0.389	0.424	0.101	0.793	0.539	1.391	0.397	1.871	4.280[a]	0.211	0.073	0.079
0.6	0.314	0.344	8.184[a]	0.804	0.547	1.738	0.482	2.338	2.813[a]	0.229	0.047	5.146[a]
0.7	0.264	0.289	6.881[a]	0.901	0.613	2.318	0.631	3.118	1.989[a]	0.268	2.969[a]	3.246[a]
0.8	0.228	0.249	5.937[a]	1.166	0.793	3.477	0.933	4.677	1.480[a]	0.358	1.707[a]	1.867[a]
0.9	0.201	0.219	5.220[a]	2.051	1.394	6.953	1.846	9.354	1.144[a]	0.645	7.507[b]	8.206[b]

Parameter values assigned: $\alpha = 0.75$, $d = 1.9$, $f = 3.1$, $g = 4.2$, $c = 0.3$, $a = 3.8$, $b = 0.68$.

K capital
N workforce
w wage rate
Y national income
Π aggregate profit
r rate of profits
D technical progress term
W aggregate wage bill
R rent

[a] Denotes $\times 10^{-2}$.
[b] Denotes $\times 10^{-3}$.

or indeed could ensure, an unlimited increase in the division of labour, the advantages would accrue only to earners of non-wage income. Were one to think of society as being composed of distinct worker, capitalist and rentier classes, what we would have is apparently a model of expropriation. However, in the economic world we wish to consider here, economic agents may earn any combination of the three income types. Income type depends on a particular economic activity rather than on a particular class. Taking this activity-based approach to incomes as the point of departure, what more can be said? Clearly the *potential* benefits of an increased division of labour exist, because of the increased national income per head. Provided wage earners are socially mobile and can enter, and thus help to break down, rentier or capitalist groupings – or, more realistically, provided increasingly specialized (i.e. deskilled) workers can gain access to rentier and capitalist incomes through institutional arrangements like pension funds and profit-sharing – then the consequences of an increased division of labour look favourable.

Now let us turn to the effects on equilibrium of shifts in capital's bargaining power. In view of what we have said in the previous paragraph, note this means not shifts in the interest of a capitalist class, but rather shifts in the advantage of owners of capital (who may also own 'land' broadly defined, and may work as employees). Table 7.2 provides the basic information. It indicates that there are some advantages in permitting an increase in capital's bargaining power. It is capital that mobilizes production, and increasing b will unambiguously increase r, K and Y. It does so by working with more labour. Technical progress D increases with the consequentially enlarged Y by bodily shifting the production function. The benefits are passed on to labour as well as to capital. For labour this implies an increasing workforce as b rises, being paid an increasing real wage rate. Adam Smith's welfare index Y/N remains neutral, it being no part of its design to reflect distribution. Possible labour–capital conflict indices like w/r and W/Π or their reciprocals are also invariant to b, further emphasizing the possible merit of permitting b to rise for the sake of an increased workforce, a higher wage, and an enlarged national income. This almost sounds too good to be true. Who are the losers in this process? Ultimately, they are the recipients of rentier income. Rent has an inverted U-shape in b; as b is progressively increased the rent is pushed down, finally reaching zero at extreme values of b when profit accounts for most of national income. However, as b rises from lower values like 0.1 to 0.4 then, even though rent also rises with profits and wages, sharing in the increase in Y, it does so at a decreasing rate. Indeed, within or without this range of b, table 7.2 indicates that the ratio of rent to national income R/Y falls steadily as b increases, implying progressive relative disadvantage for recipients of this form of income.

Table 7.2 Classical model parameterized by bargaining power of capital b

b	K	N	w	Y	Π	r	D	Y/N	W	R	w/r	W/Π	R/Y
0.1	7.441[a]	8.134[a]	1.937[a]	0.127	1.268[a]	0.170	5.072[a]	1.559	1.575[b]	0.113	0.114	0.124	0.890
0.2	0.149	0.163	3.873[a]	0.254	5.072[a]	0.341	0.101	1.559	6.301[b]	0.197	0.114	0.124	0.776
0.3	0.223	0.244	5.810[a]	0.380	0.114	0.511	0.152	1.559	0.014	0.252	0.114	0.124	0.663
0.4	0.298	0.325	7.746[a]	0.507	0.203	0.682	0.203	1.559	2.520[a]	0.279	0.114	0.124	0.550
0.5	0.372	0.407	9.683[a]	0.634	0.317	0.852	0.254	1.559	3.938[a]	0.278	0.114	0.124	0.438
0.6	0.446	0.488	0.116	0.761	0.456	1.022	0.304	1.559	0.057	0.248	0.114	0.124	0.325
0.7	0.521	0.569	0.136	0.888	0.621	1.193	0.355	1.559	7.718[a]	0.189	0.114	0.124	0.213
0.8	0.595	0.651	0.155	1.014	0.812	1.363	0.406	1.559	0.101	0.102	0.114	0.124	0.101
0.9	0.670	0.732	0.174	1.141	1.027	1.534	0.456	1.559	0.128	−1.347[a]	0.114	0.124	−0.012

Parameter values assigned: $\alpha = 0.75$, $d = 1.9$, $f = 3.1$, $g = 4.2$, $k = 0.4$, $c = 0.3$, $a = 3.8$.

K capital
N workforce
w wage rate
Y national income
Π aggregate profit
r rate of profits
D technical progress term
W aggregate wage bill
R rent

[a] Denotes $\times 10^{-2}$.
[b] Denotes $\times 10^{-3}$.

7.6 CONCLUSION

Our purpose in this chapter has been to develop an aggregate classical model with particular emphasis on the bargaining power of capital and the division of labour. The inspiration for this was sought in Adam Smith; and certainly the model constructed can in many respects be justified by appeal to *The Wealth of Nations*. It would be too much to describe what is offered here as a 'Smithian model', but it might reasonably be regarded as part of the legacy of Adam Smith.

Two new parameters were introduced. The first (k) provided a way of representing the propensity to the division of labour. The second (b) represented the bargaining power of owners of capital. The general consequences of increasing the division of labour and of increasing capital's bargaining power were shown to be auspicious. However, one should make qualifications. Conflict indices like w/r and W/Π, which assume smaller values as potential conflict rises, suggest the advanced division of labour may not be a comfortable state to be in unless wage earners also have access to rentier and capitalist incomes. Increased bargaining power for the owners of capital will systematically disadvantage recipients of rental income. As ever with the economic problem, there are gainers and losers under different scenarios, though whether one can discuss further the implications of this within the boundaries of economics, or even of political economy, is doubtful.

APPENDIX

Equilibrium values

Equilibrium values for variables in the model of equations (7.11) to (7.19) are as follows:

$$K = \frac{b\lambda}{B} \tag{7.23}$$

$$N = \frac{bd\lambda}{(1 + f/g)B} \tag{7.24}$$

$$w = \frac{bd\lambda}{g(1 + f/g)B} \tag{7.25}$$

$$Y = \frac{b\lambda^2}{(1 - k)B} \tag{7.26}$$

$$\Pi = \frac{b^2\lambda^2}{(1-k)B} \tag{7.27}$$

$$r = \frac{b\lambda}{(1-k)} \tag{7.28}$$

where

$$\lambda = \left(\frac{d}{1+f/g}\right)^{1-\alpha} \quad \text{and} \quad B = [ak\lambda - c(1-k)]$$

Now $\lambda > 0$ and we impose $B > 0$.

Division of labour parameter k

From (7.23),

$$\frac{\partial K}{\partial k} = \frac{-b\lambda(a\lambda+c)}{[ak\lambda - c(1-k)]^2} < 0$$

and similarly we get $\partial N/\partial k < 0$ and $\partial w/\partial k < 0$. Also $\partial W/\partial k < 0$ for W, $N > 0$ and $W = wN$. Now

$$\frac{Y}{N} = \frac{1}{1-k}\left(\frac{d}{1+f/g}\right)^{-\alpha} \tag{7.29}$$

from which

$$\partial(Y/N)/\partial k > 0$$

For $b, \lambda > 0$ and $0 < k < 1$, we have $r > 0$. Further, $\partial r/\partial k > 0$. From (7.26),

$$\frac{\partial Y}{\partial k} = \frac{-b\lambda[a\lambda(1-2k) + 2c(1-k)]}{\{(1-k)[ak\lambda - c(1-k)]\}^2}$$

which is negative for k small and positive for k large in the range $0 < k < 1$.

Bargaining power of capital parameter b

Directly from (7.23) to (7.28) we have $\partial K/\partial b$, $\partial N/\partial b$, $\partial w/\partial b$, $\partial Y/\partial b$, $\partial \Pi/\partial b$, $\partial r/\partial b > 0$. From (7.29), $\partial(Y/N)/\partial b = 0$. Similarly, W/Π does not involve b, being

$$\frac{W}{\Pi} = \frac{d^2(1-k)}{g(1+f/g)^2[ak\lambda - c(1-k)]}$$

Hence $\partial(W/\Pi)/\partial b = 0$. Similarly, $\partial(w/r)/\partial b = 0$. Finally, $D = kY$; hence $\partial D/\partial b > 0$.

NOTES

1 Our model is classical in that it is inspired by the writings of Adam Smith, and satisfies the characteristics of classical analysis identified by Dasgupta (1985).
2 As in Eltis (1985) we assume that total capital is made up of fixed capital and circulating capital. The distinction is not crucial to our analysis. Indeed, we would agree with Ricardo's later view that the distinction is a matter of degree rather than kind (e.g. the wheat which a farmer sows is a relatively fixed capital compared with the wheat used by the baker for making loaves). See Meacci (1985).
3 In Smith (WN, p. 343) there is a clear statement of a relation such as $F(.)$, as he argues that 'annual produce' (Y) increases with 'the number of . . . productive labourers' (N), with 'an additional capital' (K), and with 'a more proper division . . . of employment' (D). Land (T) is not explicitly mentioned by Smith at this point, and typically this resource is taken as given, though its augmentation, for example by colonization, can occur over a time scale spanning societal stages.
4 See Harris (1978, p. 45) for the distinction between a macroeconomic rate of profits and the rate of profit of a particular sector. As he emphasizes, the former can *only* be analysed in a macroeconomic model of the aggregate variety.
5 As Smith (WN, p. 66) put it: 'The profits of stock . . . are regulated altogether by the value of the stock employed, and are greater or smaller in proportion to this stock.'
6 Note that in $N^D(.)$ capital includes a component of circulating capital which can be approximately reduced to labour embodied. Provided the ratio of fixed to circulating capital is approximately constant, increases in circulating capital, given the real wage, will be associated with increased labour demand. See Hicks (1969, pp. 151–2): 'It is not the whole capital employed in industry but only the circulating part of it, which is strongly correlated with the demand for labour from industry (still at a constant level of real wages). So long as the proportion of fixed to circulating capital remains constant this of course does not matter.' See also his footnote (p. 151).
7 For example, Myint (1948) and O'Brien (1975).
8 Though this possibility of distributional conflict is given detailed treatment in Smith, it is an aspect of his work which is generally neglected. It has not to our knowledge been given formal mathematical expression by reference to Smith's work in any published form until here in this chapter. In Dasgupta (1985), it is argued that the harmonious consequences of the operation of the 'invisible hand' apply to the allocation of resources, but not to the functional distribution of income.

8
Disequilibrium and Increasing Returns

8.1 INTRODUCTION

In chapter 7 the attributes of stationary state values of variables in an aggregate Smithian model were examined. In chapter 6 an aggregate model was also used, this time to give explicit expression to the growth path of social product over time. Now we shall return to a theme introduced in chapter 4, arguably the most important theme, which explores growth and accumulation at the sectoral level, under the assumption that growth is a disequilibrium process driven by increasing returns. We do so for two reasons.

Firstly, there is a tendency for writers on Adam Smith's analysis of growth to emphasize either its 'cheerful' (growing) or 'dull' (declining or stationary) aspects. By contrast, Smith himself actually analyses – though perhaps not all in one place – what one would today call a complete 'growth trajectory', in the course of which growth, decline, and ultimate stationarity all occur. We will argue that it is both unnecessarily analytically restrictive and textually inaccurate to emphasize any one aspect of this growth process to the neglect of others.

Secondly, an essential aspect of growth, as analysed by Smith, is that it progresses at a rate which is neither uniform over time nor uniform across sectors of the economy. Smith's is a disequilibrium form of growth, driven by the increasing returns which are consequential on the division of labour, with advance in one sector being a prerequisite to advance in another.

A certain amount of formal notation may help make the approach adopted become clearer to the reader. Consider an n-sector economy at period t with sectoral growth rates $g_1(t), g_2(t), \ldots, g_n(t)$. In our view, an appropriate representation of Smithian long-run equilibrium is the stationary state in which there is a zero growth rate in each sector. Formally, stationarity is attained in period τ if $g_1(t) = g_2(t) = \ldots = g_n(t) = 0$ for all $t \geq \tau$. However, before this stationary state is reached, we have typically $g_1 \neq g_2 \neq \ldots \neq g_n$, implying unequal growth rates across sectors. Finally, growth is not merely unbalanced across sectors, but progresses at a variable rate over time for each sector, this being represented by the functional dependence of each growth rate on time, $g_i = g_i(t)$ ($i = 1, 2, \ldots, n$). This notation has been made precise, even pedantic, in order sharply to differentiate the view taken here from that adopted in a number of distinguished analyses of Smithian growth. In Eltis (1984) the sectoral aspect of Smithian growth is suppressed; a single aggregate production function is used, and for given parameters the growth rate is invariant over time. Thus a single constant g is implied. In Samuelson (1977) a more complex picture is presented of an n-sector economy. However, growth rates are the same across all sectors: $g_i = g$ for all i. Furthermore, this growth rate is constant over time until land scarcity plummets the economy into the stationary state with all sectoral growth rates falling to zero: $g_i = 0$ for all i. Only in Samuelson (1978) is a more satisfactory picture presented in which the economy follows a trajectory of variable growth, both over time and between sectors, in its approach to the stationary state.

In the sort of disequilibrium situations that are being contemplated in this chapter, markets may not be cleared, actual and desired levels of inventories may not coincide, and short-period expectations may not be fulfilled. Models of this sort have been considered in Jorgenson (1961) and most notably in Hahn (1963). They have in common, however, the retention of the assumption of constant returns to scale. By contrast, we shall argue that increasing returns and disequilibrium are characteristic of Smithian growth. Recently, Blitch (1983) has drawn attention to Kaldor's recognition of the extraordinary insights of Young (1928) in his extensions of Adam Smith. Kaldor (1972) himself made a further contribution to our understanding of the Smithian theory of economic progress, and in Kaldor (1985) there is an elegant and extended restatement of the earlier argument. There is no doubt that in his enthusiasm to amplify the merits of Smith and Young, Kaldor overstated his own case and made some ill-judged attacks on certain aspects of neoclassical general equilibrium theory. Hahn (1974), in his inaugural lecture at the University of Cambridge, was mercilessly to snipe at Kaldor for his errors. Certainly there were errors on Kaldor's part, of which the most significant was his suggestion that increasing returns are *necessarily* destructive of an Arrow-Debreu type of general equilibrium. In fact, certain limited occurrences of increasing returns are permissible: which is perhaps to say no more than that if the extent of increasing returns is limited, then the consequences are not substantial. However, it is clear that what Kaldor had in mind – and this is very much in keeping with Smith – was a situation in which increasing returns were pervasive and of considerable consequence. In section 8.3 a device will be introduced that enables one to represent the consequences of the division of labour by an appropriately specified 'implicit' production function which displays increasing returns to scale. If increasing returns are strong, the conventional stable equilibrium of general equilibrium analysis can be transformed into an unstable equilibrium.

The nature of Smith's growth analysis as we would present it is now evident: its core is a sectoral model, with many if not all sectors subject to increasing returns, and growth taking place at a rate which is variable through time and across sectors, in response to sectoral disequilibria. The final outcome of all this is stationarity.

These two sentences alone define an analytical framework of immense complexity. Smith, of course, expounded it in purely literary terms, free even of numerical examples. It is apparent that Smith did consciously think in terms of systems, these being 'inventions of the imagination' (EPS, p. 105), and that he applied his theory of scientific systems to the construction of an economic system.[1] He drew an analogy between systems and machines, saying: 'A system is an imaginary machine invented to connect together in the fancy those different movements and effects which are already in reality performed' (EPS, p. 66). Though he was not averse to the mathematical analysis of systems, he recognized the limitations of this method: 'It rarely happens, that nature can be mathematically exact with regard to the figure of the objects she produces, upon account of the infinite combinations of impulses, which must conspire to the production of each of her effects' (EPS, p. 95). Having observed how the astronomers had laboured in vain to discovery constancy and regularity in the motion of the heavenly bodies, he is compelled to remark that they were perhaps expecting too much, for it is 'to be found in no other parts of nature' (EPS, p. 96). It is appropriate, therefore, to look at Smith's analysis of growth in terms of an imaginary machine, or as we would say today, an economic model. Such a model might be mathematical, though in this form it is unlikely to capture many aspects of reality.

The purpose of this chapter is to propose a method of modelling Smith's growth analysis which is faithful to the original and involves some significant extensions. Its origins lie in Young (1928) and Kaldor (1972), and the method is essentially that of sectoral disequilibrium growth. Such a treatment is not intensely mathematical, although it is certainly analytically rigorous, but it offers, we suggest, the most illuminating means of expounding and extending Smith's growth analysis.

146 *Disequilibrium and Increasing Returns*

8.2 THE YOUNG-KALDOR EXTENSIONS OF SMITH

In September 1928 Allyn Young read his presidential address to section F of the British Association in Glasgow. His topic, 'Increasing returns and economic progress', was fundamental and very deep – perhaps too deep to be appreciated in his day. Subsequently published in the *Economic Journal*, the paper had as its core an analytical construction which even his leading disciple, Nicholas Kaldor (1972, p. 1243), found 'at times . . . obscure'. The basis of increasing returns in Young's analysis was the division of labour.

However, Young endowed the concept of the division of labour with a broader meaning than one finds in Smith. Specifically, Young (1928, pp. 537-9) extended it to industrial differentiation, and to the realizing of more roundabout methods of production. This line of analysis has been elaborated and amplified by Kaldor (1970, 1972, 1985) in a variety of publications over the last fifteen years. Most notable of these was the Scottish Economic Society Lecture delivered at the University of Aberdeen, where Kaldor (1970, p. 340) emphasized the significance for growth of the

> existence of increasing returns – using that term in its broadest sense – in the processing of activities. These are not just the economies of large scale production, commonly considered, but the cumulative advantage accruing from the growth of industry itself – the development of skill and know-how; the opportunities for easy communication of ideas and experiences; the opportunity for ever-increasing differentiation of processes and of specialization in human activities.

In his earliest paper Kaldor was particularly concerned with the way in which increasing returns might not lead to all regions benefiting from interregional trade. Subsequently, Kaldor (1972, 1985) emphasized the conditions necessary for expansionary intersectoral or interindustry trade, and this theme has been taken up in Reid (1975, ch. 7, 1979) and in chapter 4 in this book.

In Smith the analysis is incomplete, but certainly the extensions provided by Young and Kaldor are in harmony with Smith's view, and constitute a logical development of them. Young's analysis runs in sectoral terms, with the interplay of reciprocal supply and demand leading, he claims, to growth of a cumulative sort. Kaldor (1972) has demonstrated that Young's analysis too is incomplete, lacking a theory of effective demand. Such a theory is supplied by Kaldor, again working within a Smithian framework.

Exploring further these extensions of Smith, we will return to the extended and precise analytical note to Young's article. Rather than rejecting it as 'obscure', we will regard it as being of central importance. A careful study of

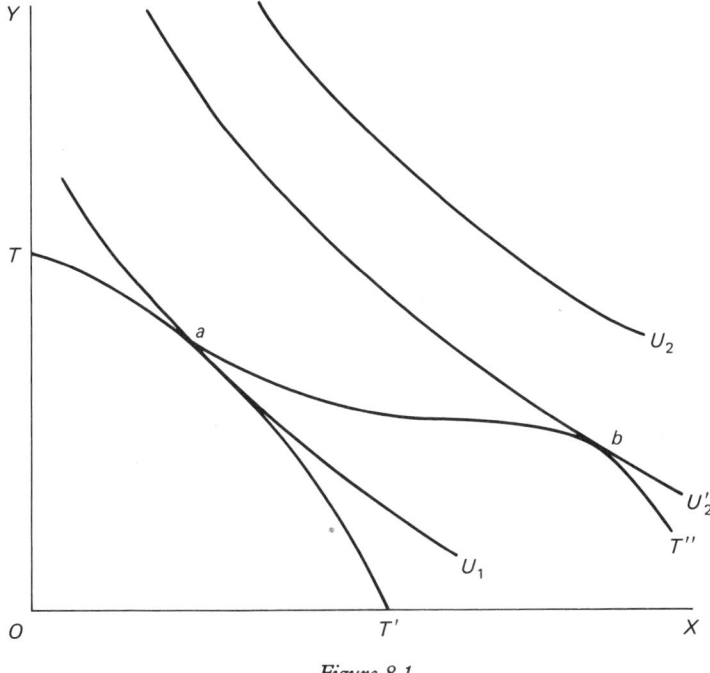

Figure 8.1

this note reveals that the whole analytical construction of the article proper is woven around a set of devices due to Pareto (1927).[2] From our standpoint, the note is full of promise, for it starts with a construction that depends on a sectoral view of the economy, namely the production possibility frontier.

Suppose that goods X and Y are produced from the same set of factor inputs of capital K and labour N according to distinct production functions. Under the assumption of an increasing opportunity cost of producing X in terms of Y as relatively more X is produced, the production possibility frontier will have the form TT' in figure 8.1. In Pareto a line such as TT' is always regarded as a possible path through the commodity space. Whether a path is, or is not, possible depends, in his terminology, on 'obstacles' to transforming one commodity into another. These 'obstacles' are defined by the form of the production functions. Superimposed on the same diagram are collective indifference curves $U_1, U_2, \ldots$

Of course, the indifference curve construction is not found in Smith, and in employing it Young is clearly engaged in rather a radical extension of Smith. However, as Hollander (1973, ch. 4) has argued in persuasive detail, Smith

148 *Disequilibrium and Increasing Returns*

certainly extensively employed a theory of choice, and his lack of a narrowly defined concept of marginal utility should not be construed as his rejecting the notion (so central to much of economic analysis) that utility is a necessary condition for exchange value. More recently Gee and Jarvis (1984), in their formal specification of a Smithian model, have represented the preference structures of labourers and landlords by explicit utility functions. There does, therefore, seem to be some merit in Young's suggested extension. In terms of Pareto's terminology, *maximum ophelimity* is attained at the point a in figure 8.1. This is a familiar way of representing general equilibrium in a two-good, two-factor economy and is a standard device in trade theory, welfare economics and so on. With Young and Kaldor, both of whom are concerned with logical extensions of the Smithian scheme, this device is used as a point of departure, for their concern is with disequilibrium.

Young (1928) directed attention not at the stable equilibrium point a in figure 8.1, but at ways in which the production possibility frontier can be modified in order to move away from equilibrium. Young talked (p. 533) of 'the counterforces which are continually defeating the forces which make for economic equilibrium' and emphasized (p. 528) that, in the growth process which he analysed, 'movements away from equilibrium, departures from previous trends, are characteristic of it.' This movement away from equilibrium is made possible by the division of labour, and this modifies production functions so that strongly increasing returns become manifest. In figure 8.1 this is represented by a modification of the production possibility frontier TT' to the form TT''', which exhibits at least decreasing opportunity cost in the neighbourhood of the initial equilibrium point a.

The circumstances under which this effect can arise are worthy of further consideration. Certainly they are not treated at all by Kaldor, and perhaps even in Young they are imperfectly understood.

8.3 THE IMPLICIT PRODUCTION FUNCTION

In this section we introduce a device that has already been hinted at earlier, especially when using a production function with a lagged dependent variable, and ask the question: what will this production function look like when the time-phased aspects of production are ignored? Because previous discussions have focused on an aggregate production function, as in chapters 6 and 7, the sectoral implications of this sort of device have been ignored. It is to these that we now turn.

Let the production functions for each sector be written:

$$Y = F(K, N; M) \tag{8.1}$$

$$X = G(K, N; H) \tag{8.2}$$

where M and H are parameters representing the consequences of the division of labour, Y and X are commodity outputs, and K and N are capital and labour inputs. Marginal products of capital and labour are assumed positive and diminishing: F_K, F_N, G_K, $G_N > 0$ and F_{KK}, F_{NN}, G_{KK}, $G_{NN} < 0$.[3] Furthermore, the marginal product schedules are assumed to shift positively with positive variations in the division of labour parameters. Thus we have F_{KM}, F_{NM}, G_{KH}, $G_{NH} > 0$. This corresponds to the situation in figure 3.3, illustrating the argument of Samuelson (1978) that inventions can shift the MPP curve positively. Here, however, this process is continuous rather than intermittent. The simplest way of expressing this is to make the division of labour terms themselves dependent on the level of output (i.e. on the extent of the market). Thus we can rewrite (8.1) and (8.2) as

$$Y = F(K, N; M(Y)) \quad \text{with } M' > 0 \tag{8.3}$$

$$X = G(K, N; H(X)) \quad \text{with } H' > 0 \tag{8.4}$$

Now, assuming invertibility of (8.3) and (8.4), we get

$$Y = f(K, N) \tag{8.5}$$

$$X = g(K, N) \tag{8.6}$$

In the recent international trade literature on increasing returns, functions like (8.5) and (8.6) have been described as *implicit production functions*. In the presence of the division of labour effects indicated above, questions of the existence (or otherwise) of increasing returns using the standard homogeneity technique should be addressed to these functions f and g rather than to the functions F and G of (8.3) and (8.4).

To illustrate the method adopted, consider the production function for Y given by F, and write F in the separable form

$$Y = M(Y)\Phi(K, N) \quad \text{with } M' > 0 \tag{8.7}$$

Now if Φ is linearly homogeneous in K and N, and $M(Y)$ has an elasticity of less than unity, then the corresponding implicit production function, say

$$Y = \phi(K, N) \tag{8.8}$$

exhibits increasing returns to scale, a result given by Helpman and Krugman (1985). As an example, consider the production function with parameters A, α:

$$Y = AK^\alpha N^{1-\alpha} M(Y) \tag{8.9}$$

where $M(Y) = Y^{0.5}$. Thus the relevant elasticity is $(dM/dY)(Y/M) = 0.5$, which, as required, is less than unity. Note that were M a fixed constant, the production function in (8.9) would appear to exhibit constant returns to scale, as the sum of the exponents on the capital and labour variables is unity. However, inverting to get the implicit production function gives

$$Y = A^2 K^{2\alpha} N^{2-2\alpha} \qquad (8.10)$$

Now the sum of the exponents on K and N in (8.10) is 2, implying increasing returns for the implicit production function, even though the original parameterized production function apparently exhibited constant returns before the division of labour effect was investigated.

Now it is known that increasing returns are a necessary but not a sufficient condition for convexity in the production possibility curve, a matter which has been given detailed treatment by Bator (1957) *inter alia*. What is being assumed in figure 8.1 is that the increasing returns, due to implicit production functions at the sectoral level of the above form, are sufficiently strong to induce the decreasing opportunity cost segment on TT'' between a and b. There clearly now is a potential advantage to be sought if increasing returns of this nature can be obtained, for the path from a to b is what Young (1928, p. 541) calls a 'preferred route', using a metaphor much employed by Pareto. What was a stable equilibrium at a has been transformed into an unstable equilibrium. However, the argument is not quite as simple as this. Young argues that the achievement of this extent of increasing returns is not costless, and that the costs of moving along the preferred route ab depend not only on the distance moved in commodity space, but also on the rate at which this movement takes place. Clearly there is no simple way of accounting for these costs of movement away from equilibrium. It is suggested by Young that they can be accommodated by supposing that the indifference map becomes 'contracted' by costs. Thus, given any point in the commodity space, a lower level of utility is attained at that point *after* a modification of the production possibility frontier because of the cost incurred in achieving it. One is, therefore, making the whole preference field *path dependent*; this concept is difficult, which perhaps explains why Kaldor regarded it as obscure. However, this is to say not that the notion is faulty, but rather that it is not readily translated into simple geometry. One can capture the flavour of the argument by considering the stable equilibrium point b in figure 8.1 at which a utility level of U'_2 is attained. Now this utility level is relevant to a preference field defined for the point b. Before the route from a to b was undertaken, the utility level corresponding to U'_2 was attained on the indifference curve U_2 *from the perspective of the initial equilibrium point a*. Likewise, the utility level associated with b having been achieved, and the cost of moving from a to b having been incurred, the utility level initially attained on indifference curve U_1 will now be attained on a contracted version of this indifference curve to the south-west of U_1 (not shown). Of course, it is not necessary to this argument that the new stable equilibrium point b should ever be achieved: indeed this is to weaken Young's conclusions, for it would signal an end to economic progress. What we suggest is that strong increasing returns of the above nature provide a continuous incentive for moving along a preferred route through the commodity space, and away from any potential static stable equilibrium. In the longer term, this tendency would be reinforced by the discovery of new resources or the growth of population which would tend to move the production possibility frontier further out into the commodity space.

8.4 THE ROLE OF THE MERCHANT

There remains a significant difficulty with this analysis, which Kaldor (1972) first attempted to solve. Young argued that, provided the increase in supply of a commodity led to an increase in demand for all other commodities, growth would be cumulative. Kaldor pointed out that for this to occur, *total income* must be rising and not merely expenditure on a particular commodity. In order to explore the conditions under which this would occur, Kaldor put emphasis on a figure who had already been significant in Smith's analysis – the merchant. Smith realized that the merchant was crucial to the development of the commercial stage of societal development, and that 'the slow progress of opulence' had been partly caused by the general contempt towards merchants: 'Trade of a merchant . . . was depreciated in the beginnings of society . . . This mean and despicable idea which they had of merchants greatly obstructed the progress of commerce. The merchant is, as it were, the mean between the manufacturer and the consumer' (LJ, p. 527). In more modern terminology, Kaldor (1972, p. 1247) locates the source of 'inside demand' in the activities of the merchant: it is he who reconciles the frequent discrepancy between flow supply and flow demand by varying his level of stocks. The emergence of the merchant (as, even, the emergence of the philosopher) is in itself a consequence of the increasing division of labour as society evolves:

> A merchant in Glasgow or Aberdeen who deals in linen will have in his warehouse Irish, Scots and Hamburg linen, but at London there are separate dealers in each of these. The greatness of the market enables one to lay out his whole stock not only on one commodity but on one species of a commodity and one assortment of it. (LJ, pp. 355–6)

It is false of Kaldor to assume that Smith neglected the function of the merchant, but certainly true that, lacking a theory of effective demand, he was not able to perceive the role of merchanting activities in sustaining growth. And yet all the elements are there in Smith's writings. He gives very full consideration to the activities of merchants in markets for which prices are prone to fluctuations: 'The operations of the speculative merchant are principally employed about such commodities. He attempts to buy them up when he foresees that their price is likely to rise, and to sell them when it is likely to fall' (WN, p. 133). Elsewhere, he talks of 'traders and artificers' for whom 'it was the manifest interest of every particular class of them, to prevent the market from being over-stocked, as they commonly express it, with their own particular species of industry' (WN, p. 141). In the same way as it was proper for Young to regard his paper on increasing returns and economic progress as 'variations on a theme from Adam Smith', so also it is appropriate for us to view Kaldor's emphasis on the merchant as a further variation. Kaldor argued that provided the expansion of supply consequent on the division of labour leads to an increase not only in the volume but also in the value of stocks held by merchants, this increase in induced investment leads to an income flow which generates an increase in the effective demand for other goods. In turn, this rise in the effective demand for other goods creates in those markets further opportunities for the division of labour, and thus leads to further increasing returns.

The above argument requires a final refinement. What has been said so far about 'inside demand' emphasized competitive markets, which we shall characterize as agricultural and subject to constant returns. Imperfectly competitive markets we shall characterize as being concerned with manufacturing activities, which are subject to increasing returns. In such markets, it is the firms that generate 'inside demand' by varying their own levels of stockholding. If production varies in response to sales, then an increase in demand will lead to an increase in both fixed and circulating capital in the face of a rundown of stocks, provided producers expect markets to grow. It is this increase of capitals that is the induced investment which enlarges effective demand. This distinction between manufactures and agriculture, with the former offering the more plentiful opportunities for the division of labour, is entirely in keeping with Smith. The identification of different forms of induced investment, the one taking place for commodities in response to excess supply, and the other taking place for manufactures in the face of excess demand, is the distinct contribution of Kaldor, but one which logically follows on from a Smithian view of economic progress, with its emphasis on sectoral disequilibria. This extension of Smith brings with it a cautionary note, and in a more modern context suggests that the 'cheerful' view cannot be supported in an unqualified way. There are two untested assumptions in Kaldor's extension of Smith.[4] Firstly, can it be assumed that merchants will increase not just the volume, but also the value of stocks in the face of excess supply? Secondly, will manufacturers necessarily be sufficiently confident to respond to excess demand by capital formation? Both assumptions depend on a view which sees capitalist development as being at least orderly if not equilibrating, without prices for commodities ever collapsing, and with expansionary long-run prospects for manufacturers.

8.5 CONCLUSION

There is much that can be drawn from the writings of as great a genius as Adam Smith. Further, there is much that one might wish to draw from him, so great is his authority. However, this brings with it the danger of misinterpretation, which might do as much damage to great economists of today as to Smith himself.

This chapter advanced the argument that any modern restatement of Smith must consider a full growth trajectory, embracing both the 'cheerful' and 'dull' phases of economic development. Furthermore, it should be expressed in sectoral terms, though not, as in the modern classical approach referred to in Chapters 2 and 3, with technologies having constant returns to scale and with uniform growth rates across sectors. Finally, it should see growth in disequilibrium terms, as in Smith it is clearly advance in one sector that creates the possibility of advance in another.

Having earlier dismissed many types of modelling of Smithian growth as inappropriate, we suggested an approach which both attempts to be analytically tight and avoids sidestepping the heart of the matter: disequilibria between sectors. The Young-Kaldor extensions of Smith are faithful to the original, constitute a genuine analytical advance, and offer scope for further development. Modelling sectoral disequilibria is fearfully difficult, and may require recourse to simulation methods if a model of any size is constructed. Gee and Jarvis (1984) have already made a preliminary excursion into this difficult territory. The route will no doubt be hard and long, but the direction now at least is clear, and is open for all the stout-hearted to follow.

NOTES

1 For a recent statement of this view, see Raphael (1985).
2 Here we are referring to the translation by Ann Schwier of the 1927 French edition of Pareto's *Manual of Political Economy*.

154 *Disequilibrium and Increasing Returns*

3   The specification of such marginal productivity relationships has been surrounded by controversy. The device is used in Samuelson (1978) and its legitimacy was examined in great detail in Hollander (1980). The discussion by Smith in his first book of *The Wealth of Nations* is taken to be one 'into which the implications of diminishing returns are fitted as a special case' by Hollander (1980, p. 560). Hollander then proceeds to give four extensive passages in favour of Smith's recognition of diminishing returns, one of which is the familiar colony quotation relevant to the specific case of diminishing agricultural returns.

4   Kaldor expressed them as requirements on expectations: a certain inelasticity of expectations regarding prices; and a certain elasticity of expectations regarding sales. These are really long-term expectations, and for the growth process to continue they must be fulfilled. Clearly the fact that stocks are in the short term being held at unanticipated levels means that short-term expectations are not necessarily being realized.

9
Classical Economics in a Post-Industrial Society

9.1 INTRODUCTION

We saw in chapter 1 how Adam Smith's stadial analysis could be adapted to a sequence of stages like feudalism, mercantilism, industrialism and post-industrialism. The last stage was first analysed by Daniel Bell in the summer of 1959 in a seminar at Salzburg and was subsequently given a detailed treatment in Bell's *The Coming of Post-Industrial Society: A Venture in Social Forecasting* (1974). The emphasis has since shifted to concentrating on the emergence of service-based economies in developed countries, but the insight of Bell remains valid, whether we call the new societal order 'post-industrial', 'the global service economy'[1] or whatever. In the type of advanced economy we are now considering, the primary resource is human capital and the primary institutions are public and private universities, including corporate universities, the wider class of academies of learning, and public and private (include corporate) research units. In the sort of terminology that Bell (1974, p. 116) favours, post-industrial society is characterized as a game between persons using an intellectual technology based on information. More graphically, David Birch, who has emphasized the role of small firms in the emergent post-industrialism, has said: 'Our economies are changing. Growing and making things are not nearly so important as thinking things up. We are developing brain-intensive rather than capital-intensive or land-intensive economies.'[2]

In considering this contemporary development from a classical perspective, we are apparently faced with one enormous technical impediment. Service activities were regarded by Adam Smith, and a number of major classical economists who were to follow him, as unproductive activities. As against this, we have a major classical intellectual tool for explaining and analysing post-industrialism: that most Smithian device, the division of labour. This classical concept, when extended appropriately, would see post-industrialism as the manifestation of a most advanced division of labour. As we saw in chapter 5, it involves the 'specialization in know-how' of Arrow (1979) or 'the division of thought' of Casson (1988). It was difficult for Adam Smith to anticipate industrialism, but his work certainly showed insight into the coming order and in some measure he anticipated its characteristics. It was, of course, impossible for him to have insight into post-industrialism, and to anticipate any of its characteristics. Whilst this is true, two major parts of his intellectual apparatus can be carried through into the current order: the idea that societal evolution is progressive and can be analysed in terms of a sequence of stages; and the idea that a major force behind economic advance is the division of labour, with its potential for productivity advance being its virtue and its potential for over-specialization its possible vice.[3] Thus, even for an age which it never anticipated, classical analysis can be extended in a way which makes it relevant to the contemporary period.

9.2 EXTENSION OF THE DIVISION OF LABOUR

Historical research by Foley (1974) has suggested that in the writings of Plato, which Smith knew well, there are anticipations of the division of labour. On reading the relevant passages, one is inclined to think that this stretches a point. But as McNulty (1975) has pointed out, to the extent that anticipations of the division of labour are in the Ancients at all, they are used to characterize society as stratified in a caste-like way, with each man doing that one thing which is natural to him, and hence producing more goods of better quality, all to the service of domestic tranquillity. In Smith, by contrast, the division of labour is fundamentally a source of growth, and is really concerned with anything but tranquillity. It actually is a disturbing effect, which brings about growth by creating new possibilities for the organization of production. Blaug (1968, p. 39) put the point well when he characterized the division of labour in Smith as being so broadly defined 'as to include everything we would nowadays call technical progress'. Indeed in the current stage of post-industrialism, which is knowledge based, Adam Smith's 'mechanical, chymical, astronomical, physical, metaphysical, moral, political, commercial, and critical philosophers' whom he talked of in the 'Early draft' (LJ, p. 570), have come into their own.[4] Bell (1974, p. 221) can write: 'The chief resource of the post-industrial society is its scientific personnel.' Smith's discussion of the third advantage of the division of labour – invention – leads him to identify the emergence of just such a specialized class of citizens, who are 'philosophers or men of speculation, whose trade it is . . . to observe every thing; and who, upon that account, are often capable of combining together the powers of the most distant and dissimilar objects' (WN, p. 21). As a consequence of this emergent class of specialists, 'the quantity of science is considerably increased' (WN, p. 22).

Now in Smith's day, the role of scientific invention was probably not great in advancing productivity and stimulating growth. As Groenewegen (1977) has pointed out, much of the productivity gain from the division of labour which attended the transition from a domestic putting-out system to a manufactory system in eighteenth-century England was largely an organizational effect. Domestic workers controlled their own pace of work and frequently took days off as they wished, and there were extensive opportunities for appropriating part of the stocks of materials which owners had intended to be used for production. Not only this, but the average holding of stocks, being distributed amongst the homes of many outworkers, was high. When activities were undertaken all within the manufactory, many productivity gains were realized. Circulating capital was reduced, because stocks were not required to be so high once concentrated in a single location. Transport costs were reduced. The loss of materials by theft was reduced. The workforce was more punctual in attendance and less liable to absenteeism and drunkenness. The work itself was more closely supervised and monitored. It is a moot point whether fixed capital must have increased in this transition process. Certainly there was fixed capital investment in manufactory buildings, but tools and equipment would have been economized upon, as workmen could now share implements rather than each requiring his own full set. Clearly, in the argument that the manufactory system raised productivity by advancing the division of labour, it is not necessary that this was attended by increased fixed capital intensity. Blaug (1968, p. 40) reminds us that the manufactory was an emerging institution at the time Smith wrote, employing three to four hundred people, and numbering no more than thirty in the whole of Britain. Thus to have even a sense of its potential significance was something of an achievement. It was at least an anticipation of the stage of industrialism.

However, from the perspective of our current post-industrial stage, it is perhaps even more remarkable that Smith's analysis of the third advantage of the division of labour anticipated the emergence of specialized natural philosophers who would make a great contribution to science. We do not really know whether Smith was familiar with inventions that were becoming important for cotton textiles manufacturers in his day, like Kay's flying shuttle, Hargreaves's spinning jenny and Crompton's spinning mule.[5] It would seem unlikely that he did *not*, as he knew influential scientific figures of the eighteenth century like James Watt; but he did not write about them. Even so, he recognized the importance of science, and the emergence of scientific specialists whose inventions could greatly enhance productivity. Though this may have seemed at the time the least important aspect of his division of labour theory, the unfolding of events has ultimately endowed it with far greater significance. It gives classical economic analysis further contemporary relevance from, perhaps, an unexpected source.

The emphasis on the growth of scientific knowledge in the current stage of economic development has also been a part of the literature on the scientific-technical revolution. The concept has its roots in the work of Bernal (1965) on *Science in History*. It suggests that, in the early twentieth century, science became an output which was an aspect of production. Weizsäcker (1973) has shown how this idea can be made a part of a division of labour model in which the economy has two sectors.[6] In one sector the output is goods, and in the other (which Weizsäcker calls meta-production) it is new knowledge. The latter enhances productivity in the former. The production of new knowledge is itself contingent on specialization, and the greater the numbers working on this product, the greater the potential for increasing productivity. A characteristic of the meta-production sector, unlike the production sector, is that there seems no intrinsic reason why the marginal contribution of a knowledge producer should ever be pushed to zero. The benefits of the 'division of knowledge', as Weizsäcker (1973, p. 106) calls it, appear to be unbounded. Indeed, the increased supply of specialization in knowledge may create its own demand.[7] The emphasis on knowledge in terms of technical scientific knowledge may be too narrow. The work of Babbage (1832) on devising an appropriate division of labour to produce mathematical tables, using no more than unskilled clerks or even mechanical computers, suggests an advantage in what Casson (1988) calls a 'division of thought' in the processing of information. A production process requires a central system which operates by acquiring and acting on information, and the latter is susceptible to the division of thought. Pushing this argument even further, a specialization in certain mental tasks may emerge within the large corporate firm. Under it, some personnel concentrate on day-to-day decision-making, others on strategic planning and so on, all having in common that they apply thought processes of judgement to complex informational problems. This generalization of the division of thought to matters of judgement goes beyond the specialization in technical-scientific skills that Weizsäcker, Bernal, and in some measure even Bell have emphasized. It suggests, for example, that entrepreneurship should be treated as an aspect of the advanced division of labour. Clearly, entrepreneurial *activity* has been around since the market was developed as a human institution. However, it was often carried out by one man who was also engaged in many other activities, like the provision of finance capital, and the management of production. What the advanced division of labour makes possible is the role of a purely specialized entrepreneurship. Indeed, this pure role itself could be subject to further subdivisions of labour – that is, greater specialization. As the division of labour takes advantages of gains which may be achieved by cooperative activities, so the costs of achieving this cooperation must rise, and the emergence of specialists in organizing this cooperation – entrepreneurs – is also implied. A weakness of Adam Smith's analysis of the division of labour and the competitive process is the slight attention he gave to entrepreneurship. Because he failed to contemplate a division of labour sufficiently advanced for the pure entrepreneurial function to be undertaken by a single individual, he continued to compound it with the role of the capitalist or the worker.[8] Today, in post-industrial society, the extent of the division of labour is so great that the entrepreneurial function is increasingly important, both as an emergent form of specialization in its own right, and as a kind of cement binding together the rapidly multiplying other forms of specialization, especially in scientific and technical areas. The relationship is really inevitable, because greater specialization in general involves a surrender of a portion of one's earlier commitment to coordination. The relinquishing by many specialists of this aspect of earlier job descriptions leaves behind a collection of coordinating tasks which must be undertaken by a new sort of individual: one who specializes in coordination itself, the entrepreneur. Of course the economic problem remains. Cooperation, as displayed by advanced division of labour, raises the value of the production of the cooperating parties. It also increases the costs of coordination. Thus an *optimum* division of labour can be conceived of, which balances these marginal revenues and costs.[9] However, beyond the economic dimension there are other costs, like an erosion of trust between increasingly specialized individuals. Part of the coordinating function should be to lower mistrust, but this can be difficult (or, put alternatively, expensive) if the division of labour encourages the establishment of different ethical codes by specialized groups.[10] The balancing of ethical needs of such groups requires appeal to a concept like justice, which may not be fully reflected in law. This is especially so in the case of the advanced *international* division of labour. A lack of shared ethical values, between countries, may encourage injustice; and this may not be readily nullified by an appropriate system of law, for international law often lacks appropriate mechanisms of sanction. This sort of argument has been particularly emphasized by writers in the tradition of Marxian political economy, as represented by Caporaso (1987). They would see the extension of the division of labour domestically as leading to a social division of labour (e.g. with boss and worker distinctions), with an implied subordination of one social group or class by another. Extended to the international division of labour, again a pattern of subordination is implied, leading to effects like the so-called North–South divide.[11] However, in Adam Smith's analysis there is no necessary *social* division of labour; an economic agent may perform labouring, rentier *and* capitalistic functions. This is perhaps not typical, but it is possible, and the overlaps are recognized. Thus we are told: 'An independent manufacturer, who has stock enough both to purchase materials, and to maintain himself to carry his work to market, should gain both the wages of a journeyman who works under a master, and the profit which that master makes by the sale of the journeyman's work' (WN, pp. 70–1). Effects like this tend to operate against the emergence of a clear-cut, class-based division of labour, with class being associated with economic function. This is not to deny that the division of labour fosters a variety of groupings. They are formed to enjoy the advantages arising from cooperation, and have a tendency to enhance their own ethical systems. However, these groupings are not based on simple socioeconomic distinctions like capitalists or workers. The great diversity of such groupings, and the possibility of overlap between them, implies a pluralistic society in which complete consensus is difficult to reach because interests are so diverse. Conflict is ever present, but less sharp than in the Marxian scenario precisely because it does not manifest itself in very large oppositional social groupings.

Finally, we must attempt to resolve the apparent paradox that *competition* and the advanced division of labour so often go hand in hand, yet the division of labour is, as we have characterized it, essentially a *cooperative* process. Hirshleifer (1977, p. 36) has, we believe, the best resolution of this paradox when he points out that the cooperative division of labour is actually a reaction to the intensity of competition when many attempt to occupy the same competitive niche. The intensity of competition can be reduced by each individual doing different things, thereby diminishing interpersonal rivalry *and* extending group resources. There is no reason why we should limit discussion of the division of labour to a competitive (i.e. free market) economy, for it can be a feature of hierarchy or what Ouchi (1980) calls 'clans'.[12] However, in this volume, the emphasis is on market mediated activity, and therefore our next task must be to return again to the competitive process that keeps the market alive.

9.3 THE COMPETITIVE PROCESS

At various points we have already referred to aspects of the competitive process. Thus in chapter 1 we contrasted the process of competition with the outcome of competition (and its implied efficient allocation of resources). In chapter 2 we indicated how *market price* was established in the short run by a process of competition within a single market, and *natural price* by a wider process of competition, taking more time, and embracing factor market adjustments as well. Finally, in chapter 4, we saw firms engaged in a competitive process which involved pressing on with output and pushing down costs (and price) in order to gain – and maintain – a competitive edge over rivals. We start this section, therefore, with some advantage in terms of prior signalling of our intentions, but with the clear disadvantage of having to treat competition in a way which may seem unfamiliar, and even unorthodox.

A necessary starting point is with the ethical framework within which competition in the economic sphere takes place. In competition as Adam Smith saw it, and as we would see it too in today's post-industrialism, there are 'rules of the game' in the market place. Firstly, there are some aspects of human conduct which are not part of the market nexus. One rule of the game is therefore to distinguish between activities which may sensibly be market mediated and those which may not. Social obligation, for example, the subject of a later section in this chapter, may not sensibly be treated in a market framework. Secondly, within the market itself, conceived of as a social device for improving welfare by the pursuit of self-love or self-interest, there are standards of conduct. Being in the market does not mean that problems of moral judgement vanish, though by the deliberate design of the system they are greatly simplified. Political economy, being 'the science of a statesman or legislator' (WN, p. 428), is not concerned with explaining the nature of moral judgement, though it cannot rule out applying moral judgement to market acts. Thus in *The Theory of Moral Sentiments*, having already explained the nature of moral judgement in terms of the sympathy, or otherwise, of the impartial spectator, Smith proceeds to apply moral judgements to 'the race for wealth', in which a man may 'run as hard as he can . . . in order to outstrip his competitors', but may not 'justle or throw down any of them' for this is 'a violation of fair play' (TMS, p. 83). It will lose the sympathy of the impartial spectator. We know from earlier discussion that by experience of making moral judgements in this way, rules or norms emerge. They may become the basis for laws, prohibiting breach of contract or breach of property, for example. Or they may provide the basis for ethical norms, which if violated will incite disapprobation. In market activities, as other human activities, acts may be judged. At the one end of the scale of wrongs there is theft of property, a serious wrong with appropriate punishments; then follows breach of contract, a clear wrong remediable by law; and at the other end there is sharp business practice which, though perhaps not subject to legal sanction, certainly is subject to social sanction, set in motion by the disapprobation of businessmen.

Merely seeking gain in the market process is not in itself a cause for disapprobation, and is certainly no ground for formal legal sanction. Indeed, the market as an institution is endowed with a framework that intends to make the pursuit of individual self-interest desirable from a global social perspective. For this reason, the pursuit of gain within a free market may be seen as an aspect of virtue. Furthermore, the extension of the domain of free markets, providing as it does both scope for an enlarged division of labour, and the pursuit of a socially constrained form of gain, is presumptively welfare improving.[13]

Let us turn now to look in a more detailed way at competition as a process. We referred above to Smith's analysis of 'the race for wealth' (TMS, p. 83), which conveys the sense in which he talked of competition. When there is an excess demand for a commodity, we are told that amongst traders 'a competition will immediately begin' (WN, p. 73) which will increase market price. At several points Smith actually talks of 'the competitors' as if referring to a race. They may be more or less eager for competition, depending on the importance of the commodity concerned in their overall budget.[14] Smith's analysis of the determination of market price, particularly in the *Lectures on Jurisprudence* (e.g. LJ(A), p. 358) is much as later writers of the Austrian school would express it. There is a negatively sloped demand function, dependent on price, which is determined subjectively; hence it matters not at all if wants may be judged 'real' or 'capricious'. There is a given supply.[15] Finally, demand depends not just on price, but on the wealth (income, endowments) of the demanders, both absolutely and in a distributional sense.

There are to be found, as Stigler (1965b, ch. 8) has indicated, five conditions for free competition in Smith. Firstly, competitors should seek their own interests independently. Thus collusion, overt or tacit, is ruled out, though it is admitted that the tendency to collusion is difficult to overcome. Smith (WN, p. 145) observed the tendency for traders, when gathered together 'even for merriment and diversion', to end up in 'a conspiracy against the publick', meaning some device to benefit the producer as against the consumer. He considered it was difficult to stop tendencies to collusion in a society which valued liberty, though he suggested that a number of facilitators of collusion which were not designed with that purpose in mind (e.g. public registers) could be dispensed with. At least regulation should not inadvertently lower the costs of collusion. Today we are as aware as ever of the tendency for collusion, and even innocent looking devices which appear to do no more than exchange information can facilitate the coordination of collusive groupings. Smith was perhaps too negative about the consequences of incorporation, but his observation was that it frequently led to price increases which were never subsequently undersold by the forces of free competition (WN, p. 144). He emphasized the difficulty of maintaining collusion without incorporation, for one dissenting member could break up the scheme. With incorporation, which he regarded as working rather like a multiplant monopoly, penalty schemes can be devised for maintaining collusive discipline, and these 'will limit the competition more effectually and more durably than any voluntary combination whatever' (WN, p. 145). It should be noted that Smith really had in mind exclusive incorporation, which effectively meant the monopolization of a trade, though he also was uneasy about what he called 'the corporation spirit', this being a form of voluntary association or agreement which limited free trade by jealously guarded secrets, and about restrictive labour practices. His reluctance to contemplate any form of combination is perhaps extreme, because it quite clearly restricts possibilities for the further division of labour *within* the enlarged firm and potential efficiency gains thereof. Indeed, elsewhere (WN, p. 277) Smith shows an awareness of this advantage. One concludes that the form of rivalry envisaged for free competition by Smith admits to some tendency at least for firms to exchange information amongst incumbents, but not to share it with new entrants. To prevent this sort of thing would involve acts which might subvert liberty. However, to provide firms with devices (be they formal legal structures, or apparently neutral statutory registers which can be used for other purposes) which can facilitate collusion should be no part of government activity. The abolition of the Register of Business Names in recent years in the UK, provided an example of government removing a potential facilitating device for collusion.

The second condition for free competition is that rivals should be sufficiently numerous to limit tendencies for market price to be held above the natural level.[16] There is no specific guideline on how many is sufficient to bring this about, but there is clearly no suggestion that *large* numbers are required, as in the modern theory of perfect competition. The view is that active or eager, actual or potential, competition is what is required, this being more important than simply numbers of competitors. Smith uses phrases which express disapproval of devices which limit the numbers of competitors artificially (WN, p. 79 and p. 146), but there is no suggestion that numbers have to be *large*. More important, they should be *unrestricted*. There is a presumption that very few competitors, like two, make for limited rivalry, and that *some* increase in numbers is likely to promote greater rivalry. Thus in considering the grocery trade within a town (WN, p. 361) Smith regards two grocers as likely to supply goods at lower prices than one, concluding further that 'among twenty, their competition would be just so much the greater.' Such intensification of competition can lead to some firms going out of business, but 'it can never hurt the consumer or the producer' (WN, p. 362).

164 *Classical Economics in a Post-Industrial Society*

This particular part of *The Wealth of Nations* is suggesting that the numbers of rivals sufficient for competition should be great enough to make liquidation a real possibility for at least some firms.

The third condition requires that competitors should have access to knowledge of market opportunities. This is not the same as saying that competitors are *fully* informed, or that they are *equally* informed (or equally ignorant). There is always a relative degree of ignorance and an unequal distribution of knowledge amongst traders. Smith was aware of the importance of market information, though it did not have such a crucial place in his analysis as in the later work of competitive process theorists like Hayek and Mises. He is aware of the tendency for high prices to be kept secret by those who might profit from them (WN, p. 77), but thought that 'secrets of this kind ... can seldom be long kept; and the extraordinary profit can last very little longer than they are kept.' Thus competitors are alert to market opportunities, which, once detected, are rapidly but not instantaneously exploited. In the competition to exploit these market opportunities, some will be more successful than others.

Fourthly, there should be no restriction on competitors from acting on market opportunities. Smith's general view was that mercantilistic restrictions were an impediment to that system of natural liberty which would lead to a harmonious outcome. Impediments to natural liberty, or restrictions on competition, included corporate privileges and restrictions on entry to occupations and on labour mobility. Indeed, Smith was of the view that any new law for the regulation of commerce should be 'long and carefully examined, not only with the most scrupulous, but with the most suspicious attention' (WN, p. 267). His fear was of what we would today call 'regulatory capture'.

Finally, and fifth in our list of conditions for free competition in Smith, is that time is necessary to achieve an efficient allocation, with wages brought into line, adjusted by the 'net advantages' of different occupations, and profit rates equalized. Thus Smith says (WN, p. 132) that 'this equality in the whole of the advantages and disadvantages of the different employments of labour and stock, can take place only in the ordinary, or what may be called the natural state of those employments.' It takes some time to achieve these natural states, and also, referring back to our third condition above, knowledge of the relevant market opportunities. We are told with reference to wages, for example, that 'this equality can take place only in those employments which are well known, and have been long established in the neighbourhood' (WN, p. 131).

Let us summarize. The market process allows the expression of self-interest in its virtuous form. There are five requirements for the market process: independent seeking of gain; sufficient rivals to make competition eager, and bankruptcy possibly; access to knowledge of market opportunities; freedom from artificial restraints to pursue one's gain; and sufficient time to allow resources to move to their best uses. Now none of these requirements is unreasonable in a post-industrial economy, though further discussion is necessary. In their own time they were eminently reasonable, for as Stigler (1965a, ch. 2) has argued, they corresponded fairly closely to observable conditions. In this sense they were a forerunner of conditions later suggested by Clark (1940, 1961) and others for 'workable competition'.[17]

The virtuous aspect of self-interest, as expressed in an appropriate market framework, is probably more acceptable as a starting point than it ever was. Impediments to economic developments in those major nations since the Second World War that have favoured very little market activity, have led to a more pragmatic attitude in the 1980s. The Soviet Union and the People's Republic of China are expressing a new interest in the advantages of market provision of goods, and can see benefit from the viewpoint of society in permitting the individual pursuit of self-interest in appropriate market frameworks. In creating opportunities for market mediation of some transactions, these countries are, as Buchanan's (1976) argument suggests, creating public goods, where here the market is viewed as a kind of institution, in the same sense as the legal system is an institution (and a public good). Viewed in this way, the market is becoming a relatively favoured institution. Furthermore, advocates of the market who would perhaps have emphasized its efficiency advantages at an earlier point, are now more conscious of the need to discuss virtue, as Smith would have put it, in the same context. Thus Demsetz (1977), in discussing social responsibility in the enterprise economy, writes: 'The analysis of the free enterprise economy as that economic system to which we *should* aspire does impose a predetermined moral framework within which to work, for it implies that the good society limits the use of legal sanctions, expands the opportunities for choice by individuals, and, therefore, places the responsibility for behaving ethically on its citizens.'

Given this widespread acceptance of market activity as an expression of constrained virtue, the establishment of the first condition for the competitive process, the independent pursuit of gain, is not difficult in the climate of post-industrialism. Indeed, given the new feature of a very advanced division of labour, which encourages the division of thought and specialized entrepreneurship, the condition is more readily satisfied than in Smith's time. A further factor encouraging this is the crumbling of the 'deference structure'[18] which he thought essential to societal stability, caused by the rise of meritocracies. This change encourages the pursuit of one's own advantage rather than that of a master or superior. Smith very much emphasized the importance of independence of competitors, tending to argue that any form of association rapidly led to collusion and complete monopolization. It overlooks the sense in which one can pursue advantage independently by voluntary association with others. This does not involve a surrender of independence, for one can choose who one associates with, depending on the benefits, and of course the costs, of forming such associations. The most obvious and important example of such an association is the firm. Viewing the firm as a coalition, in a game-theoretic sense,[19] members of it participate on a voluntary basis, and decide independently whether it is advantageous to cooperate, given various outside options involving membership of other coalitional firms. It is also the case that mergers of firms can be analysed in this way. It does not follow that this implies high levels of market concentration. Indeed, as Reid and Jacobsen (1988) have recently argued, if innovation is an important vehicle for pursuing gain, there may be transactional *dis*advantages to being a large firm, and small firms will be the preferred form.

Numbers of competitors have been treated very unrealistically in many academic theories of competition. Because Smith deployed no theory of the firm, it was difficult for him to indicate his view. When he did refer to numbers of competitors, he usually had in mind merchants, workers or other single individuals. If not considered singly, then often the opposite extreme was analysed, with merchants combining in corporations and skilled workers in guilds. Actually, this alone gives clear guidance on how firms should be treated, and it is evident that a very large number are not required for free competition. This is partly because the division of labour encourages the emergence of product differentiation, and each firm is in a sense a weak monopolist, but also because, as workable competition theory emphasizes, at least some contesting of markets by actual or potential rivals is usually enough to bring about effective competition. The latter argument has recently been given rigorous statement in the contestability literature,[20] but something like this result has been accepted by industrial economists for decades. It is accepted that, in such market structures, all or at least some firms are not far from just breaking even, and that disturbances to the market may result in some marginal firms going out of business. This prospect of business failure is actually an essential part of the incentive structure of free competition. It would not be paradoxical to say that business failure is necessary for business success.

The knowledge requirements of free competition were given relatively less attention by Smith than other requirements, but later work on competitive processes has increasingly emphasized informational matters.[21] We saw that Smith recognized the possibility of information being guarded jealously, but thought competition would always defeat this stratagem. What he did not sufficiently emphasize is that short-run informational advantages actually keep the process of competition alive. The seeking of informational advantage by the entrepreneur goes on because it confers temporary monopolistic benefit, with its ensuing profitable consequences. The alternative assumption, which should be abandoned in a post-industrial era, is that economic agents are completely knowledgeable about market opportunities; this is the assumption adopted in the theory of perfect competition. It is not simply the gross unrealism of this assumption that is a problem, for models have to be constructed using assumptions which are in some measure unrealistic. Rather, it is that the assumption directs attention away from an essential aspect of market activity. As Hayek (1955) has expressed it, given a division of knowledge between economic agents and a consequential initial incompatibility in intentions and expectations, the purpose of activity in the market is to acquire the relevant knowledge to make intentions and expectations compatible. Even the so-called 'economics of information' literature, as exemplified by Stigler (1961), does not quite grasp the implication of this, for it presents agents as making rational decisions about how much information they want to acquire as though they knew already what information would be useful. The crucial point, so clearly delineated by Kirzner (1979, p. 139), is that the market presents possibilities for discovering knowledge whose existence was previously unknown. This class of knowledge provides the basis for spontaneous, unintended learning, which when handled adaptively can be used to reconcile intentions between economic agents, in conjunction with planned, intentional learning. The latter can be absorbed within the normal cost–revenue framework, but the former, being spontaneous, cannot; it just strikes one afresh. Entrepreneurship can be regarded as precisely the capacity to benefit from this form of knowledge. In today's post-industrialism it is much more obvious than in yesterday's industrialism that the market is an institution for processing detailed information. This is encouraged by the fact that many goods and services now sold are informational in character, and the skills of marketing, advertising and salesmanship that go with selling these goods are also information based. But actually, it was always true that markets facilitated information flows. The difference now is that the volume of information flowing is vastly greater, thanks to technological change involving television, desk-top publishing, computer networking etc. and occupational change involving the emergence of entirely new jobs (what might be called 'job innovation') like systems analysis, occupational counselling, management consultancy etc.[22] Equally, entrepreneurs have been around for centuries, at least since the Middle Ages when they were responsible for carrying through to completion large construction works like cathedrals. But now their scope has been vastly extended, precisely because of the value, in this increasingly information-oriented society, of the entrepreneurial function of successfully using knowledge that has not been deliberately acquired.

Smith's fourth requirement for competition was freedom from artificial constraints, by which he meant the dismantling of mercantilist restrictions. Many treated this condition as a doctrine, with a purpose in itself. *Laissez-faire* had the important connotation of 'let's get on with it.' The Manchester School was not a movement of intellectuals, for example, but a group of businessmen who preferred to act as agitators rather than scholars.[23] Some businessmen were narrowly self-interested and hoped for lower costs and higher demand; some looked for a complex web of world trade that would discourage wars, and some for improved working-class conditions. Thus the free trade movement was a practical rather than intellectual movement. Indeed, it would even be wrong to conclude that Smith's favouring of the removal of artificial restraints on trade amounted to a *theoretical* argument for the optimality of free trade. This is really a post-Walrasian result, and is enshrined in the Heckscher-Ohlin-Samuelson model. However, the hankering after such a result has earlier roots, and was part of the intellectual vulgarization that Smith's work suffered. Nicholson (1895, p. 18) put the matter very aptly when he wrote that 'the popular opinion that Free Trade is in all cases *theoretically* the best, although in particular cases it may be *practically* the best course to make exceptions, is exactly the reverse of the teaching of Adam Smith.' Further, free trade has 'the overwhelming advantage of perfect simplicity'. Nicholson (1895, p. 19) concluded by admiring in Smith 'the reasoned judgement . . . that Free Trade is the working system, most conducive to national prosperity'. We note here particularly Nicholson's term *working* rather than *theoretical* system. This summary has proved extraordinarily prophetic of current developments in trade theory. Helpman and Krugman (1985) have been important trade theorists in developing the new literature on intraindustry trade, product differentiation and increasing returns. These would all be features of a Smithian form of competition. But they have been shown to be destructive of neoclassical general equilibrium results on the optimality of free trade. This new literature suggests that sophisticated forms of intervention may be desirable, theoretically speaking. However, the difficulty in determining what such courses of action should be, the possible costs involved, and the problems of monitoring and controlling the system, are potentially so great that Krugman (1987), in the most definitive theoretical analysis currently available on this topic, has concluded that free trade is still the most pragmatic policy recommendation one could make. It does seem, therefore, that for our age, given current scientific knowledge, freedom from artificial restraint is a sensible requirement.

Finally, we refer to the fifth, and last, condition for free competition –

sufficient time for resources to move to their best uses. If economic agents are initially unable to carry out part of their plans, as is characteristic of disequilibrium, they will revise these plans. This implies a process of learning; and acquiring new information and analysing it requires time. Thus adjustment to an equilibrium, in which expectations or plans of economic agents are compatible, is a process in real time. Smith gave considerable attention to impediments to adjustment which were the consequence of artificial restriction. Statutes of apprenticeship and corporation laws, he felt, could raise prices above their natural levels almost indefinitely (WN, p. 79). Further, 'particular accidents, sometimes natural causes, and sometimes particular regulations' (WN, p. 77) could for many commodities keep market price above natural price for a long time. For example, he thought that particular accidents could enhance market price for many years (WN, p. 78). For some commodities a permanent excess demand could keep market price above natural price 'for whole centuries together' (WN, p. 78). Though adjustment times are no doubt shorter today than they were before industrialism, the general point of Smith remains valid. This implies that frequently, perhaps typically, one is not observing a general equilibrium at all, but rather a process adjusting to general equilibrium.[24] Further, as knowledge can be acquired and processed so rapidly in a post-industrial society, the conditions of consumption and production may be changed before the equilibrium initially being approached is actually attained. Indeed, one of the most effective ways to circumvent restrictions is to innovate, either in terms of the method of producing known goods, or by the introduction of new goods altogether. There is naturally a tendency, therefore, for the equilibria towards which the system is moving to be themselves displaced. These displaced equilibria are also an aspect of the competitive process, for they too offer opportunities for profit. As a characteristic of post-industrialism is the use of theoretical knowledge to control technology, it is to be expected that the equilibria towards which the system tends become the focus of attention with a view to *avoiding* their arrival. New technologies, new tastes, new goods and new markets go hand in hand and generate new opportunities for making profit. Though our capacity to adjust to new equilibria is no doubt faster than before, our capacity to innovate has also risen, so the market process is still vigorous. This view would see no advantage in instantaneous adjustment to equilibrium, for this would remove the required elapse of time in which entrepreneurial profit may be made, and without it the system becomes stationary. Of course, instantaneous adjustment is in any case a fiction.

9.4 INSTITUTIONAL EVOLUTION

We have talked of the market process, the equilibria towards which it tends, and finally the motivation for avoiding or shifting these equilibria. As the market is an institution, and we have already discussed how markets may be modified, we have anticipated in the previous section what is to be our new concern, institutional evolution. Indeed, on a macroscopic scale, we have already talked at length in chapter 1 of institutional evolution in terms of a sequence of stages of society. In this chapter, however, the stage is taken as given (namely post-industrialism) and what we are concerned with is institutional change in the small.

Smith himself did not talk of evolutionary change, though his work is not incompatible with the evolutionary arguments which have influenced the writings of the likes of Coase (1976), Hirshleifer (1977) and Sobel (1979). At a purely biological level, Smith noted (TMS, p. 77) that self-preservation and the propagation of the species, are the 'great ends' of all animals, including man in particular.[25] Hirshleifer (1977, p. 17) too would see man's behaviour as being a product of biological inheritance. However, it is a large step to go from man himself as subject to evolutionary forces, to the institutions of man as being subject to the same or similar forces. Hirshleifer's argument would be that the extension and refinement of the system of property rights implies a kind of progressive adaptation over time. It reduces the need for direct conflict over resources or possessions, and releases time which may be used to seek mutually advantageous employment of property, thus achieving a more advanced division of labour.

However, this is to make the evolution of a very important institution, the market, look like a sequence of spontaneous adaptations. This would be the view taken by libertarian anarchists like Rothbard (1977), who argue that the state need not have the role that Smith envisaged for it. In Smith, the state, as expressed by the powers of the sovereign, would provide defence, a system of justice and a taxation system. Thus a nation which has the power to repel aggressors provides the domestic stability which is necessary to the fostering of market activity. The framework within which the market operates involves an appropriate system of legal entitlement and justice. And finally, revenues raised by taxation would be used to provide public goods which otherwise would not be produced because of the free rider problem. Though the powers of the state here are still not great, because they do not extend to interference in the functioning of any individual markets, they are certainly not minimalist. Most important, the state has a role in prescribing the conditions under which institutions, of which the market is one example, will operate. This framework does not spontaneously evolve. By contrast, in the world of Rothbard's *Power and Market* (1977, p. 8), 'a truly free market is totally incompatible with the existence of a State, an institution that presumes to "defend" person and property by itself subsisting on the unilateral coercion against private property known as taxation'. There would be no taxation, and thus no public provision of goods. Defence, police and judicial services would be privately supplied in freely competitive markets. It is argued that in such a world, order would emerge spontaneously, and this would be true, for example, of property rights. There would be a system of law, but its provision would be private, and litigants would appeal to privately competing courts for judgements over matters like entitlement to property. Here, the evolution of the market as an institution would be spontaneous, much as envisaged in Hirshleifer's analysis deriving from sociobiology. The domain of the invisible hand is greatly extended because it is not simply that the market as an institution provides a socially beneficial outcome through unplanned actions, but also that the very framework of law within which its transactions take place, and the domestic security within which it flourishes, are themselves changing by unplanned actions to bring about a desirable social order. Essentially, the argument is that if the invisible hand works in markets, then if *all* activity were to be market mediated, its beneficent effects would be extended globally. The view of Hayek (1973), for example, is that the evolution of law as a good is governed by unintended beneficial consequences, as is any other good.

The libertarian view is, however, an extreme one and appears to be both inconsistent with history and incompatible with Smith. There is no doubt, as we noted in the stadial analysis of chapter 1, that specific individual economic acts can have unintended global consequences. For example, the desire by feudal proprietors to buy the luxury goods being provided by newly emerging markets ultimately led to the transfer of property rights to a new class of tenants. No doubt this was an unintended consequence. However, the modification of the law of property rights which emerged in the face of these new economic circumstances is better viewed as the rational response at a collective level to changed conditions rather than as the spontaneous evolution of law. The cardinal point is that the development of laws and institutions is frequently, indeed commonly, a conscious collective process, rather than an unconscious individualistic process. Though the libertarian literature is growing apace[26] in this post-industrial era, and finds part of its inspiration in classical economics, especially the economics of Adam Smith, its expressed desire for no state activity whatsoever does not seem to be a statement about practically possible worlds. There is no doubt, however, that its uncompromising radicalism has heightened awareness in policy circles of the advantages of market over bureaucratic mediation of economic exchange.

A more accurate portrayal of Smith's position in modern terms would be to say that he advocated the method of comparative institutional analysis. Here, the focus is on feasible, or practically possible, institutional forms and their properties. An example of this method is contained in his discussion of the stationary economy of China, which had acquired 'that full complement of riches which is consistent with the nature of its laws and institutions' (WN, p. 111). However, he observed that the outcome may not have been optimal, in that 'this complement may be much inferior to what, with other laws and institutions, the nature of its soil, climate, and situation might admit of.' The reference to 'laws and institutions' is telling in each quote, for the indication is that they are determinants of societal welfare. Further, they may be objects of deliberate control. Thus a country which is protectionist, admitting foreign vessels into only a limited number of ports (effectively imposing an import quota), would limit the volume of trade by the adoption of these, rather than less restrictive, laws and institutions (WN, p. 112). As another example, if the property rights only of owners of large rather than small amounts of capital are well protected, there would be an underprovision of capital, a limitation on trade, and an artificially high rate of interest (WN, p. 112). Rosenberg (1960) has gone perhaps as far as logic will permit in arguing that Smith was attempting to define in *The Wealth of Nations* the exact and detailed specification of an *optimal* institutional structure. No doubt Smith's comparative institutional method was aimed at determining whether one system of laws and institutions was as efficacious as another. Thus he favoured the extension of free trade over mercantilistic restrictions for the benefits that would follow, in terms, for example, of increased income per head. However, he was arguing not that free trade was optimal, but rather that it was *workable* and would improve welfare.[27] Rosenberg is right to emphasize the importance of institutional design being explicitly controlled to harmonize the pursuit of individual self-interest with the broader goal of promoting societal welfare, but over-optimistic in suggesting that an ideal arrangement of law and institutions is possible. Indeed one may doubt whether optimality is even a coherent concept in this context.

In the quotes from *The Wealth of Nations* in the previous paragraph, two points were made concerning laws and institutions: firstly, that they determined societal welfare; and secondly, that they could be deliberately controlled to the end of increasing welfare. In the same place (WN, p. 112) Smith added two further points concerning laws and institutions: thirdly, that they may be more or less effective in promoting welfare; and fourthly, that they should be open to the use of all citizens. In an important essay Buchanan (1976) shows that these four statements of Smith provide the basis for what modern economists would call the provision of 'public goods'. Parallel to Smith's four statements, one observes that public goods, firstly, enter into the utility functions of citizens; secondly, can be supplied in assigned amounts according to decisions taken on behalf of the community; thirdly, may be supplied in a fashion which is more or less efficient; and fourthly, may be made use of by all members of the community. To clarify further on the last point, public goods are non-rivalrous, in the sense that one person's use does not limit another person's use, and non-excludable, meaning that it is impossible to deny access to their use. In strict treatments they would also be regarded as non-rejectable, meaning that non-consumption of them is impossible, even if desired. Thus defence and the law are non-rivalrous, non-excludable and non-rejectable, but visits to the Royal Scottish Museum are merely non-rivalrous and non-excludable. Some goods have both public and private elements (e.g. education).

However, quite clearly defence, and the laws and institutions which protect and enforce individual rights and contracts, are examples of public goods. It was these that Smith emphasized. A feature of the growth of state activity, especially in the post-industrial stage of societal development, has been that public provision has gone much further, and that the framework of law has been overextended to the point at which new laws may become public 'bads' rather than public goods (e.g. in terms of regulations controlling small business conduct). Even in a complex legal order, it has been argued by the 'new' welfare economists, voluntary market activity may fail. Goods may be provided in the wrong amounts at the wrong prices (due, for example, to monopolization) or markets may be missing altogether. In such a situation, it has been argued, specific intervention may be dictated, which may run from statutory regulation to direct state control, and in the case of missing markets to state provision and control *ab initio*. However, much that has been provided by the government for these sorts of reasons could in principle be supplied by the market, if property rights were more efficiently assigned. The legal system plays a role here, as an institution for internalizing externalities. This precisely illustrates the flaw in the Hayekian argument that evolutionary advance in laws and institutions will occur spontaneously. We know that the relevant markets are *not* missing because, under post-industrialism, private provision of many goods which are also publically provided goes on – in transport, education, health care, parks and library services, for example. Spontaneous adaptation of the law relating to property rights has not emerged to shift this balance towards private provision. A feature of the advance of post-industrialism has been the rise in relative importance of the tertiary or service sector. Government has been a major, and perhaps unnecessary, contributor to this. Its activities have extended markedly beyond the core category of government services (e.g. defence, police, fire, public administration) to a wide range of consumer services that, to a variable extent, could be privately supplied (e.g. passenger transport, health, education, welfare, and recreational services). Now the growth in the service sector appears inevitable. Over forty years ago, Colin Clark (1940, p. 7) stated the empirical law that 'the proportion of the working population engaged in secondary industry appears in every country to rise to a maximum and then to begin falling, apparently indicating that each country reaches a stage of maximum industrialisation beyond which industry begins to decline relative to tertiary production.'[28] Whilst this historical trend appears inexorable, and is really a manifestation of the advanced division of labour, the public provision of goods, especially in the service sector, is by no means inevitable. On further analysis, it will be found that much public provision is not for goods which display public attributes in the precise sense of the term used above. What Smithian analysis hands down to us in this post-industrial era is the notion that laws and institutions provide a means of determining the extent to which economic exchanges need be private or public. Bearing in mind that goods may be provided in a more or less efficient way, comparative institutional analysis dictates that the form of provision should be determined by the efficiency of provision. To effect changes in this public/private balance, one cannot hope for the unplanned emergence of a framework which fosters greater efficiency, of the sort that Hayek (1973) and the libertarians envisage. Rationality and judgement, using a comparative institutional framework, must be consciously used to determine a new framework. Where the goods in question have genuinely public attributes they will not be spontaneously provided by the market, and individuals in the market place are powerless to provide them. Here, collective action is required. However, in many cases, public provision should be cautiously examined to ensure that public 'bads' which restrict natural liberty are not being inadvertently supplied.

Economists have long favoured the method of borrowing theories from other sciences. One popular parallel is that between economic competitive selection and Darwinian natural selection in biology.[29] A recent analysis of Matthews (1984, p. 115) concludes that: 'It is doubtful whether competitive selection of an economic kind will be very effective in shaping that part of the evolution of institutions – likely to be a significant part – that is determined by governments.' This is not to deny the mutual connection between economic change and institutions. However, there is only one government at a time, and there is in consequence no test of fitness as against other governments. Even if government could be tested in this way, selection processes probably work too slowly to be of service in delivering to us fit government types. Rather, the route forward seems to lie in the rational analysis which government can undertake of itself as an institution, and of the institutions and laws whose forms it can influence. This requires an analysis which is not narrowly economic but embraces, as Matthews (1984, p. 115) has put it, the development of ideas in ideology, religion and science. Institutions evolve, but this is a conscious, rather than unconscious, process.

9.5 ALIENATION AND ITS AMELIORATION

Adam Ferguson, to many (e.g. Lehmann 1930) the father of modern sociology, gave us the first clear statement of what we now know as the doctrine of *alienation*[30]. Duncan Forbes, editor of Ferguson (1767, p. 46) expresses thus the content of alienation: 'In creating the complex structure of civilizations, man has created something, without anyone willing it, in which he can no longer recognize his humanity, which is no longer a society in which he shares, but something which stands over him alien to him; and if he is divorced from his community he is divided against himself, and no longer whole.' Ferguson's argument was that the division of labour would cause a gulf in society between a managerial class and the rest, who would become parts of an engine of production. We have already seen how Smith, a contemporary, friend and admirer of Ferguson, viewed the benefits of the division of labour, arising from the increased dexterity, saving of time and opportunity for invention that it facilitates. To this we must also add the incentive advantages of the division of labour.[31] However, like Ferguson (and indeed other contemporaries such as Lord Kames and John Millar), Smith was aware that the advanced division of labour could also have negative effects. Whilst Smith developed the theme of the advantages of the division of labour in book I of *The Wealth of Nations*, in book V he was closer to Ferguson, Lord Kames and Millar in pointing out disadvantages. To Smith, as a consequence of increasing specialization, 'the employment of the far greater part of those who live by labour, that is, of the great body of people, comes to be confined to a few very simple operations', and so they become 'as stupid and ignorant as it is possible for a human creature to become' (WN, p. 782). In societies which were described as barbarous, Smith observed, every man was versatile and inventive, whereas the apparent penalty of civilization was to diminish greatly the variety and complexity which most men face in their working lives. Thus 'all the nobler parts of the human character may be, in great measure, obliterated and extinguished in the great body of the people.' Though increasing specialization made society a source of 'almost infinite variety', cognizance of this was confined to 'those few, who, being attached to no particular occupations themselves, have leisure and inclination to examine the occupations of other people. The contemplation of so great a variety of objects necessarily exercises their minds in endless comparisons and combinations, and renders their understandings, in an extraordinary degree, both acute and comprehensive' (WN, p. 783).

The ameliorative factor that Smith suggested was education. Indeed, so essential was this that public provision would be appropriate: 'The publick can facilitate, can encourage, and can even impose upon almost the whole body of people, the necessity of acquiring those most essential parts of education' (WN, p. 785). What Smith envisaged as a syllabus – the capacity to read, write and calculate, and some understanding of elementary mechanics and geometry – does not seem extensive. But it should be taken in the context of its time, when youngsters went up to university at thirteen or fourteen years of age. Public education then was essentially primary education, with secondary education being undertaken at the universities. Smith also favoured probationary periods when people entered the professions (after university, generally at the age of eighteen or older), during which 'the state imposed upon this order of men the necessity of learning' (WN, p. 796) with science and philosophy being the subject matter. Science was described as 'the great antidote to the poison of enthusiasm and superstition' (WN, p. 796). These very specific guidelines on education were highly progressive in his day, and the emphasis on scientific and technical skills is prophetic of much later historical developments. Thus part of the characterization by Bell (1974, p. 43) of post-industrialism entails the strengthening of the role of science, and what he calls cognitive values[32] (broadly what Smith would have called philosophical values); the development of decision-making as a technical skill (as in current cost-benefit analysis, investment analysis, portfolio selection, and a variety of 'expert systems', e.g. in medical diagnosis); and the emergence of a 'technical intelligentsia' (similar to Smith's 'mechanical, chymical, astronomical, physical, metaphysical, moral, political, commercial, and critical philosophers': LJ, p. 570).

As the analytical framework of chapter 7 indicated, the advanced division of labour is associated with an increased social product and social product per head, and also an economizing on labour inputs. This will be reflected in a shorter working week, and thus more leisure. Colin Clark (1940), for example, has documented the systematic reduction in the working week in the leading world economies over long spans of economic history, covering the periods of industrialism and the earlier part of post-industrialism. This trend has continued, though the UK has not displayed this property quite so markedly as some other major post-industrial nations. The issue that Smith addressed, of increased specialization within the workplace, and the resulting dangers of alienation, at the same time as the emergence of a high-income economy with greater leisure, is therefore of increased relevance in the era of post-industrialism. The role of education is both to counteract the unfortunate consequences of advanced specialization and to use increased leisure time in a more cultivated fashion.

If an individual is regarded as potentially alienated, one must ask what the situation of non-alienation is to look like if the condition is to be remedied or ameliorated. In the writings of Smith we do have considerable guidance. Referring to *The Theory of Moral Sentiments* and *The History of Astronomy*, one can[33] characterize Smith's unalienated state as one which facilitates the pursuit of art, beauty and refinement in a society based on justice, prudence and benevolence, in the company of citizens with active capacities for wonder, surprise and imagination. So great is Smith's support for this outcome that he suggests:

> The state, by encouraging, that is by giving entire liberty to all those who for their own interest would attempt, without scandal or indecency, to amuse and divert the people by painting, poetry, musick, dancing; by all sorts of dramatic representations and exhibitions, would easily dissipate, in the greater part of them, that melancholy and gloomy humour which is almost always the nurse of popular superstition and enthusiasm. (WN, p. 796)

This does not amount to an argument for public provision of the arts, but it certainly argues for the state actively removing all impediments to their appearance; and could justify the state provision of training in these skills. More likely, Smith would have argued that private provision had incentive advantages. For example, he remarked that 'those parts of education, it is to be observed, for the teaching of which there are no publick institutions, are generally the best taught. When a young man goes to a fencing or a dancing school, he does not, indeed, always learn to fence or to dance very well; but he seldom fails of learning to fence or to dance' (WN, p. 764).

However, as well as considering leisure, and its civilized use, as an antidote to alienation, one has to look at the workplace itself. Whether Smith had a consistent or contradictory view on the implications for alienation of the advanced division of labour within the factory has been a source of extensive debate by West (1964, 1969, 1975), Rosenberg (1965) and Lamb (1973). Two misconceptions seem to have given rise to this debate. The first is that it is thought necessary that all consequences of the division of labour should be either good or bad. Few institutional changes have simple consequences like good or bad, and here we may note that changing the division of labour is an aspect of institutional evolution. In considering the consequences of change, one balances good against bad, and of course looks for a positive net benefit if the change is to be considered worth having. It is not at all contradictory to assert that increased dexterity, time-saving and invention are positive effects of advances in the division of labour, and alienation, loss of coordination, and moral degeneration are negative effects. One can extend or modify the positive and negative effects in a number of obvious ways, but this will not affect the comparative institutional method one applies to compare one division of labour with the other. One seeks that division of labour with the greatest net benefit. In this sense, one can think in terms of an optimum division of labour. The second misconception is to require that Smith's views on alienation necessarily have a strict affinity with any other views, be they those of Adam Ferguson, Karl Marx, Lord Kames or whoever. Clearly there are interrelations, but Smith's views are distinct, and provide a basis for analysis and discussion in their own right. Lamb (1973) may challenge the interpretation of West's various papers on alienation with respect to the Marxian categories of powerlessness, isolation and self-estrangement with a view to establishing that all three, rather than just the last, were significant in Smith. However, this does not advance our knowledge of Smith or suggest how his work may be modified or extended. For Marx, the division of labour could on balance be good or bad, but in the free market system it was thought to be necessarily bad. In this societal framework all aspects of the division of labour were thought to violate man's true nature, be he rentier, capitalist or worker. For Smith, the division of labour in the free market system, as in other systems, could be good *or* bad. Unlike in Marx, the division of labour did not have alienating effects in *all* sections of society (thus that division of labour which led to specialists like philosophers was not alienating); and further, even if in some sectors the effects were negative, the beneficial consequences (like growth in income per head) might make the acceptance of a certain division of labour on balance a sensible act. And, of course, this last point is reinforced by the possibility of correcting for the negative effects of alienation by education.

Let us set aside, therefore, internal disputes over real or imagined contradictions within Smith, and concentrate on whether alienation of the sort he discussed could, or can, be ameliorated. His emphasis when talking of alienation was on repetitive, highly specific 'detail' work in manufactures. His remedy was compulsory education. There was no suggestion that alienation could be ameliorated in the workplace itself.

Under post-industrialism a movement has developed[34] which appears to favour less specialization rather than more, both in a vertical sense (e.g. by decision-making through a hierarchy) and in a horizontal sense (e.g. according to tasks assigned in the workplace). It is known as the quality of working life movement, and may be regarded as a reaction against traditional principles of work organization which attempted to administer the advanced division of labour efficiently. The movement opposes the notion that there are inevitable benefits from all advances in the division of labour. However, the movement is not simply a reflection of a social philosophy. It also suggests that limiting the division of labour can lead to efficiency gains. It would accept workers' evaluations of their situations in terms of job satisfaction and employers' evaluations in terms of productivity. Of all the alternative schemes of work organization, as analysed by Hales (1987), for example, that of job rotation seems to be the most effective based on these criteria, with quality circles (essentially self-monitory groups for quality control) being the least effective. Actually job rotation is but one aspect of the quality of working life approach, it being part of horizontal despecialization. The latter also embraces job enlargement, which mean adding new tasks to job descriptions. Horizontal methods of reducing monotony encourage greater work variety and entail workers manning flexible, multifunction units. Its complement, vertical methods, aims to increase workers' autonomy and enrich the job. This involves more participation and devolvement in decision-making and strategic planning. It would reduce the rigid specialization of managers in strategic planning and workers in the execution of tasks. *Per contra* to the quality of working life literature, I regard these effects as other than despecializing. They are actually an aspect of a more advanced, but new form of, division of labour. Older, traditional skills become obsolete or subject to automation, and are replaced by new skills which place a greater emphasis on judgement, communication and coordination. The quality of working life approach is many things – a social philosophy, a job evaluation method, and a work efficiency technique. In its concern for efficiency, it has a bearing on the possibility of ameliorating the alienation which can accompany the division of labour, without sacrifice of output. In this sense, it is a refined method of searching for the optimum division of labour in a framework which interprets costs and benefits in a broad sense.

A major structural change since Smith was writing has been the growth of tertiary or service sectors in advanced economies. McKee (1987) has pointed out that seven out of ten new employment opportunities in advanced countries are service oriented. Many of these jobs are very different in nature from those in manufactures that were the classical subjects for analyses of the division of labour. In keeping with the post-industrial age in which they emerge, they are often information, knowledge, communication or software oriented. There are circumstances in which jobs of this sort can be as alienating as jobs in manufacturing which are highly specialized, but the presumption is against this, as communication is frequently at least an aspect if not a major component of the job descriptions. This is true of services in finance, insurance and recreation, but perhaps most obviously so in what some trade unionists call 'pink-collar' jobs,[35] meaning by this person-to-person services like hairdressing,

180 *Classical Economics in a Post-Industrial Society*

entertainment and restaurants as well as medicine and education. In these, the human interaction required for communication is intrinsic, which also makes these jobs less liable to be displaced by technological advance. Whilst unskilled factory floor work has become increasingly specialized, planned on principles of 'scientific management' (Taylor 1911), and hence potentially alienating, this has encouraged automation and ultimately the mimicking of machine operatives by programmable robots. This process of deskilling more routinized manufacturing activities has 'solved' the problem of alienation by simply removing repetitive, humdrum tasks from job markets; but it has created new problems of technological unemployment, and the need to reskill displaced workers. It is also true that technological progress is creating new types of jobs as well as destroying old ones. If we regard production as an activity which can be broken down into a large number of simple but elementary tasks, what automation does is to mimic a subset of these tasks. What is not the subject of mimicry will be performed by human labour. There is a vast number of ways in which these remaining tasks can be recombined to generate a great variety of entirely new job descriptions. Workers may need to be reskilled to perform these jobs. There are also new types of jobs being created for the production and distribution of entirely new commodities. That is, parallel to product innovation there is job innovation. Both of these effects will generally raise the knowledge content of the tasks performed in the new jobs.

As an example and amplification of the above, consider the analysis of technological trends and employment in financial services undertaken by Mothe (1986, p. 58). He stylizes the change in the labour skills hierarchy as in figure 9.1. In all the financial services considered – banking, insurance,

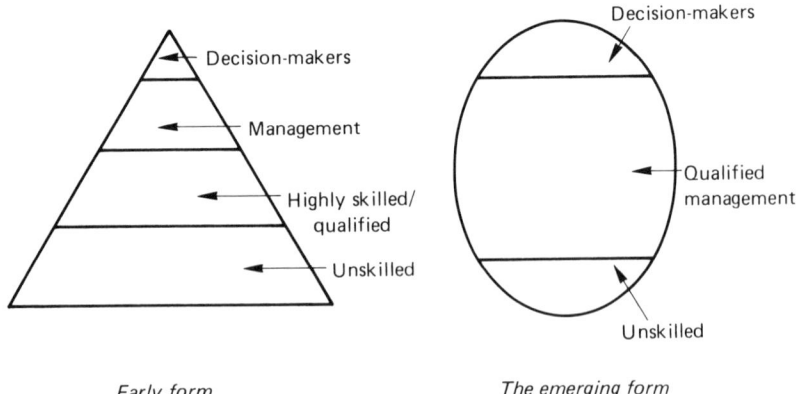

Figure 9.1 The labour skills hierarchy

building societies, computer services and business services – productivity has been greatly increased by developments in microelectronics. In particular, it has broken down many of the distinctions between managers and skilled non-executive personnel. Certain skills have become automated or obsolete because of computer developments and advances in microelectronic hardware, but this has been compensated for by new requirements for exercising judgement. Referring to the emerging form on the right in figure 9.1, it will be observed that the potentially alienating unskilled jobs have decreased proportionately compared with the old form. In their place have emerged new jobs with a higher knowledge content, more opportunity for exercising judgement, and more provision of advanced adjuncts to decision-making, involving computer software and new information and communication systems. The old 'bad' jobs have been deskilled, and the new 'good' jobs involve less alienation. Decision-making, given the wide variety of new markets that financial services are now getting involved in, particularly since deregulation of the City, is now a proportionately more important aspect of the 'configuration of jobs'. The right-hand schema is still hierarchical, with decision-makers at the top, qualified managers in the middle and unskilled workers at the bottom. However, compared with the earlier organizational form it is *less* hierarchical; two levels have been assimilated into one, and the pyramidal structure has been modified to an oval, with a much greater concentration on discretionary types of activities in the middle. The emerging form is not a consequence of a lesser extent of the division of labour, for clearly it has increased, involving a new form of specialization which is largely in the exercise of judgement and decision-making. Thus division of labour advances, but alienation is diminished. Cross (1985), in his analysis of the emergence of the 'flexible craftsmen' in electrical engineering, develops a similar but more elaborate comparison of old and new organizational forms. For example, 'man as an extension of the machine' under the old form becomes 'man as complementary to the machine' under the new form; 'maximum task break-down, single narrow skills' becomes 'optimum task grouping, multiple broad skills'; 'external controls (supervisors, specialist staffs, procedures)' becomes 'internal controls (self-regulating sub-systems)'; and, more briefly, 'low risk taking' becomes 'innovation' and 'alienation' becomes 'commitment'.

9.6 SOCIAL OBLIGATION

Much of the emphasis in this book has been on the market nexus. However, at an early point it was made clear that market activity was only a part of the totality of social activity. The market was seen as a social device for so constraining self-love that its consequences were beneficial rather than pernicious. In a Smithian framework, however, there are other aspects of morality.

The most indispensable aspect of morality is the requirement for justice. What constitutes justice should be reflected in the laws that govern society. Thus laws governing market activity aim to achieve the goal of justice. However, Smith likens the rules of justice to the strict rules of grammar, and other virtues to the weaker rules or guidelines which enable the writer to attain 'what is sublime and elegant in composition' (TMS, p. 175). If we are to have a society which goes beyond the observance of strict rules of justice, we must live according to additional but less well-defined principles, which at least offer the possibility of attaining the 'sublime and elegant' in a metaphorical sense.

The arid existence of a man who does no more than respect the strict canons of justice is well described by Smith in *The Theory of Moral Sentiments* (p. 82): 'The man who barely abstains from violating either the person, or the estate, or the reputation of his neighbours, has surely very little positive merit. He fulfils, however, all the rules of what is peculiarly called justice . . . we may often fulfil all the rules of justice by sitting still and doing nothing.' Even a man who runs his own business in most scrupulously just fashion, certainly thereby creating benefit for himself and society, would, in doing this alone, be living a life of very limited virtue. He would be 'barely innocent' and 'can merit only that his neighbours in their turn should respect his innocence, and that the same laws should be religiously observed with regard to him' (TMS, p. 82).

What we wish to be reminded of briefly in this, the final section of the book, is that virtue in the market place is, by design, of a very restricted form. It has the advantage of being readily observable, and governed by strict rules which may be legally enforced, but its prominence and precision should not lead to an exaggeration of its moral significance. Here we introduce a term which Smith did not use, *social obligation*,[36] to refer to the motive force behind those virtuous acts which a socialized individual may confer on society – through institutions, families or persons – without being strictly required to do so, and without any necessary expectation of reciprocation. There are no strict rules for such social obligations. Smith criticized the casuists for trying to prescribe precise rules for all aspects of virtue as engaging in 'frivolous accuracy'. He thought 'that they attempted, to no purpose, to direct by precise rules what it belongs to feelings and sentiment only to judge' (TMS, p. 339). In attempting to formulate rules of conduct one would be guided by the impartial spectator, and once established those rules would assume the nature of a sense of duty. Smith's 'beneficence' provides a good example of a social obligation. It is 'always free, it cannot be extorted by force, the mere want of it exposes to no punishment' but 'it may disappoint of the good which might reasonably have been expected, and upon that account it may justly excite dislike and disapprobation' (TMS, p. 79). Though the impartial spectator would approve the performance of a social obligation, its non-performance would not lead to punishment, or necessarily even overt expression of disapproval. Of a lack of obligation, Smith said: 'Nobody imagines that those who might have reason, perhaps, to expect more kindness, have any right to extort it by force. The sufferer can only complain, and the spectator can inter-meddle no other way than by advice and persuasion' (TMS, p. 81).

A weakness of the construction of an outline of post-industrialism by Bell (1974) is that it ignores the domain of social obligation. As its provision can clearly be affected by 'advice and persuasion', it is conditioned by communications and education – two of the major facets of post-industrialism. Bell's assumption was that non-market activity must be planned bureaucratic activity, and he looked forward to an extension of the public sectors of all advanced, service-dominated economies. When Smith said 'he is certainly not a good citizen who does not wish to promote, by every means in his power, the welfare of the whole society of his fellow citizens' (TMS, p. 231) he did not imply that the state had to be involved, though clearly this is not ruled out. Under post-industrialism there is extensive scope for voluntary individual action, coordinated if necessary, to raise societal welfare. This includes good neighbourliness, community work and charitable activities. The contributions to these activities can be pecuniary or in kind, and may come from private individuals, public bodies, or private institutions of either the commercial or the trust variety. Smith talked of a 'love of our country' (TMS, p. 231) which arose from a recognition that the security and protection which citizens and institutions enjoy arise from the state. We have not used this term, for it would be uncomfortable to the modern reader, even though Smith was certainly no jingoist and was also willing to be sharply critical of the constitution of a state.[37] However, what Smith was concerned with was something like what we have been calling 'social obligation'. We may conclude with Smith's own words, putting man and his capabilities in proper perspective: 'The care of the universal happiness of all rational and sensible beings, is the business of God and not of man. To man is allotted a much humbler department, but one much more suitable to the weakness of his powers and to the narrowness of his comprehension: the care of his own happiness, of that of his family, his friends, his country' (TMS, p. 237).

9.7 CONCLUSION

As in the rest of this book, our concern in this chapter has been with classical economic growth. The new aspect is that we have explored its relationship to a phase of economic growth, the post-industrial, which classical economics certainly did not experience or even anticipate.

Despite the new phenomenon of post-industrialism, it was found that classical economic growth analysis still had relevance as a conceptual framework. The extension of the division of labour to permit the emergence of many scientific, technical and commercial specializations was comprehensible in this framework. It has permitted the emergence of specialist skills in communications, information handling, and coordination. This has facilitated the entrepreneurial role, which received relatively little attention in classical analysis, but is now of greater importance. The exercise of entrepreneurship is important to competition, viewed as a process, which is the approach to rivalry favoured by classical analysis. Essential to the exercise of informed business judgement, which is what entrepreneurship involves, is the discovery of new ways of doing things and new things to do, as well as simply cheaper ways of accomplishing known patterns of production. In the post-industrial era, the development of communications technology and of data retrieval and processing capabilities has been an important facilitator of entrepreneurship so defined.

As the market's form has developed, so the institutions which determine its form – and hence the market itself, regarded as an institution – have evolved. In the post-industrial era, an earlier preoccupation has been with market failure. Indeed, this was still true when Daniel Bell wrote his famous book defending the classification of post-industrialism. However, the development of institutions to handle market failure has led to progressive disenchantment. Further, the overenthusiastic application of public goods arguments to state provision of goods which do not really satisfy the requirements of the pure case, has put intolerable strains on central government budgeting. The precise corrections necessary to mitigate market failure are highly complex, subject to constant change, and therefore in many cases practically unknowable. Institutions aimed at correcting such failure are themselves prone to 'capture'. The extension of market mediation, attempting to internalize externalities, is another route to improving the function of markets. This process itself requires evolution in the laws and institutions which govern market conduct. In this, and in decisions over the public/private division, government plays a role. Indeed, by contrast to libertarian arguments, which seem unworkable under post-industrialism, government can play a leading or initiating role in improving the efficacy of markets, and indeed of government itself. Parallel to market failure is government failure, and achieving improvements in both, and a better balance between the two, is a matter of comparative institutional analysis. Adam Smith favoured the development of education for a variety of reasons, and undoubtedly one of them was that it makes a better-informed, more efficient government possible.[38]

Another more familiar reason for favouring the development of education, including its public provision in some measure if not entirely, is to ameliorate the negative consequences of the advanced division of labour. Under industrialism these could be acute, particularly in manufacturing activity which involved repetitive, unchallenging work. However, post-industrialism has seen the disappearance of many of these jobs through the development of advanced manufacturing technologies. New jobs have emerged which in a literal sense involve more specialization, but in packages or groups of tasks rather than single activities, which reduce tedium and allow greater scope for autonomy. The quality of working life movement has shown that productivity increase can go hand in hand with more satisfactory working conditions *and* the development of high levels of specialization.

Finally, although the competitive process fosters growth and technological advance, and both have the potential to enhance human welfare, market activity, we should be reminded, is only a limited aspect of virtue, and indeed is only virtuous at all if the correct institutional framework for ensuring justice is established. Beyond what is strictly required by justice in the market, and indeed beyond what is strictly required by justice in social intercourse in general, is social obligation. As leisure increases under post-industrialism, the fulfilment of individuals will depend not only on their capacity to spend wisely their enhanced incomes, but on their capacity to meet obligations which though not mandatory are important in making the world a more moral and civilized place in which to live.

NOTES

1 This is the terminology used by Ronald Shelp (1981) in his *Beyond Industrialization*.
2 Quoted from article by Birch in Giersch (1983, p. 16).
3 We say 'possible' vice because advanced specialization can create opportunities for reskilling which make work less, rather than more, alienating. Such jobs might involve more opportunities for interpersonal contact, and the exercise of judgement, for example. This is quite apart from positive policies taken to oppose the consequences of alienation, which come under the general heading of 'job enrichment'.
4 The 'Early draft of part of *The Wealth of Nations*' is reproduced in LJ and is an attempt by Smith (dating early in 1763) to extract material from his jurisprudence lectures at Glasgow University for a book on political economy. In several respects, its treatment of the division of labour is more detailed than that contained in WN.
5 For general background, see Webb (1980, pp. 111–17). The case of the cotton trade is particularly important, because it was the first to become fully mechanized. Kindleberger (1976), in a somewhat ungenerous appraisal of Smith in relation to his anticipation of industrialism, is critical of Smith's omissions of inventions made between 1766 and 1775. However, they were

not all obviously going to succeed, and some took a considerable time to be adopted. Kay's flying shuttle, which made handloom weaving faster and less onerous, was invented in 1733 but not generally adopted for another quarter-century. The acceptance of new technology was sporadic and delayed. Webb (1980, p. 112) notes that hand nail-making persisted in the Black Country north-west of Birmingham until the 1870s; and framework knitting in the 1840s, when the object of a government investigation, was found to be using a technology that had not changed in 250 years.

6   See the discussion on this in chapter 5.
7   The assumption here is that an even finer division of labour is associated with the production of an increasing range of goods, which are consumed eagerly by customers whose tastes become increasingly diversified as their incomes increase. The argument is a slight extension of that given in chapter 8, which confined itself to a *fixed* range of products: here, that range is being extended.
8   See Kirzner (1979, p. 42).
9   We have seen in chapter 5 that Casson (1986) provides such an analysis of the optimal division of labour. It can be applied within the firm or, as he uses it, to explain the international division of labour. One should distinguish between the possibility of an *optimal* division of labour at a point in time, and the possibility of a continuing process of the division of labour. The latter will be encouraged by a rising marginal revenue from cooperative activities involving increased division of labour and a falling marginal cost from increasingly efficient providers of coordination services.
10 Arrow (1979) therefore argues that a society which has become wealthy by the advanced division of labour may paradoxically be one of discontent, even if income per head appears high. The reason is that the marked fragmentation of society, which the advanced division of labour encourages, fosters the development of a diversity of moral norms. As norms multiply, so a consensus on moral values becomes increasingly difficult.
11 According to which, high-technology activity goes on in the North of the globe (essentially in the advanced post-industrialized economies), and the activities formerly performed by workers in these economies, now deskilled, are instead performed in the South of the globe by underprivileged workers (e.g. intensively worked, young, female labour).
12 'Clan' is Ouchi's (1980) graphic terminology for corporate culture, which is a device for minimizing opportunism without resort to hierarchy, essentially through organizational socialization.
13 This statement should be handled with some delicacy. It is not to deny the theoretical validity of the Lancaster-Lipsey general theory of the second best, according to which the progressive satisfaction of conditions required for first-best Pareto optimality is not necessarily welfare improving (Reid 1987b, ch. 7). Here we are talking about the extension of the scope of the market process, rather than the scope of first-best optimality conditions.
14 The more perishable the commodity, furthermore, the more intense is the competition.
15 Hollander (1973, p. 115) provides a justification for a negatively sloped demand curve, but is wont to believe that the supply curve is positively sloped, rather than vertical as I suggest. This is because Hollander (1973, p. 119), in the case of supply, emphasizes the possibility (which is no more than hinted at by Smith) of holding a variable amount of supply in inventory rather than bringing it to market. This seems to me to be simply an analytical confusion, of the sort that later discussions (like Wicksteed 1933) fully clear up. In other words one must distinguish between total stock of a commodity and the amount which may be offered for sale at any given price, which must also take account of possessors' demand at that price.
16 See chapter 2 for more on the distinction between market and natural price. Roughly speaking, the former is determined by short-run supply and demand influences, the latter by long-run supply alone, which is based on labour costs.
17 See Reid (1987b, ch. 7) for a modern treatment of workable competition, and some new suggestions for extension of the concept.
18 See Lindgren (1973, pp. 64–5) for a discussion of deference structures, which in Smith put an

emphasis on distinguishing marks of superiority like age and fortune. Of course, whilst a meritocracy is disruptive of this type of deference structure, it does in some sense put another kind in its place, though arguably a more flexible and adaptable one.

19 See Reid (1987b, ch. 6) for an extensive analysis along these lines in the Austrian tradition.
20 The basic reference is Baumol, Panzer and Willig (1982). A summary account and critique is in Reid (1987b, ch. 8).
21 See Kirzner (1973, 1979).
22 Parallel to the control of technology to develop new electronic communication systems and the like, Bell (1974, p. 14) in his analysis of post-industrialism sees the creation of what he calls 'new intellectual technology'. It is embodied in a type of human capital which particularly equips its possessor to engage in various types of complex decision-making, where pattern recognition and judgement are called for.
23 See Grampp (1960) for an analysis of the various interest groups who contributed to the active lobbying of the Manchester School.
24 For the purposes of discussion it is helpful to regard the universal establishment of natural prices in all markets as a Smithian general equilibrium. The fact that it is a general equilibrium is more important than the fact that prices are 'natural', for today we have a way of looking at value which does not require reference to *absolute* values (e.g. in terms of labour), which of course are linked to natural prices in Smith. Marginal analysis indicates that even *relative* values which are based on subjective utility enable us to define a general equilibrium.
25 This suggests that Coase's (1976) dismissal of the role of God or divine guidance in bringing about natural harmony in the Smithian schema, and the insertion in its place of 'natural selection', would not be a strained interpretation.
26 And has a number of public platforms like the Institute for Humane Studies and the Cato Institute.
27 See the author's *Theories of Industrial Organization* (Reid 1987b, ch. 7) for a modern discussion of workable competition, and the effecting of welfare-improving rather than welfare-optimizing policies.
28 According to Clark, this maximum can be detected for the USA in 1920, for Great Britain in 1901, for France in 1901, for Germany in 1925, for Canada in 1911, for Japan in 1920 and for Switzerland in 1910. Our own view would be that qualitative aspects of post-industrialism should also be looked for, especially in terms of the development and use of communications technology. This would imply dating the onset of post-industrialism to a much more recent period. For more recent international data on services see Nusbaumer (1987).
29 See, for example, Alchian (1950), Hirshleifer (1977) and Matthews (1984).
30 The term 'alienation' or the doctrine thereof have anticipations going back many centuries before this. Put briefly, alienation means estrangement. Classical writings and early Christian theology developed the doctrine. By the nineteenth century it had become secularized. Hegel used the term *Entäusserung*, meaning self-alienation; and Marx, as a young Hegelian, used the term *Entfremdung*, in which form it lost its philosophical meaning and assumed a sociological one. Alienation in Marx was used to denote what he claimed to be a distancing of workers from the objects of their labours, namely the goods they produced.
31 See Rosenberg (1976) for a discussion of the relevant section from Smith's *Lectures on Rhetoric and Belles Lettres*, notably lecture XXVIII, Monday 7 February 1763 (pp. 170–7).
32 Cognitive values are inherent in intellectual labour, as opposed to manual labour. Modern writers on the extensive role of services under post-industrialism express this as the distinction between 'software' and 'hardware' (see Nusbaumer 1987, pp. 31–3).
33 See West (1975) for more detailed discussion of this.
34 This discussion is influenced by the treatment of Hales (1987).
35 See Wilkinson (1983), where e.g. Clive Jenkins is quoted as having used this terminology.
36 Adam Smith did not use the term 'social obligation', though he certainly talked frequently of obligation. The term is introduced to permit discussion of acts which are often neglected in the free market literature, but which are not incompatible with Smith's moral philosophy. In using the term 'social obligation' we do not intend to suggest that we adhere to the civic

humanist interpretation of Adam Smith's writings as represented, for example, by Hont and Ignatieff (1983).
37 Though he advises the citizen, 'like Solon, when he cannot establish the best system of laws, he will endeavour to establish the best that the people can bear' (TMS, p. 233) rather than becoming 'intoxicated with the imaginary beauty of [an] ideal system' (TMS, p. 232).
38 See Freeman (1969) for a development of this argument.

Epilogue

There is no single conclusion that can be reached in a work of this sort, for many themes have been explored. But perhaps precisely for that reason, concluding remarks are necessary to draw the discussion to a logical close. What will have been apparent is that the main source of inspiration for our analysis of classical economic growth from a contemporary perspective has been Adam Smith.

This is not to suggest that 'it is all in Adam Smith' – as Alfred Marshall did, before having exactly the same said of him! Smith lived in a stage of societal evolution which was, arguably, two stages before the one we are currently experiencing. Our economic worlds are different, and the route we took through economic history to our current point is a relevant determinant of how we would analyse the economy today.

Nevertheless, if one feels, as I do, that Adam Smith set out a comprehensive research agenda that is progressive, it is possible to do original work which is in the tradition of Adam Smith. Such work does not aim to be imitative of Smith, nor does it attempt to carry over Smithian ideas from over 200 years ago to a new arena. What it does say is that there are many ideas in Smith which are still potentially fruitful, but largely underdeveloped in an analytical sense. One might cite here, for example, the analysis of the competitive process and the incorporation of the effects of the division of labour in a long-run growth model. Unquestionably the reason why these developments have not yet taken place is that the leading authorities on Smith have frequently been more concerned with reminding us of wherein precisely lies the greatness of Smith's work (no doubt a laudable activity in itself), to the neglect of initiating research which explores further what we would today call the Smithian 'research agenda'. Perhaps only in development economics has this yet been done. A subsidiary reason is that many of the analytical problems that Smith addressed were simply very difficult to handle rigorously. Quite properly, we now live in an age when one has to confirm precisely what one feels on an intuitive level 'ought to be so'. This makes progress slower, but more certain. Because of the Walrasian research agenda on general equilibrium, we now know enormously more than we did a century ago about equilibrium systems and stationary states. Both of these are in Adam Smith, but the form in which he stated them could not have led to subsequent theoretical developments in the absence of the figure of Walras. However, part of Smith's neglect of such issues was his far greater emphasis on disequilibrium and growth. The great weight of his analytical attention was directed at these issues. As the Walrasian research agenda draws to a conclusion and attempts to advance it further increasingly display characteristics of degeneracy, scientific economics turns its attention to alternative or rival research agendas. What this volume has aimed to do is to present the Smithian agenda as progressive, with much yet to be achieved. We have limited attention to some aspects of economic theory, where clearly much remains to be done, but applied econometrics, economic policy analysis, the economics of politics and economic history, amongst others, also have a part to play in this unfinished agenda.

References

Abraham-Frois, G. and Berrebi, E. 1979: *Theory of Value, Prices and Accumulation.* Cambridge: Cambridge University Press.

Adelman, I. 1962: *Theories of Economic Growth and Development.* Standford: Stanford University Press.

Alchian, A. A. 1950: Uncertainty, evolution, and economic theory. *Journal of Political Economy*, 58, 211–21.

Andrews, P. W. S. 1949: *Manufacturing Business.* London: Macmillan.

Andrews, P. W. S. 1964: *On Competition in Economic Theory.* London: Macmillan.

Anspach, A. 1976: Smith's growth paradigm. *History of Political Economy*, 8, 494–514.

Arrow, K. J. 1962: Economic welfare and the allocation of resources for invention. In R. R. Nelson (ed.), *The Rate and Direction of Inventive Activity: economic and social factors*, Princeton, New Jersey: Princeton University Press, 609–28.

Arrow, K. J. 1979: The division of labour in the economy, the polity, and society. In G. P. O'Driscoll (ed.), *Adam Smith and Modern Political Economy: bicentennial essays on The Wealth of Nations.* Ames, Iowa: Iowa State University Press.

Arrow, K. J. and Hahn, F. H. 1971: *General Competitive Analysis.* Edinburgh: Oliver and Boyd.

Atkinson, A. B. 1969: The timescale of economic models: how long is the long run? *Review of Economic Studies*, 35, 137–52.

Babbage, C. 1832: *On the Economy of Machinery and Manufactures.* London: Charles Knight.

Bacon, R. and Eltis, W. 1976: *Britain's Economic Problem: too few producers.* London: Macmillan.

Barkai, H. 1969: A formal outline of a Smithian growth model. *Quarterly Journal of Economics*, 83, 396–414.
Bator, F. M. 1957: The simple analytics of welfare maximization. *American Economic Review*, 47, 22–59.
Baumol, W. J. 1959: *Economic Dynamics* (2nd edn). New York: Macmillan.
Baumol, W. J. 1962: On the theory of expansion of the firm. *American Economic Review*, 52, 1078–87.
Baumol, W. J. 1982: Contestable markets: an uprising in the theory of industry structure. *American Economic Review*, 72, 1–15.
Baumol, W. J., Panzer, J. C. and Willig, R. D. 1982: *Contestable Markets and the Theory of Industry Structure*. New York: Harcourt, Brace, Jovanovich.
Bell, D. 1974: *The Coming of Post-Industrial Society*. London: Heinemann.
Bernal, J. D. 1965: *Science in History*. London: Watts.
Billet, L. 1976: The just economy: the moral basis of *The Wealth of Nations*. *Review of Social Economy*, 34, 295–315.
Birch, D. 1984: The contribution of small enterprise to growth and employment. In Giersch, H. (ed.) New Opportunities for Entrepreneurship. Tübingen: Mohr (Paul Siebeck) 1–17.
Blaug, M. 1968: *Economic Theory in Retrospect* (2nd edn). London: Heinemann.
Blitch, C. P. 1983: Allyn Young on increasing returns. *Journal of Post Keynesian Economics*, 5, 359–72.
Braverman. H. 1974: *Labour and Monopoly Capitalism*. New York: Monthly Review Press.
Bray, J. 1977: The logic of scientific method in economics. *Journal of Economic Studies*, 4, 1–28.
Bryce, J. C. 1983: *Lectures on Rhetoric and Belles Lettres* by Adam Smith, Glasgow edition. Oxford: Oxford University Press.
Buchanan, J. M. 1976: Public goods and natural liberty. In T. Wilson and A. S. Skinner (eds), *The Market and the State: essays in honour of Adam Smith*, Oxford: Oxford University Press, chapter 9.
Buchanan, J. M. 1987: Towards the simple economics of natural liberty: an exploratory analysis. *Kyklos*, 40, 3–20.
Campbell, R. H., Skinner, A. S. and Todd, W. B. (eds) 1976: *An Enquiry into the Nature and Causes of the Wealth of Nations* by Adam Smith, Glasgow edition. Oxford: Oxford University Press.
Caporaso, J. A. (ed.) 1987: *A Changing International Division of Labour*. London: Frances Pinter.
Cassels, J. M. 1936: Excess capacity and monopolistic competition. *Quarterly Journal of Economics*, 51, 426–43.

Casson, M. 1982: *The Entrepreneur: an economic theory.* Oxford: Martin Robertson.
Casson, M. C. 1986: *Multinationals and World Trade.* London: Allen and Unwin.
Casson, M. C. 1988: Recent trends in international business: a new analysis. University of Reading Economics Department Discussion Paper, no. 112.
Chiang, A. C. 1974: *Fundamental Methods of Mathematical Economics.* New York: McGraw-Hill.
Cigno, A. 1975: Diffusion of innovations under imperfect competition. In R. H. Day and T. Groves (eds), *Adaptive Economic Models,* New York: Academic Press, 363–86.
Clark, C. 1940: *The Conditions of Economic Progress.* London: Macmillan.
Clark, J. M. 1961: *Competition as a Dynamic Process.* Washington: The Brookings Institution.
Coase, R. W. 1937: The nature of the firm. *Economica,* 4, 386–405.
Coase, R. W. 1976: Adam Smith's view of man. *Journal of Law and Economics,* 19, 529–46.
Costabile, L. and Rowthorn, R. 1985: Malthus's theory of wages and growth. *Economic Journal,* 95, 418–37.
Cournot, A. A. 1838: *Researches into the Mathematical Principles of the Theory of Wealth* (ed. Irving Fisher 1960). New York: Kelly.
Cross, M. 1985: *Towards the Flexible Craftsman.* London: Technical Change Centre.
Currie, L. 1981: Allyn Young and the development of growth theory. *Journal of Economic Studies,* 8, 52–60.
Dasgupta, A. K. 1960: Adam Smith on value. *Indian Economic Review,* 5, 105–15.
Dasgupta, A. K. 1961: Adam Smith on value, a postscript. *Indian Economic Review,* 5, 285–7.
Dasgupta, A. K. 1983: *Phases of Capitalism and Economic Theory and Other Essays.* Delhi: Oxford University Press.
Dasgupta, A. K. 1985: *Epochs of Economic Theory.* Oxford: Basil Blackwell.
Deane, P. and Cole, W. A. 1967: *British Economic Growth: trends and structure, 1688–1959* (2nd edn). Cambridge: Cambridge University Press.
Dechert, W. D. and Nishimura, K. 1983: A complete characterization of optimal growth paths in an aggregated model with a non-concave production function. *Journal of Economic Theory,* 31, 332–54.
Demsetz, H. 1977: Social responsibility in the enterprise economy. *Southwestern Law Review,* 10, 1–11.

Dmitriev, V. K. 1904: *Economic Essays on Value, Competition and Utility* (trans. D. Fry, ed. D. M. Nuti 1974). Cambridge: Cambridge University Press (published as *Economicheskiye Ocherki*, 1904).
Dorfman, R., Samuelson, P. A. and Solow, R. 1958: *Linear Programming and Economic Analysis*. New York: McGraw-Hill.
Duesenberry, J. S. 1958: *Business Cycles and Economic Growth*. New York: McGraw-Hill.
Eltis, W. A. 1973: *Growth and Distribution*. London: Macmillan.
Eltis, W. A. 1975: Adam Smith's theory of economic growth. In A. S. Skinner and T. Wilson (eds), *Essays on Adam Smith*. Oxford: Clarendon Press.
Eltis, W. A. 1984: *The Classical Theory of Economic Growth*. London: Macmillan.
Eltis, W. A. 1985: Ricardo on machinery and technological unemployment. In G. A. Caravale (ed.), *The Legacy of Ricardo*, Oxford: Basil Blackwell, chapter 11.
Fay, C. R. 1934: Adam Smith, America and the doctrinal defeat of the mercantile system. *Quarterly Journal of Economics*, 48, 304–16.
Ferguson, A. 1767: *Essay on the History of Civil Society* (ed. Duncan Forbes 1966). Edinburgh: Edinburgh University Press.
Foley, V. 1974: The division of labour in Plato and Smith. *History of Political Economy*, 6, 220–42.
Freeman, R. D. 1969: Adam Smith, education and *laissez-faire*. *History of Political Economy*, 1, 173–86.
Fröbel, R., Heinrichs, J. and Kreye, O. 1980: *The New International Division of Labour*. Cambridge: Cambridge University Press.
Galbraith, J. K. 1987: *A History of Economics*. London: Hamish Hamilton.
Gee, J. M. A. and Jarvis, J. A. 1984: Gauss-Newtonised Smith: a formal model of Smithian economic statics, growth and development. Paper delivered at the 1984 History of Economic Thought Conference, Guildford, UK.
Giersch, H. (ed.) 1983: *New Opportunities for Entrepreneurship*. Tübingen: Mohr (Paul Siebeck).
Goldberg, S. 1958: *An Introduction to Difference Equations*. New York: Wiley.
Grampp, W. D. 1960: *The Manchester School of Economics*. Stanford: Stanford University Press.
Gray, A. 1931: *The Development of Economic Doctrine*. London: Longman.
Groenewegen, P. D. 1977: Adam Smith and the division of labour: a bicentenary estimate. *Australian Economic Papers*, 16, 161–74.
Hahn, F. H. 1963: On the disequilibrium behaviour of a multi-sectoral growth model. *Economic Journal*, 73, 442–57. Reprinted in F. H. Hahn 1985, *Money, Growth and Stability*, Oxford: Basil Blackwell.
Hahn, F. H. 1974: On the nature of equilibrium in economics. Inaugural

lecture, Cambridge University, Cambridge. Reprinted in F. H. Hahn 1984, *Equilibrium and Macroeconomics*, Oxford: Basil Blackwell.

Hales, C. 1987: Quality of working life, job redesign and participation in a service industry: a rose by any other name? *The Services Industries Journal*, 7, 253-73.

Hall, R. L. and Hitch, C. J. 1939: Price theory and business behaviour. *Oxford Economic Papers*, 2, 12-45. Reprinted in T. Wilson and P. W. S. Andrews (eds) 1951, *Oxford Studies in the Price Mechanism*, Oxford: Clarendon Press.

Harris, D. J. 1978: *Capital Accumulation and Income Distribution*. Stanford: Stanford University Press.

Harrod, R. F. 1948: *Towards a Dynamic Economics*. London: Macmillan.

Hartwell, R. M. 1976: Comment on Kindleberger's paper. In T. Wilson and A. S. Skinner (eds), *The Market and the State: essays in honour of Adam Smith*, Oxford: Oxford University Press, 33-41.

Hayek, F. A. von 1940: The competitive solution. *Economica*, 7, 125-49.

Hayek, F. A. von 1955: *The Counter-Revolution of Science*. Glencoe, Illinois: Free Press.

Hayek, F. A. von 1973: *Law, Legislation and Liberty*. Chicago: Chicago University Press.

Helpman, E. and Krugman, P. R. 1985: *Market Structure and Foreign Trade*. Cambridge, Massachusetts: MIT Press.

Henderson, J. P. 1954: The macro and micro aspects of *The Wealth of Nations*. *Southern Economic Journal*, 21, 25-35.

Hicks, J. R. 1937: Mr Keynes and the classics: a suggested interpretation. *Econometrica*, 5, 147-59.

Hicks, J. R. 1950: *A Contribution to the Theory of the Trade Cycle*. Oxford: Oxford University Press.

Hicks, J. R. 1960: Thoughts on the theory of capital – the Corfu conference. *Oxford Economic Papers*, 12, 123-32.

Hicks, J. R. 1965: *Capital and Growth*. Oxford: Clarendon Press.

Hicks, J. R. 1969: *A Theory of Economic History*. London: Oxford University Press.

Hicks, J. R. 1972: Ricardo's theory of distribution. In M. H. Peston and B. Corry (eds), *Essays in Honour of Lionel Robbins*, London: Weidenfeld and Nicholson.

Higgins, B. 1959: *Economic Development*. London: Constable.

Hirschman, A. O. 1970: *Exit, Voice and Loyalty*. Cambridge, Mass.: Harvard University Press.

Hirshleifer, J. 1977: Economics from a biological viewpoint. *Journal of Law and Economics*, 20, 1-52.

Hoff, T. J. B. 1949: *Economic Calculation in the Socialist Society*. London: Hodge.
Hollander, S. 1971: Some implications of Adam Smith's analysis of investment priorities. *History of Political Economy*, 3, 238–64.
Hollander, S. 1973: *The Economics of Adam Smith*. London: Heinemann.
Hollander, S. 1977: Adam Smith and the self-interest axiom. *Journal of Law and Economics*, 20, 133–52.
Hollander, S. 1980: On Professor Samuelson's canonical classical model of political economy. *Journal of Economic Literature*, 18, 559–74.
Hollander, S. 1987: *Classical Economics*. Oxford: Basil Blackwell.
Hont, I. and Ignatieff, M. (eds) 1983: *Wealth and Virtue*. Cambridge: Cambridge University Press.
Ippolito, R. A. 1977: The division of labour in the firm. *Economic Inquiry*, 15, 469–92.
Johansen, L. 1969: A classical model of economic growth. In Feinstein C. H. (ed.), *Socialism, Capitalism and Economic Growth*, Cambridge: Cambridge University Press.
Jones, R. W. and Kenen, P. B. (eds) 1984: *Handbook of International Economics*. Amsterdam: North-Holland.
Jorgenson, D. W. 1961: Stability of a dynamic input–output system. *Review of Economic Studies*, 76, 105–16.
Kaldor, N. 1957: A model of economic growth. *Economic Journal*, 67, 591–624.
Kaldor, N. 1970: The case for regional policy. *Scottish Journal of Political Economy*, 17, 337–48.
Kaldor, N. 1972: The irrelevance of equilibrium economics. *Economic Journal*, 82, 1237–55.
Kaldor, N. 1985: *Economics Without Equilibrium*. Cardiff: University College Cardiff Press.
Kaldor, N. and Mirrlees, J. 1962: A new model of economic growth. *Review of Economic Studies*, 29, 174–92.
Kalecki, M. 1933: Outline of a theory of the business cycle. Reprinted in M. Kalecki 1971, *Selected Essays on the Dynamics of the Capitalist Economy*, Cambridge: Cambridge University Press.
Keynes, J. M. 1936: *The General Theory of Employment, Interest and Money*. London: Macmillan.
Kindleberger, C. P. 1976: The historical background: Adam Smith and the industrial revolution. In T. Wilson and A. S. Skinner (eds), *The Market and the State: essays in honour of Adam Smith*, Oxford: Oxford University Press, chapter 1.
Kirzner, I. M. 1973: *Competition and Entrepreneurship*. Chicago: Chicago University Press.

Kirzner, I. M. 1979: *Perception, Opportunity, and Profit*. Chicago: University of Chicago Press.
Kirzner, I. M. (ed.) 1982: *Method, Process and Austrian Economics*. Lexington, Massachusetts: Lexington Books.
Koebner, R. 1959: Adam Smith and the industrial revolution. *Economic History Review*, 2, 381-91.
Kregel, J. A. 1976: Economic methodology in the face of uncertainty. *Economic Journal*, 86, 209-25.
Krugman, P. R. 1987: Is free trade *passé*? *Journal of Economic Perspectives*, 1, 131-44.
Lamb, R. 1973: Adam Smith's concept of alienation. *Oxford Economic Papers*, 25, 275-85.
La Nauze, J. A. 1937: The substance of Adam Smith's attack on mercantilism. *Economic Record*, 90-3.
Lange, O. 1936: On the economic theory of socialism. *Review of Economic Studies*, 4, 53-71.
Larsen, R. M. 1977: Dmitriev's Smithian model. *Scottish Journal of Political Economy*, 24, 227-33.
Lehmann, W. C. 1930: *Adam Ferguson and the Beginning of Modern Sociology*. New York: Columbia University Press.
Lerner, A. P. 1944: *The Economics of Control*. New York: Macmillan.
Lindgren, J. R. 1973: *The Social Philosophy of Adam Smith*. The Hague: Martinus Nijhoff.
Lowe, A. 1954: The classical theory of growth. *Social Research*, 21, 127-58.
Lowe, A. 1975: Adam Smith's system of equilibrium growth. In A. S. Skinner and T. Wilson (eds), *Essays on Adam Smith*. Oxford: Clarendon Press.
Macfie, A. L. 1959: Adam Smith's *Moral Sentiments* as foundations for his *Wealth of Nations*. *Oxford Economic Papers*, 11, 209-28.
Macfie, A. L. and Raphael, D. D. 1976: *The Theory of Moral Sentiments* by Adam Smith, Glasgow edition. Oxford: Oxford University Press.
McKee, D. L. 1987: On services and growth poles in advanced economies. *The Services Industries Journal*, 7, 165-75.
McNulty, P. J. 1975: A note on the division of labour in Plato and Smith. *History of Political Economy*, 7, 372-8.
Majumdar, M. and Mitra, T. 1982: Intertemporal allocation with a non-convex technology: the aggregative framework. *Journal of Economic Theory*, 27, 101-36.
Marglin, S. 1975: What do bosses do? In A. Gorz (ed.), *The Division of Labour*, Hassocks: Harvester Press.
Marshall, A. 1890: *The Principles of Economics*. London: Macmillan.

Matthews, R. C. O. 1984: Darwinism and economic change. *Oxford Economic Papers*, 36 (supplement), 91–117.
Meacci, F. 1985: Ricardo on machinery and the theory of capital. In G. A. Caravale (ed.), *The Legacy of Ricardo*, Oxford: Basil Blackwell, chapter 12.
Meek, R. 1971: Smith, Turgot and the 'four stages theory'. *History of Political Economy*, 3, 9–27.
Meek, R. L., Raphael, D. D. and Stein, P. G. 1978: *Lectures on Jurisprudence by Adam Smith*, Glasgow edition. Oxford: Oxford University Press.
Mothe, de la, P. 1986: Financial services. In A. D. Smith (ed.), *Technological Trends and Employment*, Aldershot: Gower.
Moore, F. T. 1959: Economies of scale: some statistical evidence. *Quarterly Journal of Economics*, 73, 232–45.
Myers, M. L. 1976: Division of labour as a principle of social cohesion. *Canadian Journal of Economics*, 33, 431–40.
Myint, H. 1948: *Theories of Welfare Economics*. London: Longman.
Myrdal, G. 1957: *Economic Theory and Underdeveloped Regions*. London: Duckworth.
Negishi, T. 1985: *Economic Theories in a Non-Walrasian Tradition*. Cambridge: Cambridge University Press.
Nicholson, J. S. (ed.) 1895: *The Wealth of Nations* by Adam Smith. London: Nelson and Son.
Nusbaumer, J. 1987: *The Services Economy: lever to growth*. Boston: Kluwer.
O'Brien, D. P. 1975: *The Classical Economists*. Oxford: Clarendon Press.
Ouchi, W. G. 1980: Markets, bureaucracies, and clans. *Administrative Science Quarterly*, 25, 833–48.
Papola, T. S. 1967: A 'primitive' equilibrium system: a neglected aspect of Smith's economics. *Indian Economic Journal*, 17, 93–100.
Pasinetti, L. L. 1974: *Growth and Income Distribution: essays in economic theory*. Cambridge: Cambridge University Press.
Pareto, V. 1927: *Manual of Political Economy*. Trans. 1971 from the French edition by Ann S. Schwier, New York: Kelly.
Pearce, I. F. and Gabor, A. 1952: A new approach to the theory of the firm. *Oxford Economic Papers*, 4, 252–65.
Pigou, A. C. 1933: *Theory of Unemployment*. London: Macmillan.
Prescott, E. C. and Boyd, J. H. 1987: Dynamic coalitions: engines of growth. *American Economic Review (Papers and Proceedings)*, 77, 63–7.
Rajan, A. 1987: *Services – the Second Industrial Revolution?* Guildford: Butterworth.
Ranadive, K. R. 1977: *The Wealth of Nations*: the vision and the conceptualization. *Indian Economic Journal*, 24, 295–332.

Raphael, D. D. 1985: *Adam Smith*. Oxford: Oxford University Press.
Rashid, S. 1986: Adam Smith and the division of labour: a historical view. *Scottish Journal of Political Economy*, 33, 292-7.
Reid, G. C. 1975: An analytical study of price leadership. University of Edinburgh, Department of Economics, PhD thesis.
Reid, G. C. 1979: An analysis of the firm, market structure, and technical progress. *Scottish Journal of Political Economy*, 26, 15-32.
Reid, G. C. 1981: *The Kinked Demand Curve Analysis of Oligopoly: theory and evidence*. Edinburgh: Edinburgh University Press.
Reid, G. C. 1983: Adam Smith's analysis of growth: 'cheerful' or 'dull'? University of Edinburgh Department of Economics Discussion Paper 1983:III.
Reid, G. C. 1985a: Adam Smith on accumulation: a formal analysis. University of Edinburgh Department of Economics Discussion Paper 1985:VI.
Reid, G. C. 1985b: Keynes versus the classics: fluctuations and growth. *Scottish Journal of Political Economy*, 32, 315-27.
Reid, G. C. 1987a: Disequilibrium and increasing returns in Adam Smith's analysis of growth and accumulation. *History of Political Economy*, 19, 87-106.
Reid, G. C. 1987b: *Theories of Industrial Organization*. Oxford: Basil Blackwell.
Reid, G. C. 1989: Adam Smith's stadial analysis as a sequence of societal growth trajectories. *Scottish Journal of Political Economy*, 36, 59-70.
Reid, G. C. and Jacobsen, L. R. 1988: *The Small Entrepreneurial Firm*. Aberdeen: Aberdeen University Press.
Reid, G. C. and Wolfe, J. N. 1979: J. R. Hicks. *International Encyclopedia of the Social Sciences*, 18, 300-2.
Reisman, D. A. 1976: *Adam Smith's Sociological Economics*. London: Croom Helm.
Richardson, G. B. 1975: Adam Smith on competition and increasing returns. In A. S. Skinner and T. Wilson (eds), *Essays on Adam Smith*. Oxford: Clarendon Press.
Robinson, J. 1963: *Essays in the Theory of Economic Growth*. London: Macmillan.
Romer, P. M. 1986: Increasing returns and long run growth. *Journal of Political Economy*, 94, 1002-37.
Romer, P. M. 1987: Growth based on increasing returns due to specialization. *American Economic Review (Papers and Proceedings)*, 77, 56-62.
Rosenberg, N. 1960: Some institutional aspects of *The Wealth of Nations*. *Journal of Political Economy*, 18, 557-70.

Rosenberg, N. 1965: Adam Smith on the division of labour: two views or one? *Economica*, 32, 127-39.

Rosenberg, N. 1976: Another advantage of the division of labour. *Journal of Political Economy*, 84, 861-8.

Rostow, W. W. 1960: *The Stages of Economic Growth*. Cambridge: Cambridge University Press.

Rothbard, M. N. 1977: *Power and Market* (2nd edn). Kansas City: Sheed Andrews and McMeel.

Samuels, W. J. 1973: Adam Smith and the economy as a system of power. *Review of Social Economy*, 31, 123-37.

Samuelson, P. A. 1939: Interactions between the multiplier analysis and the principle of acceleration. *Review of Economics and Statistics*, 21, 75-8.

Samuelson, P. A. 1947: *Foundations of Economic Analysis*. Cambridge, Massachusetts: Harvard University Press.

Samuelson, P. A. 1977: A modern theorist's vindication of Adam Smith's growth model. *American Economic Review*, 67, 42-9.

Samuelson, P. A. 1978: The canonical classical model of political economy. *Journal of Economic Literature*, 16, 1415-34.

Saxton, C. C. 1942: *The Economics of Price Determination*. London: Oxford University Press.

Schumpeter, J. A. 1954: *History of Economic Analysis*. Oxford: Oxford University Press.

Seligman, E. R. A. (ed.) 1910: *An Enquiry into the Nature and Causes of the Wealth of Nations*, vol. 1, by Adam Smith (Everyman edition). London: Dent and Sons.

Shelp, R. K. 1981: *Beyond Industrialization*. New York: Praeger.

Simon, H. A. 1957: *Models of Man*. New York: Wiley.

Simpson, D. 1983: *The Political Economy of Growth*. Oxford: Basil Blackwell.

Skinner, A. S. 1972: Adam Smith: philosophy and science. *Scottish Journal of Political Economy*, 29, 307-19.

Skinner, A. S. 1979: *A System of Social Science: papers relating to Adam Smith*. Oxford: Clarendon Press.

Skinner, A. S. and Wilson, T. (eds) 1975: *Essays on Adam Smith*. Oxford: Clarendon Press.

Sobel, I. 1979: Adam Smith: what kind of institutionalist was he? *Journal of Economic Issues*, 13, 347-68.

Solow, R. M. 1988: Growth theory and after. *American Economic Review*, 78, 307-17.

Spengler, J. J. 1959: Adam Smith's theory of economic growth (parts 1 and 2). *Southern Economic Journal*, 25, 397-415 and 26, 1-12.

Stigler, G. J. 1951: The division of labour is limited by the extent of the

market. *Journal of Political Economy*, 59, 185-93.
Stigler, G. J. 1957: Perfect competition, historically contemplated. *Journal of Political Economy*, 65, 234-67.
Stigler, G. J. 1961: The economics of information. *Journal of Political Economy*, 69, 213-25.
Stigler, G. J. 1965a: Textual exegesis as a scientific problem. *Economica*, 32, 447-50.
Stigler, G. J. 1965b: *Essays in the History of Economics*. Chicago: University of Chicago Press.
Stigler, G. J. 1976: The successes and failures of Professor Smith. *Journal of Political Economy*, 84, 1199-213.
Sugden, R. 1986: *The Economics of Rights, Co-operation and Welfare*. Oxford: Basil Blackwell.
Sylos-Labini, P. 1969: *Oligopoly and Technical Progress*. Cambridge: Cambridge University Press.
Taylor, F. W. 1911: *The Principles of Scientific Management*. New York: Harper.
Thweatt, W. O. 1957: A diagrammatic presentation of Adam Smith's growth model. *Social Research*, 24, 227-30.
Tucker, W. T. 1964: The development of brand loyalty. *Journal of Marketing Research*, 1, 32-5.
Vickers, J. 1985: Notes on the evolution of industry structure when there is a sequence of innovations. Paper delivered to the EARIE Conference, Cambridge, UK.
Viner, J. 1927: Adam Smith and *laissez-faire*. *Journal of Political Economy*, 35, 198-232.
Walsh, V. and Gram, H. 1980: *Classical and Neoclassical Theories of General Equilibrium*. Oxford: Oxford University Press.
Webb, R. K. 1980: *Modern England* (2nd edn). London: George Allen and Unwin.
Weizsäcker, C. C. von 1973: Notes on endogenous growth of productivity. In J. A. Mirrlees and N. H. Stern (eds), *Models of Economic Growth*, Edinburgh: Macmillan, 101-14.
West, E. G. 1964: Adam Smith's two views on the division of labour. *Economica*, 31, 23-31.
West, E. G. 1969: The political economy of alienation: Karl Marx and Adam Smith. *Oxford Economic Papers*, 21, 1-23.
West, E. G. 1975: Adam Smith and alienation. *Oxford Economic Papers*, 27, 295-301.
Wicksteed, P. H. 1933: *The Common Sense of Political Economy*. London: Routledge.

Wightman, W. P. D. and Bryce, J. C. 1980: *Essays on Philosophical Subjects* by Adam Smith, Glasgow edition. Oxford: Oxford University Press.
Wiles, P. J. D. 1961: *Price, Cost and Output*. London: Basil Blackwell.
Wilkinson, B. 1983: *The Shopfloor Politics of New Technology*. London: Heinemann.
Williamson, O. E. 1971: The vertical integration of production: market failure considerations. *American Economic Review*, 61, 112–23.
Williamson, O. E. 1985: *The Economic Institutions of Capitalism*. New York: Free Press.
Wilson, T. 1976: Sympathy and self-interest. In T. Wilson and A. S. Skinner (eds), *The Market and the State: essays in honour of Adam Smith*, Oxford: Oxford University Press, 73–99.
Young, A. 1928: Increasing returns and economic progress. *Economic Journal*, 38, 527–42.

Index

AUTHOR INDEX

Abraham-Frois, G. and Berrebi, E. 73, 191
Adelman, I. 30, 53, 56, 57, 60, 62, 65, 104, 105, 191
Alchian, A. A. 187, 191
Andrews, P. W. S. 82, 84, 91, 191
Anspach, A. 49, 191
Arrow, K. J. 54, 93, 95, 97, 98, 118, 156, 186, 191
Arrow, K. J. and Hahn, F. H. 3, 15, 27, 46, 191
Atkinson, A. B. 72, 191

Babbage, C. 112, 158, 191
Bacon, R. and Eltis, W. 61, 191
Barkai, H. 53, 55, 57, 58, 59, 60, 62, 73, 106, 128, 192
Bator, F. M. 150, 192
Baumol, W. J. 31, 91, 192
Baumol, W. J. et al. 187, 192
Bell, D. xiii, xiv, 3, 155, 156, 158, 176, 183, 184, 192
Bernal, J. D. 158, 192
Billet, L. 28, 192
Birch, D. 155, 185, 192
Blaug, M. 41, 156, 157, 192
Blitch, C. P. 144, 192
Braverman, H. 95, 192
Bray, J. 192
Buchanan, J. M. 28, 165, 172, 192

Campbell, R. H. et al. 192
Caporaso, J. A. 159, 192
Cassels, J. M. 77, 192
Casson, M. C. 93, 95, 96, 98, 99, 100, 105, 106, 112, 113, 156, 158, 186, 192
Chiang, A. C. 30, 31, 193
Cigno, A. 113, 193
Clark, C. 165, 174, 176, 187, 193
Clark, J. M. 165, 193
Coase, R. W. 15, 112, 170, 187, 193

Costabile, L. and Rowthorn, R. 44, 53, 193
Cournot, A. A. 20, 193
Cross, M. 181, 193
Currie, L. 45, 94, 107, 116, 128, 193

Dasgupta, A. K. 36, 37, 44, 112, 142, 193
Deane, P. and Cole, W. A. 10, 193
Dechert, W. D. and Nishimura, K. xii, 193
Demsetz, H. 165, 193
Dmitriev, V. K. 37, 38, 193
Dorfman, R. et al. 50, 193
Duesenberry, J. S. 115, 120, 121, 142, 144, 194

Eltis, W. A. 53, 60, 61, 62, 63, 73, 112, 194

Fay, C. R. 10, 194
Ferguson, A. 5, 175, 178, 194
Foley, V. 156, 194
Freeman, R. D. 188, 194
Freud, S. 32
Fröbel, R. et al. 95, 112, 194

Galbraith, J. K. 2, 194
Gee, J. 31
Gee, J. M. A. and Jarvis, J. A. 148, 153, 194
Giersch, H. 155, 185, 192, 194
Goldberg, S. 31, 128, 194
Grampp, W. D. 33, 187, 194
Gray, A. 31, 33, 194
Groenewegen, P. D. 100, 113, 157, 194

Hahn, F. H. 72, 144, 194
Hales, C. 179, 194
Hall, R. L. and Hitch, C. J. 77, 195
Harris, D. J. 142, 195
Harrod, R. F. 117, 195
Hartwell, R. M. 8, 195

Hayek, F. A. von 30, 164, 167, 171, 173, 174, 195
Helpman, E. and Krugman, P. R. 149, 168, 195
Henderson, J. P. 44, 195
Hicks, J. R. xiii, 3, 12, 44, 47, 59, 60, 61, 63, 112, 115, 116, 117, 128, 195
Higgins, B. 53, 54, 55, 56, 57, 195
Hirschman, A. O. 40, 195
Hirshleifer, J. 160, 170, 171, 187, 195
Hoff, T. J. B. 30, 195
Hollander, S. xii, 3, 10, 16, 20, 22, 25, 35, 36, 39, 41, 44, 46, 47, 49, 79, 91, 147, 154, 186, 195, 196
Hont, I. and Ignatieff, M. 188, 196

Ippolito, R. A. 95, 102, 103, 134, 196

Johansen, L. 53, 196
Jones, R. W. and Kenen, P. B. 100, 196
Jorgensen, D. W. 144, 196

Kaldor, N. 19, 24, 35, 87, 88, 100, 105, 107, 116, 124, 144, 145, 146, 148, 150, 151, 152, 154, 196
Kaldor, N. and Mirrlees, J. 54, 196
Kalecki, M. 54, 117, 196
Keynes, J. M. 115, 116, 117, 128, 196
Kindleberger, C. P. 10, 31, 185, 196
Kirzner, I. M. 73, 112, 167, 186, 187, 196
Koebner, R. 10, 197
Kregel, J. A. 128, 197
Krugman, P. R. 168, 197

La Nauze, J. A. 10, 197
Lamb, R. 177, 178, 197
Lange, O. 30, 197
Larsen, R. M. 38, 197
Lehmann, W. C. 175, 197
Lerner, A. P. 30, 197
Lindgren, J. R. 186, 197
Lowe, A. 49, 64, 73, 197

Macfie, A. L. 27, 197
Macfie, A. L. and Raphael, D. D. 26, 31, 33, 197
McKee, D. L. 179, 197
McNulty, P. J. 156, 197
Majumdar, M. and Mitra, T. xii, 197
Marglin, S. 95, 197
Marshall, A. 21, 46, 100, 189, 197
Matthews, R. C. O. 174, 187, 197
Meacci, F. 142, 197

Meek, R. 30, 198
Meek, R. L. et al. 198
Moore, F. T. 85, 198
Mothe, P. de la 180, 198
Myers, M. L. 19, 32, 198
Myint, H. 30, 142, 198
Myrdal, G. 116, 198

Negishi, T. 20, 22, 23, 75, 198
Nicholson, J. S. 168, 198
Nusbaumer, J. 33, 187, 198

O'Brien, D. P. 9, 21, 25, 30, 32, 46, 73, 142, 198
Ouchi, W. G. 160, 186, 198

Papola, T. S. 41, 46, 198
Pareto, V. 147, 148, 150, 153, 198
Pasinetti, L. L. 30, 115, 117, 118, 119, 120, 121, 122, 123, 124, 128, 198
Pearce, I. F. and Gabor, A. 92, 198
Pigou, A. C. 116, 198
Plato 156
Prescott, E. C. and Boyd, J. H. xii, 198

Rajan, A. 113, 198
Ranadive, K. R. 3, 30, 198
Raphael, D. D. 17, 32, 33, 153, 198
Rashid, S. 112, 198
Reid, G. C. 32, 33, 53, 57, 76, 91, 92, 119, 128, 146, 186, 187, 199
Reid, G. C. and Jacobsen, L. R. 166, 199
Reid, G. C. and Wolfe, J. N. 128, 199
Reisman, D. A. 3, 6, 9, 30, 199
Ricardo, D. 142
Richardson, G. B. 20, 22, 23, 24, 35, 87, 199
Robinson, J. 11, 12, 199
Romer, P. M. xii, 199
Rosenberg, N. 16, 96, 172, 177, 187, 199
Rostow, W. W. xiii, 3, 31, 200
Rothbard, M. N. 170, 200

Samuels, W. J. 16, 18, 32, 200
Samuelson, P. A. 31, 51, 52, 53, 57, 58, 62, 65, 68, 69, 70, 72, 73, 115, 117, 144, 149, 154, 200
Saxton, C. C. 77, 200
Schumpeter, J. A. xiii, 20, 41, 104, 200
Schwier, Ann S. 147, 153, 198
Seligman, E. R. A. xv, 200
Shelp, R. K. 185, 200

Author Index

Simon, H. A. 112, 200
Simpson, D. 3, 200
Skinner, A. S. 5, 6, 7, 11, 31, 32, 35, 44, 45, 47, 112, 200
Skinner, A. S. and Wilson, T. 60, 200
Sobel, I. 170, 200
Solow, R. M. 11, 45, 112, 200
Spengler, J. J. 49, 57, 64, 113, 200
Stigler, G. J. 20, 75, 94, 95, 100, 101, 102, 162, 165, 167, 200, 201
Sugden, R. 32, 201
Sylos-Labini, P. 80, 82, 201

Taylor, F. W. 180, 201
Thweatt, W. O. 73, 201
Tucker, W. T. 92, 201

Vickers, J. 92, 201
Viner, J. 28, 66, 201

Walsh, V. and Gram, H. 42, 43, 47, 50, 73, 118, 201
Webb, R. K. 185, 186, 201
Weizsäcker, C. C. von 105, 158, 201
West, E. G. 177, 187, 201
Wicksteed, P. H. 201
Wightman, W. P. D. and Bryce, J. C. 201
Wiles, P. J. D. 91, 92, 201
Wilkinson, B. 187, 202
Williamson, O. E. 101, 112, 202
Wilson, T. 17, 18, 19, 202

Young, A. 24, 33, 87, 88, 94, 100, 105, 107, 113, 116, 124, 144, 145, 146, 147, 148, 150, 151, 152, 202

SUBJECT INDEX

acceleration principle 117
accelerator business cycle model 117
accelerator effect 116
accelerator relationship 118
accumulation 35, 43–4, 96
    industry level 75–92
activities 102
administration of justice 97
aggregate approach 35
aggregate classical model 129–33, 140
aggregate production function 4, 46, 53, 54, 57, 107, 109, 130
aggregation by analogy 104
aggregative growth models 53–64
aggressive price leadership 87
aggressive pricing policy 75
aggressive pricing strategy 77
agriculture 25
alienation 175–81
allocation 35, 96
allocation of resources 41, 142
allocative analysis 43
allocative equilibrium 20
amelioration 175–81
apprenticeship 169
arts 177
average cost curve 23
average revenue curve 23

balance of payments 9
balanced growth 51
bargaining parameter 130
bargaining power 129, 133–6, 140, 141
bargaining process 131
benevolence 15
boss/worker distinctions 98
brain-intensive economies 155
brand loyalty 92
Brownian dance 70
Brownian motion 69, 70

canonical classical model 57
canonical classical model of political economy 72
capacity extension 80
capital accumulation xii, 42, 45, 59, 60, 63, 65
capital intensity 109
capital-labour ratio 57, 58
capital-labour substitution 106
capital-output ratio 63, 119, 120, 122, 123, 125
capital stock 64, 65
ceteris paribus assumption 6, 23, 83, 103
Christianity 26
circulating capital 61–3, 109, 142, 157
classical economics 2, 115–18, 155–88

Subject Index

classical model 115–28
classical perspective 1–33
coalition 166
cognitive values 176
collusion 162, 163, 166
Coming of Post-Industrial Society: A Venture in Social Forecasting, The 155
commercial society 1, 5, 8, 30
commodity supply 40
communication 97, 180, 181, 183
comparative dynamics 124–5
comparative modelling 115, 126
comparison model 118
competition 1, 17, 19, 20–5, 29, 30, 40, 75, 101, 160
   act of 1
   atomistic 101
   consequence of 1
   free 162–4, 166, 168–9
   Smithian form of 168
competitive process 1, 3, 24, 40, 75, 160–9, 185
competitive structure 1, 2
computer services 181
concentration 82–3
conflict 98, 136, 160
constant mark-up
   and expanding demand 82, 87–9
   and stable demand 82, 84–7
constant price and stable demand 82–4
constraints 168
consumption/growth trade-off equation 43, 47
coordination 98–9
corporation 169
cost-capacity ratio 85
cost curves 81, 101
cost dominant 80
cost-plus pricing 77–9
cost-reducing technologies 75, 80, 88
cumulative causation 107
cumulative decline 128
cumulative gross investment 54
cumulative growth 112, 128

damped cyclical growth 124
Darwinian natural selection 174
decision-making 97, 158, 176, 181
decomposition of value 37
deference structure 165
demand for labour function 132
demand schedule 39
democracy of the market place 2

disapprobation 161–2, 183
disequilibrium effects 103
disequilibrium process 143–54
disequilibrium situations 88, 89
distribution 25
distributional conflict 136, 142
division of knowledge 158, 167
division of labour 22–4, 30, 32, 45, 71, 79, 115, 118–20, 131, 156, 181, 184
   advanced 160, 176–8, 185
   and bargaining power 133–6, 140
   and technical change 46, 54, 75, 91, 93–103, 109, 111, 126, 129
   consequences of xii, 20, 22, 52
   cooperative 160
   extension of 156–60
   interfirm 23
   international 94, 99, 105, 159–60
   intersectoral 24
   intrafirm 23
   optimum 99, 100, 159, 178, 179
   parameter k 133–6, 140, 141
   productivity-enhancing effect 63
   propensity to 133–6, 140
   significance of 93
division of thought 79, 156, 158
droit légitime 26
droit naturel 26

econometrics 13
Economic Calculation in the Socialist Society 30
economic systems 1, 3–13
economic theory 13
Economics of Adam Smith xii
economics of information literature 167
Economics of Price Determination, The 77
economies of scale 101
education 176, 177, 183–5
effectual demand 37–40, 64–5
efficiency gains 179
elasticity of demand 39
elimination price 83, 86
endogenous self-sustained growth 124
endogenous technical change xii, 24, 94, 103–6, 111, 129
England's Treasure by Forraign Trade 31
entrepreneurship 99, 158–9, 165, 167, 184
equilibration 35
equilibrium 136, 138, 148
   adjustment to 169

Subject Index

allocative 20
analysis 72
  existence of 120–4
  growth 112
  long-run 47, 143
  stability 120–4
  stable 9, 46, 148
  systems 19–20
  theory 72
  unstable 9, 31, 65, 110
  values 140
  see also general equilibrium
Essays on Adam Smith 60
Essays on Philosophical Subjects (EPS) 16, 19, 145
ethical norms 161
exchange economy 7
exogenous technical change 134
expanding markets 100
explosive cyclical growth 124
exponential decline 124
exponential growth 124
extent of the market 119
extraneous final consumption 50

Fable of the Bees, The: or, Private Vices, Publick Benefits 32
factor endowments 25
factor prices 25
factor supplies 40
fair play 161
falling natural price curve 32
fellow-feeling 18
feudalism 5, 6
firms 19–25, 75–92
fixed capital 142
fluctuation models 118–20
fluctuations, aggregate level 115–28
free competition 162–4, 166, 168–9
free enterprise economy 1, 165
free mobility of factors of production 40
free riders 18
free trade 168, 172
freedom 19
full-cost pricing 77
functional distribution of income xii

general equilibrium 41, 169
  analysis 44
  systems 27
  theories 3, 19, 118, 144
general rules 15
General Theory of Employment, Interest and Money 116–17

gross profits 78, 81, 85, 86, 89
growth 43–4, 46
  aggregate level 115–28
  consequences of 46
  cumulative 112, 128
  damped cyclical 124
  industry level 75–92
  macroeconomic view of 44–6
  neoclassical theory of 45
  of social product 11
  sectoral models 50–3
growth analysis 143, 145, 184
growth cycle 11
growth models 118–20
growth paths 64–72
growth rates 43, 144
growth theories 49–73
growth trajectory 4, 21, 40–1, 64, 109, 110, 143

harmony 25–9
Harrod-Domar model 61
Heckscher-Ohlin model 106
Heckscher-Ohlin-Samuelson model 168
high-level skills 99
History of Astronomy, The 16, 19, 177
history of economic thought xii

impartial spectator 14–15, 17, 18, 32
implicit production function 145, 148–51
incentives 96
incorporation 163
increasing returns xii, 19–25, 100, 143–54
indifference curve 147
individualism 18, 19
Industrial Revolution 8, 10, 31
industrialisation 9, 10, 174, 176
information availability 166
information exchange 163
information systems 181
informational advantage 167
informational problems 158
innovation 40, 81, 86, 88, 91
inside demand 152
institutional evolution 170–5
institutions 184
international division of labour 94, 99, 105, 159–60
inventions 91, 157
investment priorities 25
invisible hand 26, 44, 46, 52, 142

job satisfaction 179
justice 28, 182

Keynesian effective demand 119
Keynesian model 115–28
Keynesian school 115
Keynesianism 116 18
kinked demand curve 20, 22

labour command theory of value 52
labour demand 64
labour productivity 102
labour skills hierarchy 180
lag structure 24
laissez-faire 168
land scarcity 55
Lange-Lerner socialism 29
laws of justice 28
laws of primogeniture 5
learning by repetition 105
Lectures on Jurisprudence (LJ) xi, 5, 9, 95, 96, 156, 162
Lectures on Rhetoric and Belles Lettres (LRBL) 93, 96,
legislation 97
leisure 185
libertarianism 170–1
long-period analysis 115
long-run equilibrium 47, 143
long-run normal price 46
luxury consumption 43, 50

macroeconomic analysis 44
macroeconomic models 53
Manual of Political Economy 153
manufacturing 25, 185
marginal physical product curve 70–1
marginal propensity to consume 121, 124, 125
marginal revenue curve 22, 23
marginal utility 148
mark-up pricing 77
market activity 27
market expansion 88
market extent proxy 107
market information 9
market opportunities 164, 165, 167
market price 38, 39, 40, 161, 162
market process 24–5, 164
market rates of rent, wages and profit 37, 40
market supply 38, 39
Marxism 95, 159, 160, 178
maximum ophelimity 148
mercantilism 7–10
merchant role 151–3
meta-production 158

microeconomic analysis 44
microelectronics 181
monitoring 98–9
monopoly 100, 101, 163, 166
moral judgement 32, 161
moral philosophy 16, 18, 27
moral systems 15
morality 182
multiplier-accelerator business cycle model 117, 118

national income 132, 133, 136, 138
natural law philosophy 25–9
natural liberty 25–9
natural price 38, 39, 41, 42, 46, 161
natural rates of rent, wages and profit 37
natural resources 133
natural states 164
negative feedback 38
neoclassical theory of growth 45
new markets 100
non-linear first-order difference equation 30
North-South divide 160

0.6 rule 85–6
On Competition in Economic Theory 91
order-delivery lag 117
output-capital ratio, *see* capital-output ratio
output dominant 80

Paradox of Thrift 116
pari passu demand curve 23
partial equilibrium 41, 82–3
patent race model 92
Peoples Republic of China 165, 172
permissiveness 18
Perron-Frobenius theorem 51
person-to-person services 179
Physiocrats 19, 26, 33
pink-collar jobs 179
political economy 161
population adjustment mechanism 73
population growth 11, 53
population supply equation 62
post-industrial society 3, 155–88
Power and Market 170–1
power relationships 2
preferred route 150
price followers 76–7, 90
price in labour 36
price leadership 76–7

price relations 42
pricing policy 76
priority pattern 77, 83
process theory 72
product differentiation 166
production function 59, 64, 68, 70, 104, 106–11, 118, 133
production of output xii
production possibility curve 150
productivity 106, 179
productivity enhancement 6, 63, 98, 103, 105, 134, 158, 181
professional ethics 98
profit 54, 82–3, 131
profit function 65
profit maximization 78, 92, 99
profit rates 25, 53, 58, 59, 63, 68, 85, 89, 131, 133, 142, 164
progress of material well-being (opulence) xii
progressive specialization 102
propensity to division of labour 133–6, 140
propriety 15
prudence 15
public goods 172, 173

quality circles 179
quality of working life 179
quantity relations 42

ratchet effect 11, 36
Register of Business Names 163
regulation 162
research and development 81
restrictions 164

satisficing rules 92
savings function 59
Say's Identity 119
Say's Law 87
Schumpeterian fluctuation 70
science 176
Science in History 158
scientific knowledge 158
scientific management 180
sectoral analysis 35, 44
sectoral disequilibrium xii
sectoral growth models 50–3
sectoral model 42–3
self-command 26
self-expression 19
self-interest 1, 2, 13–19, 28, 161, 162, 164, 165

service activities 155
service sectors 179
short-period analysis 115
Smith's Theorem 101–3
social conflict 6
social control 29
social norms 17, 18
social obligation 161, 181–3
social product 4, 30, 37, 45, 55, 64, 108, 110, 121, 125, 132
social protocol 17
socialization 18–19
societal development 11, 173
societal forms 7
Soviet Union 165
specialization 105, 156, 158, 175–8, 181
stability analysis 127
stable equilibrium 9, 46
stadial analysis 3–13, 30
stadial view of economic development 1
stationary state 4–5, 57, 64–72, 143–4
Stoicism 26
subsistence level 53
subsistence requirements 52
supervision 98
supply and demand 37
supply of labour 132
surplus economy 43
sympathy 16–19

target pricing 77
taxation 170, 171
technical change 75, 91, 93, 106–11, 118, 125, 126, 134
  and division of labour 46, 54, 75, 91, 93–103, 111, 126, 129
  endogenous xii, 24, 94, 103–6, 111, 129
  exogenous 134
technical coefficients 50, 52
technical progress 79–82, 104, 105
technical skills 176
technological skills 126
technology matrix 51, 52
Theory of Moral Sentiments, The (TMS) xiii, 2, 13–19, 26, 27, 32, 161, 162, 177, 182, 183
theory of the firm 20, 76
Theory of Unemployment 116
thrift 116
thriftiness increase 124–5
thriftiness parameter 119, 123
total income 151

Trade and Navigation of Great-Britain, The 31
trading 25

ultimate limitational factor 57
Umschwungstheorie 31
unstable equilibrium 9, 31, 65, 110

valuable invention 80, 91
value surpluses 43
value theory 47
vertical integration 100, 101
virtue 165, 185
Von Neumann model of balanced growth 51
Von Neumann model with positive consumption 52

wage levels 36
wage rates 53, 63, 103, 135, 136
Walrasian system 72
Wealth of Nations, The (WN) xi, xii, xv, 2, 5–9, 13, 15, 16, 20, 22, 24, 27, 28, 30, 31, 33, 45, 59, 60, 65–7, 76, 85, 89, 93, 95, 96, 131, 140, 152, 154, 157, 160, 162–4, 172, 175, 177
welfare 134, 161, 172, 173, 183
welfare index 135, 136, 138
welfare state 17, 18